Afield

American Writers on Bird Dogs

Robert DeMott

AND

Dave Smith

Skyhorse Publishing

Skyhorse Publishing books may be purchased in bulk at special discounts for sales promotion, corporate gifts, fund-raising, or educational purposes. Special editions can also be created to specifications. For details, contact the Special Sales Department, Skyhorse Publishing, 555 Eighth Avenue, Suite 903, New York, NY 10018 or info@skyhorsepublishing.com.

www.skyhorsepublishing.com

10 9 8 7 6 5 4 3 2 1

Library of Congress Cataloging-in-Publication Data

DeMott, Robert J., 1943-
  Afield : American writers on bird dogs / Robert DeMott and Dave Smith.
    p. cm.
  Includes bibliographical references.
  ISBN 978-1-60239-776-7
  1. Bird dogs--Anecdotes. 2. Dog owners--United States--Anecdotes. 3.
Authors, American--Anecdotes. I. Smith, Dave, 1942- II. Title.
  SF428.5.D46 2010
  636.752--dc22
                                              2010002043
Printed in the United States of America

for

Jack Matthews:
novelist, poet, essayist, dramatist, historian, humorist,
lexicologist, bibliophile, teacher . . .

"No man is quite objective about his favorite dog. . . ."
—George Bird Evans,
The Upland Shooting Life (1971)

Contents

Acknowledgments and Permissions

The editors thank Tony Lyons and Nick Lyons for their sustained interest, encouragement, and advice regarding this project. In the course of moving this book from idea to reality, Ron Ellis has been a valued conspirator, sounding board, and cheerleader. Jim Harrison, Guy de la Valdène, Syd Lea, and Tom McGuane helped open doors that otherwise might have stayed closed. Joyce Bahle, Pete Fritzell, Dan Lahren, Randy Lawrence, Craig Nova, and Patrick Smith were generous and helpful in a number of ways. Dave Smith's research fund at Johns Hopkins University underwrote the preparatory editorial work provided by Textual Healing, LLC. We thank Victoria Woollen-Danner for providing an illustration for Bruce Guernsey's essay and Laurie McGuane for timely photographs. Special thanks goes to Richard Ford, who gave more than was required. The women in our lives, Kate Fox and Dee Smith, both dog lovers we are happy to say, make it all worthwhile. So has Jennifer McCartney, our able editor at Skyhorse.

We've long admired and intently pored over *Gun Dog, Shooting Sportsman, Upland Almanac,* and *Pointing Dog Journal,* more for their photographs than anything else: pictures of suave Weimaraners, vigilant Vizslas, crisply efficient German shorthairs, linebacker pointers, Llewellyns carrying themselves like young MBAs, hoity toity English and Irish setters desporting like, well, the English and Irish at an Ascot party, and all manner of the big and of the little field dogs, down to Brittany spaniels, frequent favorites these days. "Even if you knew nothing about dogs, or birds, or hunting," Tom Davis says in *To the Point: A Tribute to Pointing Dogs* (2003) "you would know beyond a shadow of a doubt," that such athletic, intelligent animals "mean business." Regrettably, although we originally envisioned a lavishly illustrated work with professionally photographed full-page portraits of writers and their dogs doing their bred-in-the-bone business, an accompanying textual component of completely original essays by a broad representation of writers along gender and racial lines, the fact is that we have had to come to accept Melville's lament in *Moby-Dick,* that there is never enough time, strength, cash, or patience to go around for even the best of intentions. Which is to say that our photographs are more homespun than polished, our lineup of contributors more monochromatic than we hoped, and that a few essays in *Afield* had prior lives which we appreciate being granted permission to reuse here.

Christopher Camuto's "Expecting to Be Surprised," transcribed by Cara Maria Cambardella (Bucknell University), originally appeared in longer form as "Expecting to Be Surprised" in his *Hunting from Home: A Year Afield in the Blue Ridge Mountains.* Athens: University of Georgia Press, 2004, pp. 218-219; 226-239.

Clyde Edgerton's essay "Bird Dog Ben" originally appeared in shorter form as "Chicken Dog" in *Garden and Gun,* 3, August/September 2009, pp. 52-53.

Jim Harrison's essay "The Dogs in My Life" originally appeared in shorter form as "Dog Years" in *Field and Stream,* 109, September 2004, pp. 78-82; 131.

Thomas McGuane's essay "The Only Honest Way to Eat Poultry" originally appeared as "A Novelist Takes Aim" in *Wall Street Journal*, March 28, 2009, p. W9.

The late William G. Tapply's essay "Burt" originally appeared in different form in his *Upland Autumn: Birds, Dogs, and Shotgun Shells*. New York: Skyhorse Publishing, 2009, pp. 31-39; 65-77.

Our deepest gratitude goes to our contributors. When we kicked off this scheme thirty months ago with only a vague notion of our intentions and goals, some were already friends or acquaintances, some were friends of friends, some were strangers, some were friends of strangers, yet we all seem to have found a common ground in our admiration for bird dogs—setters, pointers, spaniels, and retrievers—and our desire to write well about them.

Finally, we dedicate *Afield* to Jack Matthews: colleague, mentor, dog lover, onetime avid upland hunter, and, above all, valued friend, eighty-five years young, whose presence and words still inspire, enlighten, and delight.

RD, Athens, OH
DS, Baltimore, MD
December 2009

List of Illustrations

Writers Hunting, Hunters Writing

INTRODUCTION

Robert DeMott and Dave Smith

> Writing is my occupation; hunting is a preoccu-
> pation. The two so often conflict that it interests
> me when they occur together."
> —Vance Bourjaily, *The Unnatural Enemy* (1963)

Although we have been the closest of friends for four decades—poetry brought us together in 1971—we have not been day-to-day hunting partners. Yet we have teamed up so long, even if occasionally, in the woods and fields of Ohio, Maryland, and Louisiana, that it seems somehow unusual and even incomplete for one of us to go afield without the other. We have hunted each other's traditional game birds—DeMott's northern ruffed grouse and woodcock, Smith's southern Bobwhite quail (with ring-necked pheasants thrown in here and there for good measure)— over setters and spaniels named Babe, Jen, Meadow, Molly, and Finn, and others we have fooled with as well, and we have learned there are things the other would not be caught dead without—for DeMott a pair of pruning shears to snip through multiflora rose and greenbrier brambles; for Smith a towering Thermos filled with a day's supply of hot coffee. No matter how fast or slow the action, no matter how staunch or bedraggled the point, no matter how unerring or wayward the shots, our chief pleasure has always been in the shared experience of watching dogs work, anticipating the choreography of point, flush, and shot, but also looking sideways, too, carrying on animated conversations about everything under the sun, and perhaps more than anything else, storing up sustaining impressions and vivid memories to call up at times like this when the only hunt worth its name is the hunt for words.

Behind the field memories and man-dog camaraderie, words have bound us together. During an impromptu lunch beneath a clump of tag alders, or around a kitchen sink doing the unglamorous but necessary work of plucking, drawing, and cleaning a few brace of woodcock or quail for dinner, we do what old hunters always have done, we tell back the stories that contain some of the best, most enjoyable moments we have lived. Hunters hunting, dogs working, stories forming, writers writing: as processes they partake in a way of being that requires avid readiness, and they all fit splendidly, as a bird dog's head fits so comfortably into the palm of a cupped human hand.

We have no doubt that it was at some such moment in Athens, Baton Rouge, or perhaps Baltimore, speaking of writing and hunting and dogs and the ways we have braided them and considered them all of a piece during our many years of friendship, that we broached doing a book together to celebrate that bond. Each of us is certain that the other first raised the idea, but its point of origin hardly matters as neither of us has ever felt the competitive urge to upstage or one-up his pal. The idea of doing a "bird dog book"—loosely defined—floated around in our telephone conversations, emails, and hand-written letters for several years before gaining momentum. Then, in 2007, when one of us reached phased retirement after a lifetime of teaching, it was time to nudge the project forward.

In Spanish philosopher José Ortega y Gasset's thoughtful treatise, *Meditations on Hunting* (1942), he relates an anecdote about a Persian prince who abdicated his throne because his people refused to accept a ruler who did not hunt. "The young man," Ortega y Gasset writes, "had become interested in literature and was beyond hope." We don't think there is anything wrong with literature seducing people—we count ourselves among its victims. But we are relieved to be able to conduct business differently now, and novelist Vance Bourjaily's comment in his valuable but nearly forgotten nonfiction collection on hunting, *The Unnatural Enemy*, comports more closely with our attitude. Writing and hunting "so often conflict," he claims, "that it interests me when they occur together."

It interests us, too, and so we began with a simple premise—that outside the professional sporting press there were plenty of accomplished writers—novelists, poets, essayists in and out of universities—who were also just atavistic enough to hunt upland birds or doves or waterfowl seriously, perhaps even obsessively, with trained dogs. We sensed that, despite the cultural impress of political correctness, society's general swing away from field sports, and the current hot-potato debates about all aspects of ethical behavior toward the non-human world, the work of these authors—apologetic or unapologetic, untroubled or conflicted as it might or might not be regarding current discourse—would be writing that we'd very much like to see.

Following some weeks of back-and-forth brainstorming we compiled a list of thirty or so writers, ranging from the already famous to the yet-to-be-discovered, who we hoped might contribute to such a niche book of enthusiasms. We set about contacting our wish list and proposed that each of them write an original memoir-style essay of between 2,500 and 3,750 words (longer if need be, though the average length turned out to be about 3,700 words) that treated his or her relationship or experience with past or current bird dogs in a substantial, lively way, or visited some related aspect of upland hunting with pointers, flushers, or retrievers that reflected their particular passion for the sport. We also asked for photographs to salt the text.

We requested essays that were literate, artful, and informed, but not fussy, sentimental, grandiose, pedantic, or—God forbid!—academic. We wanted sure-handed narratives of process and perception, engagement and reflection, rather than how-to manuals, or what novelist Annie Proulx, herself a hunter, once called "dumbed-down hook and bullet stuff," and Richard Ford in his masterful Foreword to this collection calls "fin 'n feather" writing. We hoped their focus would be on immediate and tangible elements as a means of illuminating experiences that can be at once utterly mundane and thoroughly mysterious, but that often bring us—momentarily at least—close to the ragged edge of our otherwise intensely programmed, homogenized, techno-oriented lives.

Hunting with fowling dogs, which is our version of the age-old Ur-chase, allows us a look, however briefly, into one kind of unruly, tangled psychic and physical terrain where wild impulse and self-consciousness, raw experience and groomed language, chaos and ceremony intersect. Often (but not always) the chase leads directly to killing a living quarry, the ineluctable result of which, given a mix of skill and luck, is a dead, sometimes bloody, bird in the hand, and later in the oven. ("Hunting, like religion, is incomplete without death," novelist and respected outdoorsman Robert F. Jones once wrote. "That's why it's not a gallery game.") Few things taste better or deliver a more unalloyed experience than wild game we have killed, cleaned, and cooked ourselves (especially grouse, woodcock, teal, wood ducks—birds that simply cannot be domesticated, pen reared, or artificially farmed in any way, shape, or form). Yet we also realize that, depending on one's degree of personal sensitivity, capacity for ironic reflection, or susceptibility to guilt, there is always that signal moment, when the dog delivers a dead bird to hand, that can occasion a haunting, unresolvable mix of "self-satisfaction and self-reproach," as Texas-born novelist William Humphrey says in *Open Season: Sporting Adventures* (1986), because "you hold in your hand the creature you both love and love to kill." Each reader, we think, must deal with this conundrum in his or her own way. For some it will be an impasse; for others a gateway.

Despite a pedigreed history recorded by such shooting gentlemen as William Harnden Foster, Dr. Charles Norris, Nash Buckingham, Burton Spiller, Frank Woolner, George Bird Evans, and others, we guess that for many of us hunting over bird dogs is a messier, more digressive, less aristocratic affair than most people realize. This is a good thing, because it has no innately privileged status, no elevated claim to being any more or less worthwhile as a literary subject than a hundred other human activities we can name. Like the scent of a quail or grouse or dove no one can take in but knows exists anyway, bird dogging is no more than or no less than the metaphoric equivalent of all realistic, quotidian experiences that require our active participation, willing involvement, close observation, and probably a little faith thrown in for good measure. Plus, it's fun.

Which is to say, hunting with bird dogs and all that it entails, is but one among many of the complex grounds of being writers have always traversed. This is the *paysage moralise* of existential behavior. Whatever special status the subject acquires in this collection springs from the writer's individual set of preferred enthusiasms, his conscious decision to write through the contradictions as if—for the moment anyway— nothing else mattered. No matter where one lands on the predatory scale and killing issue, the hope, of course, is that in writing and reading about these favorite experiences we arrive at an understanding of our own complicated responsibility toward the biotic world and our privileged, causal connection with what President Jimmy Carter memorably termed the hunter's "rules of ethics, etiquette, and propriety" in his autobiographical *An Outdoor Journal* (1994). Hunters, pay attention, look to your dogs and game, and don't forget to husband yourselves, we say.

The most common launch point in these essays is a single hunter hunting with the canine(s) whose presence in the landscape (besides a reasonable number of game birds) makes field experiences not only possible but worthwhile. Whether they are on the ground in New England, the South, the Midwest, the West, or even eastern Europe, pointers, setters, spaniels, retrievers in myriad shapes, sizes, and hues are the genuine stars of this book. We doubt they know that, but would not be surprised if they did. Clearly, whatever modicum of attainment is reached in woods and fields and marsh belongs mostly to them. They do nearly all the grueling physical work and perhaps wisely leave the metaphysical, elegiac, nostalgic, lyrical stuff to us.

Allah, it is said, does not count against a person's allotted hours on earth the days spent hunting, or in the chase. "In the inevitable way of old tags," Vance Bourjaily says, "this one seems sometimes to be true: there are such hours, marvelous, absorbed, stolen from time." In that sense, then, the narratives gathered here should prolong our lives twice over—once in the writing and once in the reading. They are rites of passage, exercises in shape-shifting memory, little fables of identity, wee jokes of fate, and maybe more than anything else, songs of love that nearly always end the same, in a kind of enjoyable, sometimes bittersweet, delight, and—dare we say it—even wisdom. These are tales in pursuit of something significant yet simple, profound yet commonplace. We went to the field for pleasure, all kinds of pleasure: the dog finding what couldn't be found, the clean, unexpected shot, the solid and welcome feel and smell of earth underfoot, the leafless winter trees backlit by a setting sun, the exquisite taste of a wild bird cooked to perfection, the day burned so vividly inside us it felt like a distillation of forever, the words a fellow hunter found to describe indescribable moments, even those moments when a beloved dog died. We tell that story in our individual ways— tragically, lyrically, humorously—over and over and over, sometimes in novels, short stories, poems, or as in this collection, in the congenial form of nonfiction essays.

No one represented in *Afield* is a full time professional trainer, sporting journalist, narrow-gauge specialist, or gonzo expert in the nimrod arts. We'd bet each contributor knows that life's real work, its most central, main-line effort, lies elsewhere—in social, domestic, and aesthetic realms. That is to say we are husbands, fathers, sons, brothers, uncles, nephews, teachers, novelists, essayists, poets first and sporting gents second (we say this knowing full well the deserved reputations and elevated outdoor skill levels of many of our contributors). Hunting over bird dogs won't change national policy, stem the tide of terrorism, make people admire us more, or efface the most traumatic human stains—divorce, financial setbacks, illness, war, and death of loved ones. But because bird dogs continue to insinuate themselves into our hearts, because game birds will always lend a quotient of welcome unpredictability to our lives, and because it has given us joy to anticipate what this book might become, we now invite readers to share our pleasure.

The Beast at My Feet

FOREWORD

Richard Ford

I'll just say it: I've never liked stories about dogs. Stories about hunting dogs. Sheep dogs. Seeing-eyes. Bloodhounds. St. Bernards with casks of brandy. Dogs that could talk, count, sing arias, walk on two feet or dance the boogaloo. I remember getting into a heated discussion with my grandmother many years ago, about whether Lassie the Collie was a boy or a girl. My grandmother had her regular programs, and *Lassie* was Sunday night (we're talking tv, here). She was in the "Lassie is a boy" camp, and didn't care what a name might've meant in Scottish. She wasn't Scottish. She was Osage and held her convictions, you might say, fiercely. I was home from college at that time and knew pretty much everything in the world, and took nasty pleasure—as college students will—in goading her about those of her views which were at variance with my superior, better-informed ones. She and I could gin up our bickerings into pretty formidable feuds if we both felt foul enough. Which is what we did on the Lassie issue. At a certain frustrated moment, when pecking at each other threatened to make her miss something critical in the show, she rocketed around in her chair, fired off a pityingly corrosive glare at me and said, "I don't care what you say. You're an idiot. Lassie's not a girl. That's all there is to it. Shut up." To which I piously replied, with a smirk. "Great. That's fine. You know everything there is to know. But who gives a damn about Lassie. It's just a story about a *dog*."

I hadn't worked my rationales out very finely at the time. This was more than forty years ago. But the undercarriage of my argument with my grandmother—who was past eighty then, but not yet beyond the age at which she could be taught a useful lesson—was that if Lassie had been something other than a precocious Collie (if she'd been, say, a human being, capable of the delicate discernings humans are capable of—regret, complex joy, an interior life, duplicity. A self. The grainy stuff you'd find in a John Cheever story), then I'd have been interested in how she could, for instance, find the lost keys to the pick-up in time to escape the inferno, or how she knew a mountain lion was lying in wait in those rocks ready to jump on people, or what unheard of effort it took for her to swim the length of frigid Lake Ooganooky to tell the forest ranger that Timmy'd broken his tibia and couldn't last another night in the woods. I felt, then—I still feel—that animal stories let the air of interest out of the moral balloon. They over-simplified and rigidified the colorful variants I'd found life to be full of, and that made it worth worrying with. It hadn't dawned on me that this was precisely what kept my granny glued to the tv on Sunday nights, and why it was easy to wind her up with my dumb-ass college-boy bad manners. Like I said, she was eighty. She'd seen enough Cheeverish stuff just in the natural course of things. She'd be dead soon. Having the world seem simple, even wrongly simple, wasn't much of a sacrifice for her.

We were always a family that hunted and kept dogs for quail and Mississippi flyway ducks. My parents and my mother's parents were all from north Arkansas—and quail were everywhere up there then. My father—who died in the early sixties—used to go to a mysterious place called Bird Town, where quail were plentiful and I wasn't invited. And I have a precious, faded photograph of my pretty mother as a young woman, sitting a big bay gelding, wearing high lace-up boots and jodhpurs, just about to ride into the field, a double gun in her saddle scabbard. Eventually we all lived together after my father died—my granny, my grandad, my mother and I. My grandad ran a big old drummer's hotel in Little Rock, where we "lived in," and he kept his bird dogs in the hotel basement. These beasts were hard-mouthed old weepy-eyed, red-ass pointers who did nothing for ten months of the year but sleep, eat and snap at flies. My grandfather—a round, jovial Gildersleevian man who featured himself a consummate sport—would waltz down every evening and feed the dogs meat trimmings and marrow bones and beef drips out of the hotel kitchen, using big greasy metal bowls the dogs nosed around the floor. "These goddamn dogs eat bettern' I do, Dick," he'd say, immensely pleased as he watched them gnashing and growling and cutting their eyes at each other, guarding their grub. It wasn't at all true that they ate better than he did. No one did that. But dogs were always in our life. We hunted them everywhere, hauling them around in the trunk of his red Buick Super, into which he'd had installed a shiny metal air port so they wouldn't suffocate. We were all crazy about dogs. One, "Ole Ben," my grandfather even named after himself, so much did he love him. "Ole Ben Shelley. The Dog."

But up in room 604, where we lived in the hotel—a long shadowy hallway of connected rooms converted into an "apartment"—there were always fresh copies of *Field and Stream* and *Sports Afield* lying on the pie-crust table in the little living room, along with *Argosy*s, *Reader's Digest*s, and the Rotarian magazine. It was almost certainly from these slick sporting monthlies that I developed my disdain for dog stories. After all, I was living (and being made to work) in that great six-hundred room ocean-liner of a place, where daily and nightly the most exotic, eye-popping, sometimes dismaying, sometimes hilarious, occasionally terrifying, but never only-mildly-interesting human dramas transpired in front of my astonished eyes. Brawls, illicit couplings, florid and riotous lewdness, mournful suicides, late-night union and race debacles, abrupt police and fire department arrivals, plus the regular hum-dee-dum of that unwieldy Titanic, thrumming along with its everyday business. For me to sit down then and read Ted Trueblood or Norman Strung or Homer Circle or even old Archibald Rutledge (where'd these guys get these names?), spooling it out about faithful old "Flame" making his final mile-long retrieve of a rooster his ninety-year-old master, Mactavish, had only dropped a leg on, after which both Mactavish and Flame gorked over dead as hammers at each others' feet, proving that true loyalty knows no bounds, and man and beast are but variant shades upon life's indifferent wall—well, that didn't hold a flicker to *real* life. At least not the real life I was seeing in my day job. Ditto stories about dogs getting skunked or dogs getting porcupined or ratttle-snaked, or retrieving the decoys or chasing the bear through the camp . . . you get the picture. These slick sporting stories wanted me to concede human qualities to low creatures—think of Ole Ben, dozing down in the basement—whereas I was keeping my gaze fixed on the actual people. For another kind of boy I guess it could've worked out different. I didn't like Aesop either.

Plus, those old boys with their houndstooth porkpies and wine-rich names and Meerschaums all *thought* they were really writing about the dogs, and only as an afterthought making canny comparisons back toward the rest of us simple clods who were really just dogs in men's suits. I didn't buy it. I knew dogs. Dogs didn't commit suicide or carry guns. Dogs didn't lie or feel remorse. They definitely coupled, and sometimes risibly, but never illicitly, and they weren't a bit sorry once the deed was done (though they did usually go to sleep). Dogs and men, even in my teenage view, weren't a fit comparison. Dogs were . . . well . . . dogs.

Then, as now, I've truthfully never seen a bird dog do anything I found remotely enviable, or in the least imitative of deeds out of my own festering life. I've never seen a dog—a blooded setter or a wormy porch hound with crossed eyes—do anything more than what I'd expected him to do, and paid a good bird-dog man beaucoup dollars to train him to do. In the great majority of those thousands of hours that I've hunted over pointing breeds, what I've usually observed is a great deal *less* than I wanted, or had dreamed of, or paid for, or sought hopefully to admire or was willing to put up with. I reiterate. I'm a dog lover. But I'm not nuts.

Therefore, I don't come to the task of writing appreciative words about this book of essays by writers on their bird dogs with my head already in the right place. Better to say I've come to be convinced.

★ ★ ★

Right off the bat, I consider writing readable, interestingly detailed accounts of one's love affair with one's hunting dogs *shouldn't* be that simple. Likewise writing about bird hunting. Which is the reason so much of it—say Nash Buckingham—turns out to play the whole business for yucks and winks, with dogs performing doggy hijinx and exhibiting fantastic swami-like astuteness at which the rest of us either gape with approval or fume with rage, but otherwise take the role of second fiddle. And even if you don't have the same restrained regard for dog flesh as I do, you have to acknowledge that writing seriously (as in Chekhovian seriously) about dogs and hunting is likely to be a challenge. For one thing, dogs can't talk (at least none of mine have yet). And we don't really know much about what they think—except about food, water, sex, sleep and from time to time game birds, plus their displeasure at being yelled at, punished, ignored, or confined. However, I've noticed that both talking *and* thinking have sort of become formal staples of interesting writing in the last few centuries. Even just with hunting by itself—which offers no end of variety, mystery, stimulation, drama, contemplation *when you do it*—you pretty quickly get to the end of how many ways you can rotate the diamond *when you write about it*. In that regard—but only in that very, very *un*important regard—hunting's like sex: you *resort* to writing about it, but not because you want to quit doing it.

Really good writers—including those of us who *would* be really good writers if we knew how—seem to approach bird dog and hunting accounts by "sliding" deftly off from the routines of rock-hard points and covey rises toward "other things" which hunting doesn't so much *stand for* as stands *beside*—offering relief or a change of focus or just a colorful background. Years ago, Tom McGuane (whose vivid little essay figures in this volume) asked me if I'd ever written a hunting story. We happened to be hunting Huns at the time, near where he lived then outside of Livingston. No, I said, I'd not written a hunting story, and rehearsed all the reasons I've just been going on about. Well, Tom said, it's just that if you *were* to write one, I know a guy who's collecting hunting stories for an anthology. This fellow might welcome one from you.

Afterward, I went home to Missoula and thought about a hunting story. I thought particularly about a jaunt I'd recently made with my wife and a friend out to a small lake near Ovando, Montana, where some snow geese were reported to be stopping over. There, I'd snuck up on the great raft of them where they were conniving near the shore. When I was close enough, I stood up and made my presence known. (No dogs were involved in this.) And the whole, alarmed, squalling mass of geese just clamorously rose in the air all at once and flew around me like confetti in the wind, so that shooting two was easy.

That might make a hunting story, I thought. Only when I sat down to write it the next week, my hunting story quickly became not a story about shooting snow geese (that didn't seem really interesting enough by itself), but a story about a teenage boy revisiting a memory of his mother and her lover going goose shooting near Great Falls, Montana, and about how all the events of the day transpired to produce a flash point of a love going south in the boy's mother's life, and about how unwilling we all are to see our parents as our equals. Nothing simple at all. Still, it *was* a hunting story. People sought and shot birds, just the way I had. But hunting seemed to stay in the background. The gist of the story lay elsewhere—off to the side, or up in front of the hunting parts. In any event, the guy published it.

And just one more thing, then I'll get off myself, here. Some time in the middle nineteen nineties my Brittany, Scooter, began losing the use of his right front leg. First his paw went mysteriously limp and flopped back and forth like a hasp on a cellar door. Then after a few weeks his whole leg started to be useless. I brought him to every doctor I could find, and eventually to the esteemed veterinary clinic at Washington State University in Pullman. Rick Bass's account, "Old Dog," which leads off this collection, describes a similar event with his dog, also in Pullman. As with Bass's dog "Point," the WSU vets put Scooter through their battery of scopes and acronyms and expensive diagnostic machineries. And as with Bass, I was presently informed Scooter had cancer and that my choices regarding his future were few and simple: euthanize him right then; amputate his front leg and hope we got it before the cancer reached his spine. Or just take him back home to Montana and let him roam around however he could—hunting, pointing birds, enjoying his life until that bad day which was surely coming. Scooter seemed to be in no pain. Dogs can put up with a lot we wouldn't think of enduring. I took a day to think the whole situation over. I grieved, I ground my molars at night, felt befuddled by the unknown, effronted by fate (Scooter was only seven). I tried aimlessly to imagine what *I* would want if such a sorry hand of cards had been dealt to me. Scooter, of course, was no help. He had to do whatever I decided he had to do, and didn't even know that much.

After a long day and a long night of bruising Dostoevsky-style brain-harrowing, I decided (Kristina and I decided) that we "couldn't imagine this stout creature as a tripod" (which is what Syd Lea decided and wrote about late in this book in describing his own dog's last illness). Like Lea, we elected to let foul nature take its course—which in a few months it fouly did. Though not before Scooter had run many days in the sharptail fields and tule patches along the Smith River, days that featured him larruping around on his three good legs—his useless one flapping—finding and pointing birds and performing his dog's duties as near to perfection as he'd performed them on all four. And then, of course, in due time pain from his disease suddenly fired up and became almost instantly beyond what he could tolerate. And Kristina sent him sorrowingly off to meet his maker that very afternoon. I for some reason was in Norway at the time. I cried in my bed in the hotel.

About a year later, I found myself sitting around thinking about Scooter and what a sorry lot he'd drawn and I'd drawn, too. And I just wrote down on a piece of paper the words, "A dog with three legs." And pretty quick I'd written out a story about, yes, a man who had a dog with three legs, just like Scooter. This man, unlike myself, had a banged-up marriage that was busting apart, though he was gallantly staging a hunting trip with his wife—who already lived in a faraway city—a trip wherein the man would try to fit the marital jigsaw back together. All the while, his dog ("Scooter") was coursing around with three working legs, hunting pheasants, making everybody notice and admire and pity him. It was going to be a story, I believed, about "imperfections," and how we learn to make do in life, often under less than ideal circumstances.

Naturally, the story didn't work out. And for probably obvious reasons: too much oversimplifying correlation between dog life and human life. Too little authorial skill. It just seemed the only way I could make my and Scooter's dog story remotely "work" on the page—by Scooter's story becoming what Henry James called a "donnée," a given, a provocation to write something *else*, something to the side of the actual events that involved my wonderful dog who got sick and sadly died. I just didn't get the story far enough to the side, I guess. I'm sure a better writer could've written it. Maybe Chekhov actually did.

What I've just described has to do with writing fiction, of course—making stories artificially up out of bits of things that both did happen and many that never did, with the intention of producing something in language that the facts themselves probably wouldn't add up to on their own, and that didn't exist before I wrote it. The writing that makes up the stories in this book, on the other hand, is *non*fiction, which means that everything described as happening had to have happened just the way the writers say it did—with nothing added except the soft tissue and ligatures of construction and interpretation, all of it accompanied by the proviso that once any factual event is rendered into the "event" called language, it really can't be precisely the same as it was when it happened. Words and deeds are different acts. Though both these forms achieve truth by being persuasive.

What I notice about almost all the stories and memoirs in this book is that the writers are forever, as I said before, artfully, pleasingly sliding off to the side of the agreed-to subject—dog, man, birds-in-the-air— and applying themselves instead to the obdurate, mysterious but finally yielding life attending it. The writers here know that going forward in life is not simple but woolly business, requiring complex strategies for survival, and that two of these strategies can be serious writing and serious reading. They're willing to believe that, by describing the complex accommodations a man makes with his old arthritic Brittany in the early September dove fields of western South Carolina, a writer can open up some new and not at all simple-minded possibilities.

"When I unload Patti from the car, she is wheezing. It makes me think of the asthma I suffered from as a child," writes the novelist Scott Ely, a Vietnam veteran with his own menu of nitty survival issues, years beyond being Agent Orange'd in our country's defense. "I recall reading in Seneca that the ancients called that affliction 'rehearsing death.' Some nights she wakes me up, and I reach out to pet her until her breathing returns to normal. I can't decide if I'd rather watch her die or wake to find her dead on her dog bed. I pour her a bowl full of water and she drinks most of it. I'm eager to find her a spot in the shade. She lies down in the grass in the shade thrown by the truck, while I sit on the tailgate and eat my barbecue sandwich, some of which I share with Patti. . . . And it's then that I realize how much I would like her to live for another four or five years."

When I first read Ely's stately, mournful celebration of life, I actually *mis*read it. To me, so rapt was I by the narrator's perplex with life, it said (and will always say) ". . . how much *I* would like to live another four or five years." Kafka, that old jokester, famously wrote that a book should affect us like the death of someone we love more than ourselves. But I've never thought—as Ely doesn't either—that Kafka intended to exclude *ourselves* from the peril in his equation, or that we shouldn't be allowed to substitute life for death.

Hell's grim tyrant finds a second-row, center seat in much of the work of this book. A lot of the writers are getting on now (me) and (unlike me) are quizzically interested in how getting old feels. "I'm seriously thinking of slowly ending my hunting life with an English cocker," the poet and novelist Jim Harrison writes, "like my wife's dog Mary, whom I could easily teach to be president (or at least a senator), run a corporation or write my novels." From this you can detect that no one's insulting anyone's intelligence about the big issues. Big D death's just another member of the entourage. And no one's alleging that hunting game birds over a pointing dog (now mostly a rich man's sport, anyway) is what life's all about. It isn't. "The dogs are everything," McGuane says. But he doesn't mean that literally. It's just exuberance. "Bird dogs plead with you to imagine the great things you could be doing together. Their delight is a lesson in the bliss of living." This, however, I'm certain he does mean.

If anything, restraint, affection, good humor, precious specificity govern the writing that's here. And not the old tight-lipped, frozen-nuts Hemingway restraint, by which game is *utilized* and saying less (or, better yet, saying nothing) is superior to the general mess of imprecision of feeling when it comes to expressing the ineffable. These guys are writers first and dog guys second, and they measure words both more—and less—to the task. You occasionally, in fact, can feel them leaning into you with their sentences, working faithfully to get across what's important (precisely the pressure I come to good writing to experience).

"This was one of those afternoons in Vermont," the novelist Craig Nova rhapsodizes about an autumn day in which he shot a woodcock then had his dog run off, "that comes after a still night when the trees have mulled. The leaves make perfect circles around the maples, just like those in a garden architect's plans, and since the ground is covered with these yellow-and-pink circles, the sky and every object in the later afternoon is covered with that warm pink and yellow light. It isn't only a physical thing, but something else, too, and that color with its dusty quality, like a woman's powder, suggests a connection to other days in the fall through the decades, or centuries, or millennia."

★ ★ ★

Happily, all included here seem to have screwed down tight on the many abjectly boneheaded things hunters say in public (and in private). No one here says he likes dogs more than people (the genetic signature of the misanthrope). There's very little bragging, everybody cheerfully owning up to his own dog's foibles and to their own occasional wantonness afield. There's no grinding, bullying NRA-ish gun-toter advocacy, nor any foolishness about bird hunters really being true conservationists— Darwin's little helpers in orange caps. Everybody here acknowledges that when you go hunting you occasionally kill another creature (though, surprisingly, not that often), and this fact and the consequences of those deaths are visited on the hunters just like they'd be visited on anyone. Indeed, in these pages there's no advocacy even for hunting itself, which as you read on seems, as a topic, to recede into the middle background, in favor of watching the dogs, taking the lively air and trying to make life in the wide open stand out a bit more vividly before the murky stuff gets the better of us.

Which is good, since none of these people seem to go about hunting over dogs in anything like the same way—a fact that nicely pleads the case against the boorishness that says hunting is a pious, gnostic and exclusive club (like the Cosa Nostra or Sigma Chi), and that only a few adepts are waved through its portals. Some guys, for instance, hate it when their bird dog's nose hoovers along to the ground, whereas other guys prize a trailer. Some guys stride baronially to the field with a fancy Spanish double gun bought with movie dough, while others go out carrying pawn-shop auto-loaders with duct-taped stocks. Some dog men require the stately retrieve; others couldn't care less. Some guys *have* to train their own dogs; other guys (me) wouldn't consider it for a minute. Some guys are deep into blood lines, while others pick up "drops" found idling along the Interstate and train them to be bird machines. All of this leads to the view that if you've ever gone hunting with another human being—your wife, your best friend, your grandpa Ludlow, your law partner or your secretary—then you have to believe it's a fresh miracle that two humans can ever act in concert to realize a single end both would describe using the same words. Though you could conclude from this that hunting birds over a trained dog really isn't that difficult. Just look at the people you know who do it reasonably well.

Some things, though, are apparently forever. And in this book it's man's love of dog, against which I lodge little argument—except that I'm always slightly uneasy about saying I love my wife *and also* "love" my dog Lewy. Once again we find love to be a many-splendored—and nuanced—thing.

Which is what holds this book together and eventually makes me like dog stories better than I ever used to. Oh, sure, there are sweetly predictable excesses along the way here. Hunting dogs are routinely said to be smarter about hunting than their masters—for which I have considerable contrary evidence of the first person nature. Dogs are said by my friend Guy de la Valdène to be children—though you'd need to consult his own non-canine children to know what he means by that. Dogs, variously, are said to "smile" (dubious), to be "learn*ed*" (I'm skeptical), to understand the poems of W.S. Merwin, to be "noble," and "great," to experience indignity, to possess powers of clairvoyance, and to radiate sarcasm like a Harvard professor. They are believed to be, in other words, and again contrary to my experience, evolved beings.

The fact simply is, though, dogs are often attendees to the most signal events in our lives—all those occasions off to the side of us simply going hunting: successive so-so marriages, beating cancer, loving your son anew, writing your first song with words in it, getting old. Croaking. "What does it mean to you be almost seventy years old?" I heard a man ask McGuane a couple of summers ago. "It means," McGuane said, rather affably, "that I won't be burying any more bird dogs." We all laughed. But we all also thought: Right. There's a good thing. Even the grim reaper comes with consolations.

It's just hard to express the quiddity, what we used to call the meaning, of a mostly mute, mostly approving creature who accompanies us through our highest and lowest moments. I've suppressed so many consequential things in my life that I can only now and then limn them out—and then unexpectedly—by remembering what dog I had at the time. Sweet Montana Rose. Dixie Doodle. Little Lulu. Scooter I. Scooter II. Chloë. To fit into the right words the nature of this complex, adjunctive relationship and still do it and ourselves justice requires a privileged speech, a little excess, a few liberties taken, the random allegorization— even reverie. Literature always does that to express the ineffable. And we don't mind as long as it just seems true at the end.

A couple of years ago, I hauled myself up to the Metropolitan to take in an exhibit on the history of modern photography as revealed in the work itself. All the greats were represented at their best—Fox Talbot, Julia Margaret Cameron, Gustave LeGray. But on my bus ride back down town I happened to find an article from that day's *New York Times*, in which the writer was seeking to sum up the impact of the very exhibit I'd been seeing just a half hour before: "All used the camera," this writer wrote, "to find bigness in themselves, and in their new medium." These words struck me, and I think about them all the time now—half believing they're true about art, half believing they're not. Not always, anyway. But there's room, isn't there, in our moral pantheon for the small good thing that simply stays what it is? Hunting wild birds behind a trained dog—for those of us who still do it, us oldsters, us anachronisms—is precisely that, with the stress laid on *good*. The writers in this volume—for all they know of life, love, flora, fauna, whatever their skill-set—know this, too, and gratefully. Life's going in the direction of less for all of us. We're not dummies. We had it in full when we had it, and we loved it. What's left is maybe a remnant of what once was whole, but it's still large enough to get us up and out in the morning, large enough to celebrate, to revel in, to tell and tell again. Think of this book then in that way. As a celebration. It won't disappoint.

Old Dog

Rick Bass

I drove through parts of three states to get to the best hospital in the West. I felt good, or hopeful, from the minute I parked the car in the one wedge of available shade. Everywhere around me, it seemed, grad student-clinicians and assistants, looking imminently professional in their clean white smocks, were walking dogs across the green lawns that were of the vet hospital's domain. Sanitary trash cans and scoops were stationed regularly along the sidewalk, and each grad student walked a different breed of dog across invisible territories—each possessing its own intangible space—and each dog had its own unique ailment. Some were only hinted at by a certain limp, while others bore their afflictions, or the residue or legacy of just-excised afflictions, more visibly: a patchwork assemblage of dogdom with shaved heads and bellies, cast-plastered legs, and wide spaceship-looking protective neck cones. I felt bad about leading Point—with his own mysterious affliction so evident, swollen as he was now like a beach ball—through and past such a confederation, knowing that even Point, usually oblivious to the world of any nuances that were not immediately dog- or bird-related, would nonetheless be able to do the math on this one.

And sure enough, as we approached the wide glass double-doors, which hissed open automatically as we crossed some invisible threshold, he stopped and then slunk to his belly and refused to go any farther, nor could I pull him forward on the leash; nor did I want to, for I knew it was important that his first experience with his doctors be a good one.

I turned around and took him back to the car—he was delighted to leap back up into the front seat, stubbed tail wagging, as if to say, "Whew, boss, that was a close one, glad you rethought it. What were you possibly thinking?"

I left him in the car, cracked the windows, and went back inside to register and meet with the doctor and grad student who would be assigned to him: and I had to admit even I—practiced in such a world for forty-eight-plus years—did not feel too great about passing through those double doors.

Once inside, however, I felt better. The greeting area was clean and spacious, a vast circle with an immense skylight, through which poured radiant light. The tile floors were inlaid with the bronzed facsimiles of various animal tracks, and there were couches and coffee tables arranged leisurely throughout. In no way did it seem like a place of crisis; if anything, it seemed the opposite, and I was encouraged to realize that while illness was universal, so too was recovery—or at least here, it was, or seemed to be.

I filled out my paperwork and then was introduced to my vet, Dr. Mordecai, and his assistant, Laura. Such was their professional bearing and demeanor—concerned and attentive—that I could not quite tell at first who was the student and who was the lead veterinarian, until Dr. Mordecai explained.

The straws at which we tend to grasp when in a fear-based situation! I was still bleary from the road, trying to transition to real time, but what struck me at first was Dr. Mordecai's last name, with its proximity to the derivative for death—*he must be great*, I thought, *a kind of a Boy-Named-Sue phenomenon*—and in similar literary fashion I was comforted by his first name, Adam—certainly for the Biblical perspective, but also

Rick Bass & Auna, Point's successor.

(*Courtesy of Rick Bass*)

by my remembering that it was the first name of the super-doctor, Adam Stanton, in Robert Penn Warren's classic novel, *All The King's Men*—the Great American Novel, I would suggest, with its themes of power, corruption, innocence, time, and history.

Dr. Mordecai and Laura and I visited a bit more about the patient, and after having gone through a lengthy list of questions, they looked around and suggested that I could go ahead and bring him in for them. (Elsewhere around the lobby, other patients were sitting on couches and in cushioned chairs, visiting with their new vets, with their dogs sitting smartly at heel as their owners stroked their heads, or with their cats sitting prim in their laps, some purring and others listless, vacuous.)

"Well," I said, "I was hoping you could help me carry him in." The way they looked at each other, I could tell this was not standard operating procedure, had maybe never even happened before—if a physically capable dog did not want to go someplace, did not you merely pull a little more firmly on the leash—particularly given the leash-holder's advantage of the tiled floor underfoot?

"Just try and bring him in on the leash, and we can help," they said. They assured me they had gotten pretty good at handling all manner of animals and were up for any challenge.

To argue or protest would have been disrespectful, so I went back out to the car and snapped on Point's leash and led him back toward the hospital. And trusting soul that he was, he jogged along happily, barrel-belly swaying and sloshing as if pregnant, or like the ponderous, joyful swagger employed by certain aging sluggers who no longer have to play the field, but are instead called upon only to stand at the plate a few times each year and swat almost lazily, but powerfully, at the buzzing fastballs. On the way there, he stopped again at the various scent-markings of his predecessors, giving his nose in particular, I could tell, to the more recent signatures of dogs in estrus—and it was all I could do to pull him off such scents; as if he had all but mounted an invisible dog, so committed was he to that one place, that one space, in which nothing was visible, but in which an entire world, another world, existed.

I stood there letting him take one more sniff—I could see the doctor and his assistant standing in the lobby, watching and waiting. Point crouched, lifted his leg to spray a sprinkle of his own existence while I looked out at the arid hills and thin and heated haze-blue summer sky beyond the facility. There were fences and gates behind the big building, pasture land where the horses were kept—the real treasures, I supposed, in terms of people's finances, if not per-pound capita of heart—some of the most valuable horses in the world came here for treatment and recovery, animals that might easily be bought and sold for six-figure prices—race horses, show horses, stallions, and breeding mares—and again, clutching at straws that had no bearing on the situation at hand—either Point had myxosarcoma, or he didn't; if it was instead a tumor blocking some duct, it would either be operable and correctable, or not, regardless of the name of the vet, or the history and professionalism of the facility—I was nonetheless reassured to realize that there well could be several million dollars' worth of horses back there behind that wall, getting stethoscoped and hoof-trimmed and what-not.

I pulled harder on his leash; it was time to face the music. It was hard to believe how strong a little forty-five-pound dog could be unless you had experienced it firsthand. Compact and dense as iron, he was impossible to hold when he did not want to be held. On one hunt in southeastern Montana, he had tangled with a porcupine at dusk, and my two hunting partners and I—three grown men—had not been able to hold him down to extricate even a simple quill, nor had the vet, a fourth, once we took him in to town. Seven hundred pounds of man versus forty-five pounds of German shorthaired pointer, and it wasn't even close.

I tugged harder, and finally he released his nose-hold on that mysterious patch of ground and resumed trotting amiably alongside me. And despite the fact that we were once more approaching those double doors, he seemed utterly relaxed, was utterly trusting—believing with dog-like certainty that now that he had indicated his preference on the matter, I would not lead him back to those hissing double doors, beyond which lay malady and infirmity: nothing of which, he would have been the first to assure me, had anything to do with him.

And would that have been denial, on his part, or was it simply a fiercer and more powerful, more persistent, reality than my own?

He pulled me along toward our destination—willing, always, to cast in whatever direction I aimed him, and in his surges, his lunging hops toward such a blind destination, any destination, he seemed as strong as one of the horses out in the pastures beyond, or an ox, or a bull.

We passed beneath the porch awning, past the elegant xeric landscaping and the park benches, toward those doors, and it was not until they clicked and slid open that Point's surging lunges ceased, and he threw himself flat to the ground like a commando and began inching backwards.

I stepped forward and picked him up—with his swelling, he was a good twenty percent heavier—and for a moment, I was able to hold him, but as soon as I took a step toward the doors, he began to writhe and twist wildly, and in his wriggling, seemed somehow able to increase his body weight threefold—a trick known also to children who do not wish to be carried—as if summoning a secret partnership with the universe, in which the resister is granted, for a short while, the density of kryptonite.

I had to set him back down before he knocked me down. I called out to Dr. Mordecai—so near, yet so far away—just a few more steps!—that I had a plan, then whirled and retreated—galloped, with a grateful

Point—back to the car; and to Dr. Mordecai and Laura, it surely seemed that we had had second thoughts, had gotten cold feet, and were bailing, escaping back to Montana, where we would hunker down and let nature and destiny—whatever that was—take its course.

Instead, I loaded Point into his portable kennel—a plastic cage-contraption that filled the entire back of the Subaru—and then, like Atlas, hoisted it, with bouncy dog inside, and began struggling my way back toward the mythical double doors, where Dr. Mordecai and Laura met me, and assisted me from that point, helping to ferry the kennel (with its thrashing, shifting cargo inside) across that threshold not so much like pallbearers, but like the carriers of a potentate. Once we had reached the inner sanctum, we opened the gate (I was reminded of the chutes that spring open at rodeos, expelling the rogue saddle bronc or the bull), and as Point rushed out, we surrounded him, praised and petted him—he peered about suspiciously, suspecting dimly that some trickery had just occurred—and then led him gingerly to the floor scales for that most basic and preliminary of the admittance procedures, where he decided to resist again, lifting one foot, then two feet, rearing and rolling and doing the kryptonite thing again, and peeing great volumes on the shining-clean floor. I knew that it was a much peed-upon floor, that it was tile for a purpose—"Don't worry about that," they said, and some helpers came quickly with paper towels and disinfectant—and after trying to get even the roughest of quick-flash readings—1.7, 24, 55, 20—Dr. Mordecai and Laura decided to estimate him at forty-five pounds, which was perhaps irrelevant anyway, due to all of his fluid retention.

I picked him up and managed to carry him into the examining room, where, again, he peed voluminously, and would not hold still to have his temperature taken—again, three people, professionals, simply could not accomplish it—and I wondered—again, irrelevantly, and behind-the-curve—if there was any way they could see him as I saw him—as a loveable, noble, powerful companion, with a deep and wonderful long history of sweetness and greatness—or if they instead saw him as he was, and only in the moment: a scarred and grizzled old knee-scabbed swollen ill-mannered hound from the sticks, dragged kicking if not screaming into the big city for which he was utterly unsuited.

Even I, who knew how he was when he was in his element, was suddenly having trouble seeing him through my old eyes, and I suspected that the vets assumed he was always this way: ungovernable, unmanageable, and perhaps no longer suited for life.

It was a useless worry, a fantastic paranoia—they were professionals; their job was to treat and if possible cure illness—but still, I could not help but notice what a spectacular pain in the ass he was being.

What could I tell him—that they were here to help him? The only procedure he would even remotely allow them to perform was to listen to his chest with the stethoscope. He wasn't hostile or snappish—they saw plenty of that, I knew, so I hoped that counted for something—but still, he was *mercurial*; and were it not for the obscene bloating, I have no doubt they would have said, "Get this dog out of here, he's the strongest and healthiest we've ever seen."

Dr. Mordecai listened to Point's heart a little longer and then lifted the instrument from his ears and announced that he had a murmur, though it was far too soon to tell if that was a cause or an effect. He asked if I knew whether that was a pre-existing condition, and when I told him no vet had ever heard one before, he frowned and mulled it over, and then excused himself to go consult with some of the other vets.

I sat there in the little examining room with Point and tried to calm him, tried to distract him from his relentless pacing, though to no avail. He had always gone where I had asked him, without complaint, and I had always taken him to wonderful places—scent-filled places, game-filled places—and so this was a big change for him, for us, and I could not help but feel that part of his agitation was due to the fact that he was as worried by this inconsistency—my apparent lapse in judgment—as he was by the physical surroundings and the incarceration itself. He was not a dog to brood about relationships, but as he paced the sterile room, and as I sat on the floor trying to pet him every time he circled past, I sensed an agitation and confusion, a sustained alarm, that had nothing to do with his body's changes or his illness, and everything to do with his inability to convince me to leave.

We waited a long time, and when Dr. Mordecai came back, he was prepared: he had mapped out a schematic system of possibilities, along with a graduated scale of how to pursue and explore these possibilities, which included various cancers—some relatively fixable, others dire. X-rays would be the first course, and we'd go from there. Biopsies, tissue laparoscopies, CT scans, MRIs, and exploratory surgery were the other options, in order of increasing complexity and cost, and beyond that, chemical treatments and radiation.

I blanched, rejecting those last two out of hand—I had heard stories of people who, desperate to keep their pets alive, had spent all those thousands of dollars, and, worse yet, had subjected their animals to increased and advanced suffering—the animal unable to understand the reason, the payoff, for such reductions and diminishments—and I had never even remotely understood such decisions—had felt pity for those who followed that path.

I was desperate to do whatever could be done for Point: it was why I had come to Pullman. But I was resolved to do nothing that would diminish his quality of life. No matter what emotional comfort he provided me, a creature whose existence was so predicated upon a physical mastery of his world, with all the senses functioning with at-times hyperbolic intensity, deserved all or nothing. He was different from a person, in that regard. He was a pet, and a loving one, but was more wild than domestic.

Dr. Mordecai paused, listening to what I was saying on this count, and while it was useful for him to know each owner's sentiments as he proceeded through his diagnosis and prescription, and while he was careful not to lobby or impose his decisions or personal opinions, he did want to clarify the mention of chemical and radiation treatments.

They did work, he said, in various instances, as did the chemical treatments—not always, of course—and they were also capable of extending life. Further, they were not even remotely as expensive as they were for humans, and were much reduced in intensity and duration. Many times the side effects were not even noticeable. He spoke carefully, letting me know he was not agreeing or disagreeing with me, but simply giving me a kind of quick primer or overview of what he meant when he said chemical or radiation treatment; and I remembered this was a different breed of hospital. All vets seek to care for and heal, if possible, all animals, but this clinic had tools at its disposal that it had used before and would use again; more than any other place, perhaps, they were committed and prepared to follow something all the way to the end, until they finally vanquished even the last remnant of illness, which might in the end glow like but a single spark.

Dr. Mordecai went back to the top of the list. He was recommending at the very minimum an X-ray and a blood sample—the most basic of work-ups. I reiterated my fear of leading Point—and myself—down some slippery slope, probing and sawing and excising and stitching, with the poison, the disease, eventually swamping him. Dr. Mordecai and Laura understood my fears and concerns—that I did not want to lead him into any suffering—but they also didn't yet have the first clue as to what was wrong. Maybe he had just swallowed a damned pine cone, or a ground squirrel. Maybe this was all a bad dream, and we would yet escape this—would be out in the bright sun and summery heat, whole once more, and unconcerned. Oblivious, once more.

"I do have to warn you," Dr. Mordecai said, "Cancer is the first thing we look for or expect, in an aged dog."

I nodded, trying to hold back the tears welling. I had been preparing myself to hear that for days, but evidently I had not done a good enough job.

And how inarticulate I must have seemed, with my repeated concerns that I didn't want to make choices that would lead him into suffering. Did I come here to try to get him fixed, or not? Why couldn't I be more assertive, more aggressive, instead of all cautious and tiptoe-ish—trying to sneak up on this thing? Just shoot the damn X-ray, then go from there.

But I wanted all the answers at once. I wanted to know the future, all at once: every minute and every mile. I wanted to know things no doctor could tell me, and things that no battery of tests could provide. How long, and what quality?

They led him off on a leash—he gladly scooted through the open door, and then balked when I parted down one hallway while he was to travel down another—and I went out into the waiting room to wait.

The chairs were comfortable, and the light slanting down through high glass window-walls was pleasurable. The waiting itself was torturous. They might find anything. The blood tests would take a little longer than the X-rays, but they, too, might reveal some awful truth.

I had brought some paperwork, knowing I might be down here for days, but I couldn't begin to concentrate; I shuffled the papers in that beautiful light, in that beautiful and strangely serene facility, and just waited, still caught in that no-man's land, the territory between my old reality and the imposition of the world's greater or larger reality, being revealed to me now with an ever-broadening view. Each melting second carried me further into it, and—like Point in the hallway—I kept wanting to go back.

★ ★ ★

The wait was only a couple or three hours, during which, as I thumbed through every dog and cat and horse and parrot magazine available, turning the pages without reading or even really looking, I felt a kind of cage springing up around my heart, with a confining structure being built by the vertical spikes of fear and hope that would surge upward every time one of the white-suited doctors would stride through the sunlit atrium, white-coated, purposeful, and fully alive. But always, they were other doctors, working on other patients.

By this time my heart was locked up by those spikes of hope—spikes that seemed to be made manifest now by those coming-and-going doctors. In such a cage, my heart still could beat just as strongly, but was unable to escape.

By this point I was negotiating with the blue sky out the window: asking for only one more hunt. Best of all, one more pheasant hunt. Dove and grouse season started Labor Day weekend—thirty-two days distant. Pheasant season didn't begin until the second week of October—seventy days distant—and what would have been the greatest miracle, I told myself, would be not just one more rooster over my little speckled dog, but one more rooster rising iridescent and cackling, ring-necked and golden-eyed, crimson-wattled and blue-shanked, out of the snow—rising vertically into the deep blue sky of winter, and with the bird so colorful, against that background of snow, as to seem incapable of being something that the earth could produce or contain.

The bird would fall, of course, as they always fall, in dreams—and because I would have been preparing for the shot for seventy days, or

100—however many it took—before that first snow fell. I guess it was pretty much a prayer.

★ ★ ★

When my doctors appeared, they were striding not in useless tangents directed away from me, as had all the others, but were coming straight on, walking through that sunlight in a purposeful manner that was neither somber nor celebratory. I could tell nothing from either their gait or their countenance.

I don't remember the words they used, the sentences and phrases. They needed to run some more tests, they said, but basically the blood work was okay, and the X-rays were negative. What they thought might be going on was a leaking heart valve. "Is that something that could be fixed with surgery?" I asked, and they said it wouldn't require anything that drastic, just some medicine. Some pills, I think, and maybe a diuretic, to help keep the fluid from building up.

They may have said, "It's certainly not life-threatening"—at least not in the short term. They might have said, "No problem, we see nothing to worry about." I can't remember the words, only the confusion I felt, the massive imbalance, from having leaned so hard and so far one way, only to then be asked to lean in the other direction. Their words were a confusion, the bright atrium sunlight was a confusion, and most confusing of all was the temptation I was being offered: to take one step forward into the land of miracles.

I could hear and understand the words they were saying, but I could find no emotional registry on which to place them. It was not so much disbelief as emotional incomprehension. I could understand the science and the good luck and the consequences, but there was no place within me where those words would lodge.

They wanted to keep him overnight, they said—I forget why, now—they would run some kind of sonic heart-gram, I think, which would verify his leaky old heart. They suggested a hotel just down the road where I could stay, and they would call that night with their findings.

I told them it was possible I knew the precise day he had injured his heart valve, if that's what it was. It would have been almost a year earlier, over on the east side. We had been out hunting sharptails, and his buzz-collar had broken—had snapped and fallen all the way off, lost somewhere out in the vast expanse of dense cover we were hunting. It was early season, hot, and he found the sharptails, which began flying. He began chasing them, and without the buzz-collar, I could not motivate him to return from such joy. He ran for a long time—just as he used to do when he was a young dog—except he no longer was a young dog, he was suddenly nine years old, that year.

By the time he had pursued the last sharptail down to the bottom of the cover, a mile distant, and then had come running back up the hill—being distracted and diverted, along the way, by other scents—the September heat was blazing, he was panting like a fiend, like a locomotive, and could barely even walk. I poured him some water, but he wouldn't even drink it. We started walking back to the truck—Elizabeth and Lowry were with me—but after only a few steps, he began wobbling as if drunk, and then pitched forward into the grass.

I thought he was stone dead, then. I hurried to him, picked him up—he revived, regained consciousness, still panting mightily—and I gave the gun to Elizabeth and began carrying him out, holding him at chest-level in the deep cover, the equivalent of a fifty-pound sack of potatoes, sweat roaring off me beneath that bronze-hazed sky.

He protested being carried, however—writhing and twisting violently each time he recovered consciousness, clamoring to be set back down on the ground—desperate to keep hunting, and totally incapable of accepting what he clearly viewed as the indignity of being carried off the field. It was he who had led me across the fields, always he who charged out ahead while I followed; it had never been any other way but that, and certainly, he had never needed babying, mollycoddling, or assistance of any kind.

I had to set him down each time his writhing became too powerful for me to be able to hold him, at which point he would resume pushing forward, hunting again, but then weaving again, before pitching forward onto his face.

I got him out. We went back to the little high-plains prairie-house— little more than a small yellow box out on the plains, holding tight against all the year's elements—where he slept as if dead all night, and then in the morning he bounced up, eager and willing to go to work again, and betraying no sign of the malady that had felled him the day before.

There in Pullman, Washington, so many hundreds of miles away from his hunting grounds, the doctors shrugged. "Maybe," they said, "Maybe he hurt it that day." They might have glanced at each other for the briefest of moments, puzzled by my lack of exultation, my hesitancy to accept and embrace wonderful news. But none of those feelings were in me. The words that would supposedly have helped create and nurture those emotions were there, but instead, all I felt was extreme caution and, at best, something close to a huge relief—except that I could not trust it. It was relief without faith yet, and as such, artificial, vacuous.

The doctors nodded, seeming to understand. They had probably seen it all before. They had probably seen everything.

★ ★ ★

I checked into the hotel room, which was so similar to those eastern Montana high prairie wind boxes that I felt an acute homesickness, and a magic, too: as if, by sheer desire alone, time had been catapulted forward several weeks, so that it was already September, and hunting season. As if it were no trick at all, to spring further and faster forward in time, but that the impossible thing would always be to go back, or even hold still for longer than a blink. Not even a blink.

Like those windswept ancient cottages where we stayed in eastern Montana, this room too had a view that opened to wheat country. It was haunting—wheat, in that regard, being the fuel, the lifeblood force for my speckled dog, in that it supported the birds that supported his fiery heart—and there was a proverbial ocean of it just outside the window, but my dog was not with me, and it was not yet hunting season. Looking out the window of that 1950s-era trailer-court room (frayed chenille bedspread, black-and-white TV, decrepit, clanky air-conditioning unit, rust-stained sink and bath, but clean), the world he loved most was right there, right out the window, as if but another step away—as if opening morning was the very next day—but that was only how it looked, it was not really how things were.

★ ★ ★

I napped restlessly, sprawled on the bed with arms outflung as if having fallen there from the ceiling, still fully dressed, having not even taken my shoes off. At some point in the evening I heard a slight rumble of traffic—it was a college town—and I opened my eyes once to observe, in that blink, the approach of sunset, and then I closed my eyes without moving at all and napped again, until the jangle of the old phone brought me back up into the world, not levitating me, electrocution-style, but instead bringing me back up slowly, as if coming up from the sleep of anæsthesia: the fearsome and ultimately narcotizing chemicals of stress and grieving only gradually releasing their hold, deigning to slough and slide away like exfoliating scales of salt, or even some precious heavy metal that had been keeping me buried in the muck at the bottom of the sea. As those glittering scales slid away, plate by plate, I was able to sit up higher and higher in the bed, and perceive my accruing piecemeal return to the present reality: sick dog, strange-yet-familiar hotel room, bad situation, sore heart.

It was 10:00 PM straight up, the point at which the hotel clerk shut off her old-fashioned switchboard for the night—the call had eked through by seconds—and when I answered, it was Dr. Mordecai.

I got the impression he was calling from his home, but was still on the case—had been on the case all day, and all evening. He said that when he left the clinic earlier that evening, Point had been doing fine. Dr. Mordecai had been on the phone with several colleagues and after consulting with them, he was leaning toward thinking that the simple heart-valve hypothesis was not sufficient, was not accurate; that there was something much more serious going on; that that might still be a part of it, but was not the whole of it.

It wasn't just a wearing-out heart valve, he said, but mesothelioma, caused by exposure to asbestos—the first dog in Lincoln County, Montana, it turned out, to be diagnosed with it, the sentinel case, almost certainly courtesy of the W. R. Grace asbestos mine—but that is a different story. All dogs are born with a death sentence, they hunt for us, and then they are gone. They do not get to stay either young or strong forever. It's an old truth but still we have to relearn it with each dog.

There was no cure. I had some things to think about. I would have to make some decisions for him.

★ ★ ★

Needless to say—mesothelioma!—he didn't get better.

He is gone now and I'm still here, still eating some of the birds he got for me. Someday I will be old and diminished as well. This is the biggest problem with hunting dogs: a young man can start out with a young dog but then is still young when the dog is old. A disynchrony that, unless one is careful, can approach gracelessness.

Do old hunters work with young dogs? Is there likewise capacity for similar, or opposite, disynchrony in that relationship?

Where is the balance?

It's hard. You think it's all fun and games. What a mercy that we forget how hard it sometimes is, or can be, one day. Will be.

Last Dance for the Ladies

Tom Brokaw

This is the story of two Labrador ladies: one, an elegant, highly intelligent, and self-confident blonde, the other, her kissing cousin, a tautly shaped, raven-haired bundle of energy and anxiety. The blonde was known to a wide circle of admirers as Sage, the Wonder Dog. The cousin was called Abbie, a name assigned by her Scottish breeders before she arrived in our family at the age of two.

My wife and I have been so willing to arrange our lives to accommodate Sage and Abbie that in a vain attempt to re-claim some dignity we say aloud from time to time, "Good God, we're the kind of people we used to make fun of." It doesn't change our behavior but we do take some comfort in acknowledging our weakness in their presence.

They, in turn, demand nothing more than regular meals, soft beds, hands-on affection, and deep grass hillsides or fields of grain so they can exercise their God-given abilities to find upland birds, send them aloft and, if their master doesn't screw up, retrieve for him the shot-gunned quarry.

But I am ahead of myself.

Tom Brokaw, Abbie & Sage.

(Courtesy of Tom Brokaw)

We were empty nesters, our last-born child having departed for Duke. Meredith decided we needed a dog to fill the vacuum. She heard about a litter in Colorado sired by Chopper, the legendary avalanche dog at the top of Aspen Mountain.

Sage came from that litter first to our ranch in Montana where from her earliest age she demonstrated a unique combination of curiosity and what can only be described as canine self-confidence. She seemed to know she had royalty in her bloodline.

When Sage arrived, she was nameless and remained so for several weeks as we struggled to find the right call sign while remembering the admonition to pick a name that also serves as a command. Preferably one syllable and punchy.

We were struggling until a family friend suggested running through the spices. Rosemary and thyme may work for Paul Simon but not for a bird dog. But Sage? Yes. Perfect, especially for a dog already showing signs of innate wisdom and, besides, she was starting life nosing through the sagebrush on the surrounding hills.

Sage seemed to understand her moniker brought with it certain expectations of self-confidence and making the right choices.

Shortly before acquiring Sage I had edged back into shooting again after a hiatus brought on by the lethal consequences of 1968 when two of my heroes, Dr. Martin Luther King, Jr., and Robert F. Kennedy, were gunned down. I had moved up from the Remington Wingmasters of my South Dakota youth to my friends' over-and-under Berettas and Purdeys at their exclusive shooting clubs in New York.

My eye had not left me, and the old thrill of nailing a pheasant on afterburners had returned. I began to wonder, could this new dog become a boon companion in the field?

From her earliest days with us she was nose down and tail up whenever we wandered into the hills surrounding our ranch, endlessly curious and focused.

I called a well known trainer in upstate New York, Jerry Cacchio, who came highly recommended. He set the tone quickly. "You celebrities all think you've got a bird dog. You'll have to leave her with me for six weeks at least before we find out." We hesitated, but agreed that, however Sage turned out, the training would he helpful for her as a pet.

Three weeks after we dropped her off, Cacchio called to say, "Come get your dog." Damn, I thought, she flunked out. "No," Cacchio assured me, "You're a lucky guy. This is a smart dog. I can't teach her much more. You and I are going to spend a lot of time together."

It was a conversation that changed my life. I had a *bird dog*. Now the challenge was to get her into the field as swiftly as possible. And so began one of the unexpected but altogether harmonic experiences of my life, an annual rite of man, dog, friends, guns, and cackling roosters in the autumnal glory of the high plains or the quick flush of Hungarian partridge and sharptail grouse in the sagebrush-dotted landscape of Park County, Montana.

On our first trip back to South Dakota, my hunting pals were simultaneously skeptical and patronizing: "A New York dog, here in the mother lode of wily wild pheasants, competitive canines, thick cover, country boy shooters, and hunting as high church? Ho ho."

Two memories from those first hunts will linger forever. Sage was in a post-puppy phase, still finding her way when we hunted with friends in a sprawl of vast cornfields. I had left the main party with Sage to work her in a more isolated corner of the grain when I heard Meredith shouting to send her back. My friend Emmett had downed a rooster and the other dogs had not been able to find it in the jungle of unpicked corn spilling over the horizon.

I said simply to Sage, "Go to Meredith," and she sprinted off a hundred yards to the main party. Meredith pointed to the general area where the pheasant had gone down and said, "Sage, get the bird." Sage turned and rocketed into the standing stalks for a few moments and then came strolling out with a dead pheasant locked firmly in her jaws. Sage dropped the retrieved bird at Meredith's feet and raced back to join me in our corner of the field.

Emmett turned to Meredith and said, "You know, it's a shame that dog has to live in a New York apartment. Why don't you leave her here with me?" Nice try, no deal.

The following autumn Sage sat up in the passenger compartment of the plane I had chartered to central South Dakota as we drifted down to a small strip near Platte, a farming community in the heart of corn, soybean, and cattle country. Sage's ears were cocked and her nostrils were wide before we taxied to a stop. She was a long way from her New York home but she knew *exactly* where she was and what was expected of her.

For the next three days she put on a gold medal performance of finding, flushing, and retrieving a rich harvest of wild pheasants in corn, beans, sunflowers, grass, and tree rows, moving at a steady, fluid gait with no episodes of whining or yelping while she gave equal attention to the eight hunters she was serving.

In a deep ravine hard by the Missouri river, the prairie grass had grown so thick it created a long, winding tunnel of cover along the dry creek bed at the bottom. Sage quickly determined it was the equivalent of a pheasant bunker, and she fearlessly dove in and disappeared from view. But we could track her by the nervous movement of the grass speeding along in two distinct clumps: first, pheasants racing through what they thought was their sanctuary, followed closely by Sage.

We raised our guns, knowing this couldn't go on forever and then—boom—at one end, the roosters exploded into the cerulean sky, followed closely by a streaking blur of golden dog fur. Bang, bang— one, two roosters went down, but one managed to get airborne again, however momentarily. Sage leaped four feet into the air and snatched it back to earth.

My friend Terry Ring, the soft-spoken proprietor of Silver Creek Outfitters, Sun Valley's premier gun and fly fishing shop, turned to me and said matter of factly, "I've been doing this a long time; I don't think I've seen a better dog."

That night I retreated to my bedroom to read, and Sage went along. I was in bed with a book and Sage resting her head on my chest when a college friend looked in on us. I could tell from his expression that he would have been less jealous if I had won the Nobel Peace Prize.

From that day and night on Sage was not just my dog; she was my mistress and no one was more understanding than Meredith.

When Sage was tight by my side on the sidewalks of New York, cornfields and CRP plots of the Great Plains, sage-covered hills of Montana, and streamside as I fished through the summer months, we moved seamlessly through a zone of serenity, bound by deep mutual affection and dependence.

It was a pattern happily repeated season after season and then enhanced by the arrival of Abbie when Sage was eight years old.

On her baptismal trip to South Dakota, Abbie was confused. She'd been trained to retrieve, not to flush, so on opening day she stayed close by my side in the first field while Sage reconnoitered the landscape. After a few moments Sage simply looked back over her shoulder at Abbie, as if to say, "Okay, rookie, let me show you a trick or two."

I sent Abbie to Sage's side and then hit but did not kill a feisty rooster who immediately went into the evade-and-escape mode. As the pheasant darted off, Sage led Abbie on a serpentine track, her nose down and tail up, until they caught up to the wounded bird and brought it back to my feet.

Later on that cold and windy day I dispatched Sage to help my friends hunt a band of trees bordering a cornfield while I kept Abbie with me to work on her commands. My back was to a barbed wire fence that separated the field from a ditch and a gravel road when a cackling rooster throttled out of the tree line just as a carload of local hunters stopped on the road to watch the action. I swung my 20-gauge hard from left to right, thinking, "Please, God, don't let me blow this shot in front of the good ol' boys." It was a clean kill over the road, and the big cock pheasant went down in the deep grass of the far ditch.

I released Abbie, who took four strides, cleared the fence in a powerful, yet graceful leap, and streaked to the far side of the road where she grabbed the pheasant and returned it swiftly to my side. As she resumed her sitting position, the carload of locals broke into whistles and cheers.

I've interviewed presidents and royalty, rock stars and movie stars, famous generals and captains of industry; I've had front row seats at Super Bowls, World Series, and Olympic Games; my books have been on bestseller lists, and my marriage is a long running success. That day with Sage and Abbie is right up there when I come to reckon, "How did one guy get so lucky?"

Somewhere in the deep recesses of my mind and heart, however, I knew this couldn't go on forever. Somewhere out there beneath an ominously grey sky of late autumn in the American West, when the birds were blitzing the steady winds, the day would come when Sage and Abbie would make their final retrieve.

That each would do that with élan and dignity in her own way is one more tribute to their individual and collective place in that part of my soul I reserve for greatness that I've encountered.

★ ★ ★

When Sage turned thirteen, I knew the day was fast approaching. She was hobbled by arthritis, and her hearing was as dim as my own. Still, she maintained her essential majesty, never more elegantly than when I returned from a long, difficult trip to Iraq and stumbled into our bedroom for a recuperative nap. As I lay down I could hear Sage laboriously working her way up the stairs to our bedroom. Just as I was about to drift off, she somehow managed to struggle onto our bed and stretched out beside me, placing her head affectionately on my shoulder as if to say, "Welcome home, partner. I missed you."

A few weeks later we were back in Montana for a weekend of shooting Hungarian partridge on a snowy weekend. My friend Ron had flown in from Los Angeles, and we both knew this was going to be tough duty for my aging ladies, Sage and Abbie.

They were game but the birds were scattered by the storms and so we spent a couple of hours trudging through deep snow and up slippery hills. As we were walking back to my pickup we passed a thick hawthorn bush on a steeply pitched hillside leading into a marsh belly deep in white, wet snow.

Without a word from me, Sage did a sharp right turn and plunged into the bush. I shouted to Ron to be ready, and he clocked a partridge forty yards out in the snowy marsh grass. Sage was on the retrieve, making her way through the drifts like a swimmer stroking against the tide. She collected the little grey bird and turned back to us, the most difficult part of her journey still ahead as we stood atop the pitched embankment.

Abbie rushed down, trying to claim the retrieve but Sage just patiently turned her head until Abbie sheepishly backed off and allowed Sage to make her way steadily to our side. Ron and I were speechless.

Four days later Sage and I were in the sagebrush on another hillside. I shot a double of sharptail grouse and she, for the first time in her life, didn't know where they were. Her eyesight, hearing, and now her matchless nose were going fast.

The following summer we buried her in Montana in a grove of aspens on a hillside overlooking the river where she frolicked with me on my morning plunges and stood as a sentry while I cast for rising trout, awaiting autumn and rising birds.

Abbie lived on but she, too, began to break down, and no combination of drugs or surgery could delay the onset and penalty of withered limbs.

My hunting days were now the province of Red, another yellow Lab, a boy's boy, athletic, and another superior dog in the field. In Abbie's thirteenth year I gathered my gun, shells, and whistle from the locked closet in our Montana farmhouse and started out with Red for an afternoon of grouse.

Abbie rallied herself from the sleeping pad and gave me such a mournful look I succumbed and said, "Ok, you get to go, too." She waggled all the way to the four-wheeler where I lifted her in beside me and drove to a tall stand of bluestem and timothy bordered by chokecherry bushes leading to a sharp incline.

Red was bouncing through the vegetation, onto something, just what, I didn't know, as Abbie followed me through the waist-high grass. Suddenly, Red put up a covey of blue grouse and a separate covey of ruffed grouse simultaneously.

I killed a ruffed and winged a blue at the top of the ridgeline. Red went after the dead bird, and I said to Abbie, "Okay, old girl, we have to find the other." It was a hard, hot hike straight uphill. When we reached the top, I looked around and Abbie was missing. "My God," I thought, "she's died of a stroke or heart attack."

Then, out of the corner of my eye, I saw a black ball of fur tumbling down from the top of the hill, pushing a wounded grouse ahead with her nose. Abbie, her legs now worn out, was sliding and rolling the bird into the bushes where she could trap it against the thick roots. When she reached the bushes, she grabbed the blue in her jaws and lay down, waiting for me to retrieve them both. I pocketed the grouse, picked up Abbie, and carried her down the hill, weeping softly as I kept repeating into her ear, "Good girl, good girl."

Expecting to Be Surprised

Christopher Camuto

It should be noticed that only by hunting
can man be in the country . . . .

—José Ortega y Gasset

During the first year of their lives, bird dogs learn to their enormous disappointment that men hunt in seasons. Not seasons as dogs sense them in their fur and through their noses, but arbitrary seasons unfathomable to the canine mind. A good dog comes to accept this outwardly—he or she eventually understands that there will be no hunting in April or August—but not inwardly. Scrape a chair back at midnight on some mellow June evening and the bird dog sleeping under your desk will leap to its feet eagerly, sure that the hunt is on. Not hard to guess what it was dreaming. Patch—who is now six—still does this nearly every night, bouncing and dancing in the hallway where my bird-hunting vest is hung, trying to urge me onto a new idea, a radical practice, the Tao of dogs.

Christopher Camuto & Patch.

(Courtesy of Christopher Camuto)

You have to laugh. And you have to agree. Why not? Work is hard and, in the end, dull. Why not go out the door on a balmy June night and hunt birds in the insect-buzzing starlight, count coup on Carolina wrens and chickadees with Vega and Altair winking overhead? Get the neighbors up and start a bonfire down by the river to celebrate the new order of things, the world according to dogs. I have no doubt that would be fine. No matter how much they come to love you in that unstinting way dogs love, bird dogs must wonder to their dying day what poverty of spirit, what failure of imagination could have hold of their gun-toting partners during the months when there is no hunting.

★ ★ ★

In October we tumble out of the truck on a frosty morning. Patch dances, clanking away, as I shove water, sandwiches, shells, and some dog treats into the bird vest. I've got my brier-busting Filsons on and a wool sweater that doesn't feel warm enough at first. Grab the whistle, grab the gun and the hunting pouch, and set out through this old apple orchard to see what we can find.

This year no easy bird greets us by flushing through the twisted trees. I like those forgiving crossing shots when you can see what the grouse has in mind. Swing through the well spaced trunks until you find an opening waiting for the low-flying bird. It's more likely a grouse would bust out of the bracken and veer off high like a duck startled off a pond, leaving me to twist around and shoot at the sky. But if I'm going to fantasize, I'm going to make the shots easy.

Apple trees pruned by wind and ice take on a hauntingly wild look, and their mottled fruit tastes tart and dry, as if nature were reclaiming the idea of an apple by taking some of the well bred juiciness and prettiness out of them. The two I pick will add a tang to lunch. The orchard peters out at the head of a hollow through which a strong stream flows. The stream comes out of a rocky cul-de-sac in the side of a mountain north of the orchard, cold water from inside the mountain. Leaf-choked now, half its pools hiding like birds under cover, the stream doesn't so much flow as wait, cool water in rocky bowls, a tiny trout or two in each, dace flashing around together mirroring the flock-flight of blackbirds. Quiet and still, the idea of a mountain stream is there, and in the spring its rushing water will speak volumes, and the trout that have come through winter will wax fat on juicy mayflies. When I fish that same stream, lower down, in April, I'll hear grouse drumming up on the slope where we are headed and remember today, when we crossed the stream to hunt the ridge above.

Pleasant as it would be to walk down along the stream, we have to get up on that slope in order to quarter through a mountainside of evergreens and laurel where the birds might be. The breeze we need doesn't hold and except for getting birdy on old scent in the orchard, Patch's coursing around looks pretty aimless. But he is doing what he can with what he has to work with. I whistle him over and we slog uphill to an old logging road that follows the contour we want about a third of the way up that mountainside. I'm hoping that the birds, if they are around, are below us so that we can flush them downslope into the hollow that broadens out around that stream. Otherwise we will have to climb the mountain and quarter back high, which means, among other things, that one of my legs will be shorter than the other at the end of the day.

A quarter mile along that road, Patch gets down to business in some indifferent-looking cover I wouldn't pay much attention to if I were on my own. He's all over the place and scenting low, not finding a living center for his work but nosing through the possibilities in an orderly way. Good bird dogs are thorough, and he knows far more than I do about what's been going on here. I stay behind him to his right, where he has learned to expect me, shotgun up in front of my chest, safety off. Early in the day, the gun feels light and I'm as quick and as good a shot as I will be all day. He worries that cover to pieces for some reason I can't see, and then loops upslope, where he loses interest in his own moves.

The day warms as we hunt along. An October day in the backcountry is like a struck match—cold, hot, cold. At some point I shed my wool sweater, take a draught of water, and chomp around a wormhole in one of those wild apples. We keep to the logging road as the easiest way through the most possibilities. No sense heading into the tough stuff until we see or hear or smell a bird. When Patch whiffs sign, he'll check the woods out on either side. During the course of the season, he'll send a few easy birds to me that way, getting nearly out of earshot and then turning back with a bird between us. I'm not sure how he figured out that move. He'll push a grouse across a logging road and leave me with no excuses for missing. When I bring the bird down in the grass, he gives me the most approving look he possesses. When no bird appears, he has an elaborate way of noticing its absence.

Patch follows the wind combing through the terrain, but it gusts and shifts and then dies, leaving us in eddies where we can't do much. I follow Patch's shifting interests, readying myself when he gets intense around blowdowns and other natural openings where poplar and red maple seedlings are growing in thickly amid grape and greenbrier and other tangled growth best referred to as *whatnot*. Grouse get in stuff that's way beyond my words for things. Any plant or vine or shrub with seed or fruit will bring them for a taste. Birds are nature's most eclectic epicures. On public land, where there has been a lot of disturbance and what passes for "grouse management," there will always be coralberry growing wild and autumn olive plantings, but I'm convinced that the natural openings in mature forests do more for grouse than gimmicks involving bulldozers and backhoes. Take an early-morning walk in the Great Smoky Mountains, and you will find grouse flushing with pleasing frequency in woods that haven't heard a chain saw in eighty years. That's old-style grouse management—the undisturbed life of the woods. Grouse will take these artificial edges now if that's all you give them, but I am convinced they are deep forest creatures, more kin to black bear than quail. And when management areas are no longer managed—the con game having moved on—they become an impossible mess of exotics grown wild—too thick for even a dog to get through.

After a while, it's clear that although he is working hard, Patch is getting nothing serious out of those pines. A warm breeze from the East that feels like it has some staying power turns our heads. Much as I love being out in the Blue Ridge for its own sake, I hate for a day of grouse hunting to degenerate into merely an armed walk. Patch comes to heel on the road, and we confer at the head of a boggy opening that leads down toward a hollow we haven't hunted. That will put us back into the wind. Modest as these old mountains are, and as often as we've been here, we can always find a new place to explore. Sometimes, the earth seems turned differently to the sun, and you find another way into a landscape full of small surprises that were waiting there all along.

We ease around a spring hidden in sphagnum moss and ferns with those little ground pines and club mosses that have a Jurassic look to them spreading all around. There's witch hazel and yellow birch, haw and buckthorn, spicebush, little cedars, and spindly white pines bordered by ranks of ratty post oaks that are small but probably ancient. It looks right for game, the wind is in our faces, and it's a downhill gig. Patch looks over his shoulder at me like this could be the place.

It's a mess getting through there—sometimes what looks open isn't open at all and sometimes biodiversity can be a real pain in the ass. A knee-high tangle keeps me hobbled. Briers grab at the gun and pull at my arms and shoulders. The boggy ground gives way at every step and I feel guilty at every tear in the moss mat. I can feel my wool socks sopping water. My vest hangs up on every other bush. I have to spin and twist from the hip, like a slow-moving running back. Hard to stay steady for a bird. Hard to give a damn about the birds. Patch threads through the post oaks, hitting dead ends of his own. But he is not giving me his *What's the point of this?* look, so we might be on the track of something. You earn your chances bird hunting and you get into the country in ways that are less than lyric. Busting cover is part of the price of admission, if not the most elegant part of the game.

In a couple of hundred yards, the spring seep finds itself a rocky streambed and a bench of land thick with cover under a broken forest opening that looks as birdy as a Robert Abbett painting. Patch cuts himself loose and I whistle him right back in no uncertain terms. I like the reluctance in his obedience, but I need to catch my breath. I want him working close and slow—none of that bird-busting puppy behavior that he slips back into sometimes. I'm looking for a point and a hold, not the joy of the chase. If I could, I'd show him an Abbett painting of a setter working just in front of a companion who is ready for the bird hidden in the composition.

★ ★ ★

Despite the value of prior experience, I probably hunt better in new places, where I move along without any preconceived notions about how the day should go. Hunting grouse, you are expecting to be surprised.

That's a fine way to spend a day, and a hard thing to do for six or eight or ten hours. On a good day you flush two or three birds in the places I hunt—that's ten or twelve *seconds*, figuring three or four seconds between the *Wha?* of a grouse getting up and the *Shit!* of its being gone. That's ten or twelve seconds out of 28,800 in eight hours of hunting and, of course, the kicker is you don't know when the feathers are going to fly. If you really want to flush a grouse, put your gun down and start to take a pee.

Old haunts are marked with previous years' surprises, which will never repeat, no matter how many times you play the tape over in your mind. You can't hunt well with a narrative already laid out, any more than you can write well with too many preconceptions about how a stretch of writing should go. You never know what is waiting for you in the language that will come to mind on a given morning. You have to hunt grouse word by word, as it were. There is no story, just the woods, Patch worrying the cover with fantastic energy until he freezes on point. *Bird!* In hunting, every moment counts, and you need to be ready for whatever flushes from the new day unfolding in front of you and the dog.

★ ★ ★

Patch gets into a tunnel of greenbrier and, watching him work, I have no doubt we've hunted to where we need to be this morning. "Birds, Patch, birds, easy, easy." He's on good scent, but the bird is not there. I let him do his intelligence gathering, his hunting bell clinking purposefully. When there is a bird at stake, Patch will tear himself up in the thick stuff, beat the tip of his tail bloody with a kind of canine excitement that goes from being an elegant extension of my hunting to an awesome display of his own raw hunting powers. He never goes off on his own anymore, but when I see him really getting into it, with his instincts firing pure desire, it's clear he could hunt better without me.

But Patch works at my pace—his highest compliment to me—and now that he's on birds I can stay in the open, keeping my feet free to position for a shot. He works through a few ghost birds, crosses the small stream, which I can hear trickling softly whenever he stops to consider his next move. The day has warmed up, and the heavily scented air is all autumn; the brushwork of the gods in the woods is, as always, quite well done. Would art have come up with nature without the example of it?

The forms? The colors? The deft pathos with which life dies down to its root at the end of the year? Not thoughts I have while waiting tensely for a bird to flush, but thoughts I have writing this, remembering working autumn cover.

Patch does move up on a grouse, which flushes before his flowing point freezes into the stance a painter would capture. Life is not quite like art. But his body language has given me all the warning I need, and I'm set to cover the tough angles into the timber on our right and still be able to swing back toward that beautiful opening in the autumn woods on the left. The bird goes high and left but doesn't get far, its suddenly crumpled flight one of the starkest images of the year, an image of a hard harvest in the yellow woods. I'm excited with adrenaline and relieved to have dropped a bird we came this far to find, but before I even start to bring the gun down I see that Patch did indeed flow into that classic point. And he's not waiting for me to paint his portrait. The second grouse flies low into the timber and, shooting beyond my skills for once, I use the tightly choked second barrel to stop it at the edge of the woods into which it tried to escape.

A poor man's double, I guess, and the only time I've done that. Patch went for the second bird first and waited for me, looking down at it with some sense of the occasion. A true forest creature, ruffed grouse, feathered with the browns of acorns and the red of spicebush and dogwood berries, tail feathers banded black and white like the fins of brook trout. The bird was tumbled over on its back, one wing outstretched oddly, caught reaching in death for one last gout of air. When I picked it up, I could see bloodstains on the sugar maple leaves where it had come to rest. I let Patch get his whiffs and then folded the bird's wings, felt the airy heft of it absent the miracle of its life. I was sobered by my success but unrepentant. I was out in the backcountry with Patch on an October day that flamed in root and branch with the beautiful mortality of things. We were hunting, and hunting comes to this.

Life comes to this, since we depend in one way or another on the lives of other creatures to maintain the vanity of our own existence. That, I think, is the ground on which all life can be said to be sacred, using this word in a purely secular way. Things are sacred because they are. Hunting, so prosaic in its scene and accoutrements, will take you to the bright heart of life and death and measure you against what you think you know about that. It will reveal to you feelings unnamable as the colors of autumn leaves, baffling as the scent of split wood or the tang of wild apples. There are moments, hunting, when you have that uncanny feeling that you are about to remember something very important, like a faded dream is reforming in your mind. That dream or memory doesn't quite coalesce, and you are left only with the rustling autumn day around you. Of course, that is the memory, that is the dream, those rustling autumn hours in the mountains and the feathery colors of a bloodstained grouse, so familiar and so strange in hand, warm bounty of the season that is disappearing around us as we hunt.

I set Patch, no natural-born retriever, to find the first bird in the grassy opening where he gave me that easy shot. He snuffles and circles his way around to it. I sit down on a rock to enjoy what we have accomplished. To suddenly have two plump birds to clean and tuck in the vest is as bountiful a moment as I have ever had afield. I feed Patch a giblet out of hand—warm wild food, sacred as food gets—but save the rest, since he doesn't like to eat in the middle of a working day. I'm so well off—the season suddenly complete in a way—I feel like sitting on a rock and getting started writing a novel or some other impractical task. It's noon and we're done. We'll hunt on, free now to hunt the day itself, but I am not eager for another bird. We are hunting well. That is already in the bag. We have more than what we came out for, more than we deserve today, but birds perhaps we earned on other days when we kept faith with the idea of hunting but returned home empty-handed.

This rivulet we have followed leads not to the watershed's main stream but to a small creek I've hunted down in the past. This two-bird detour connects a small swath of the landscape I didn't know with the part I know well. So my backcountry holdings have been enlarged by thirty acres in addition to the two birds. The creek takes us back up to a faint extension of the logging road we started out on maybe a mile farther on from where we left it. We hunt all the way back up. I'm at half throttle, but Patch is in his midday groove, worrying the laurel slicks. Once on the overgrown road, the path of least resistance takes us on toward the rim of the bowl-shaped watershed we are working. Although unfamiliar terrain is a help in keeping an open mind, I like hunting in watersheds I know nearly as well as the humble woodlots of Highland Farm, ancient hollows deep in the mountains that seem like home, that are home at certain times of the year, some wild extension of the idea of home, like those tart, dry apples from an orchard abandoned long ago. Maybe Patch had the right idea when he was a puppy careening into the world as if it were all home. Today, we've hunted five hours into the mountains, following our inclinations and the scent of wild birds brought to Patch's nose on a random breeze. We hunted in a new place where we had never been before and then worked our way back to familiar ground until we found ourselves lounging on a rock outcrop where we've lingered dozens of times before and seen something different each time.

★ ★ ★

Good hunts come to vistas. I like getting up on the high ground and being able to see the shape of the land around me, especially the distinctive outcrops of granite and greenstone that underwrite the highest peaks. The Blue Ridge substitutes toughness for grandeur, a quality of age in mountains. These worn, old mountains may not look like much from a distance. But you get up in their hollows and you learn to appreciate the unassuming but rugged landscape into which they have weathered. On the ridgelines, where ancient rock juts rudely toward the sky, you feel you have gotten up on the working edge of time itself. At home, where ticking clocks presume to measure what is immeasurable, we sometimes forget how wild time is. Hunting in the backcountry, you feel the hours keenly and see them as fine and strange as the spiry yellow witch hazel blooms that we have encountered at every turn today, or as full of promise as mountain ash in fruit that hangs heavy in the wind up here.

There is no finer visual contrast than the beauty of fall—the color of a year of forest life molting eagerly before your eyes—set against a skyline of two-billion-year-old rock whose purpose is to resist change grudgingly and gracefully. Somewhere between the fluttering fall of this year's leaves and the stolid life of granite from Precambrian times, when Earth was strange as Mars, we find a scale of time that suits our own needs and purposes. We hunt in and around the life of things, and despite the birds we've killed today, we are part of the life of things. Perhaps the still-warm birds in my game bag are proof of that. From the point of view of the woods, the birds we killed are gone and we are a strong intrusion. From the point of the granite from which we watch the sky for ravens, we are not even present. Watch granite from the granite's point of view and you will feel yourself disappear.

The ravens we often find here do not disappoint. They are up, a gang of them, playing in the cool daylight, cronking their guttural cry. Ravens use the air as no other birds do. Strong fliers, their great talent is the stall, the way their broad wings and tails enable them to hang in the air battling each other for fun, counting coup with wing strokes and feinted beak jabs until one bird gives up, folds itself, and tumbles straight down to another invisible plateau, from which it makes a stand in the air.

Go back far enough in history and you will understand that to see character—and virtue—in animals is not necessarily to personify. It is to remember that, in wise cultures, animals guided human nature and informed what, ideally, human beings might be. We do not project virtue into animals. Long ago they projected their virtues into us. Despite the claims of culture, perhaps the best of our character is in what we have in common with animals. And, insofar as we have spirits, that, too, comes from our kinship with the things of this earth.

It's not true, what José Ortega y Gasset asserts, that *only* by hunting can you get to know country, *be in* country. Poets and artists and pure-hearted lovers of nature, who are often aghast at the idea of hunting, know the country as well as Patch and I do. But this is how we do it, how we have found what I hope is an honest place in a landscape we love, and where, I hope again, we leave more than we take.

When Patch gets restless, we push on. Deer hunting is my gig. Grouse hunting is his show. Back in the woods, it's all about following Patch as he tries to worry birds out of the land. I follow, tired and feeling every step now.

There is a roughness to hunting that suits us, man and dog—what the wild carvings of a fiddle are to the orderly strains of a violin, a strain of music closer to the beckoning in the percussion of a grouse drumming in the woods. We hunt maybe as a way of going over to the other side of things for a while, dancing by old fires, each of us a little more wolfish than we would otherwise be. In the end, I can't speak for Patch, but hunting seems to question and answer something in me I would rather not deny and forces me to 'fess up to my inherent selfishness as well as

my mortality. If you love the tragic gaiety in nature, to borrow a phrase
from Yeats, there is nothing sad in that. It's rather invigorating to take
life for what life is, as a hunter hunting, if you will. Heaven is indeed
underfoot, as Thoreau suggested, crunchy and loud in the fall, the air
full of earthy perfumes and shards of hazeless light that look like shining
windows in the woods. I can't imagine not hunting birds with Patch in
October, following grouse wherever the grouse lead.

While you hunt, home and away trade places, and you learn
things you would otherwise never know. There is a dark side to that, the
violence of gunfire and the birds we kill and take away, the beautiful birds
especially, not to mention our own hours, which are gone forever. That
aftertaste is pretty sharp after a day in the woods. But those hours would
have flushed wild anyway. And neither birds nor bird dogs nor human
bird hunters live forever. That's part of the fine, wild edge of things, too,
and not a lugubrious thought. Afield, we see them go—birds and hours
careening through the bare hickories and the leaf-rattling oaks headed
for the safety of the soft-boughed pines.

★ ★ ★

It's getting late and we have our birds, but on the long way back Patch
and I stop at one last stretch of good cover where we might flush a
bird just for the sake of hearing it escape. I hunted alone for several
years before I acquired Patch. I'd roam the ridges and put up some birds,
mostly at random. That was good hunting in its way, but I never liked
staying out until dark when I was alone on the trackless ridges. The
familiarity of familiar places disappears at night. I've slept many nights
in the backcountry, but I still get an uneasy, shivery feel with darkness
coming on—a touch of what Huck Finn, watching the broad river
that was his home and not his home, called the "solid lonesomeness" of
things. For me it was the sudden feeling that I didn't really belong in the
backcountry, that I had either hunted too far or not quite far enough and
had been caught out, at sunset, on ground that wasn't mine.

With Patch for company, I don't mind dusk catching us far from
the truck as we hunt for one more flush of a wild bird in a wild place,
just the sound of wings that proves that we are hunters hunting, that we
belong in the woods.

Dog Days

Guy de la Valdène

The Farm (Tallahassee, Florida), April 2009

On some superficial level, I understand the time it took the live oak outside my window to grow from a sapling to a tree that manufactures shade. But I am overwhelmed when informed that the fossils of grey partridge unearthed by paleontologists in the caves and middens of France and Hungary a century ago were more than 1,000,000 years old and that those birds were a preferred food of our forefathers, the Cro-Magnon.

In my seventh decade, I brood about the passing of time and the short lives of my dogs, but I don't know how to reconcile my years as a conscious being with the calendar of the birds I most like to hunt.

Half a century after my first dog, I still marvel at how quickly they learn to recognize cover, the manner in which they point and retrieve birds, the indolence of males marking territory, the smutty presentations of bitches looking to breed. I love the everyday quirks in a dog's character, its habits, its independence, the insouciance of

(Courtesy of Guy de la Valdène)

Brigitte Bardot, Guy de la Valdène's French Brittany.

its sprawling slumber, and the accepting drop of a dog's ears at the approach of a trusted hand.

When I reach a reassuring hand to a sleeping shoulder next to me, I'm always a little surprised when the dog doesn't acknowledge my caress or join in my unease. Perhaps they, too, worry in their dreams. I wonder if dogs know they are growing old, or whether they understand the inevitable progression of diminished capacities. What do they think when they can no longer jump into the back seat of a car or, like me, hurt at the end of the day?

Anymore, I don't ask more of my dogs than what their genes dictate. I hate the stubborn ones who refuse to acknowledge my commands, but I have grown to forgive. It didn't used to be that way. But as a good poet friend of mine wrote, "I have come to regret being right about anything anymore."

Consequently, I don't care if a pointer holds its tail at twelve o'clock or a retriever drops a bird at my feet instead of in my hand. And although no one appreciates perfection more than I, I'm not a good dog trainer for the same reasons I am not a Republican: I endorse all forms of social anarchy.

I only wish I were capable of displaying the joy of living as profoundly as my dogs.

France, Fall and Winter 1964/65

My first pointing dog was a black-and-white Llewellyn setter bitch bred in Turin, Italy. Her gentle black eyes and long nose were set in a cameo of fine facial bones. She was a true Italian princess, both desirable and unstable. Her name was Odia, and like most of the pointing dogs I would later own, she knew how to make me regret the impulsive nature of my desires and miss the gentle disposition of my Labradors.

From Odia, I learned how to yell at a dog from a distance, a misplaced anger, which achieved the same blank response I would receive from the television set after blaming it for losing a football game. But I also witnessed for the first time the heart-stopping glory of a dog that, purely for reasons of genetics and lust, transforms the act of hunting into an art.

My friend Simonelli, my mother's plumber, and I would watch in wonder as Odia tip-toed at top speed through the beet fields of our valley, seemingly unaware of the tightly planted oval roots until suddenly she would stop, her body obedient to an innate command. Odia was as exhilarating to watch as the Mille Miglia road race through the mountains of Italy long ago. She was a nimble dog who seemed to float effortlessly inches above the ground, never landing in trouble, quick as a mongoose. I killed partridge and quail behind her in the alfalfa fields of Normandy for two seasons before giving her to Simonelli when I married and moved to the United States.

My first bird dog taught me that personalities dictate decisions, which in turn affect events. Most of the time, Odia paid little attention to me. When she did trap the scent she was looking for, her mindset went from that of hunter to an exquisitely trained athlete, a gymnast looking to stick the landing with authority, regal, always expecting a perfect score.

Those moments in the field were new to me and wonderful because of the lunacy of a dog's commitment to stop at the mere suspicion of a bird in hiding. It was magical and stirred something old and delightful in me. I applaud the first man who taught his dog how to extend the momentary pause inherent in predators before they attack, and rewarding his dog for its patience.

Odia taught me to identify cover, to exploit the wind and its possibilities, to harmonize the tempo of a hunt to her behavior, and to celebrate her discoveries by taking advantage of them quickly. At first, I felt alien, walking in front of Odia, her nervous system attuned to the proximity of birds. I was transfixed by her intensity, and like the greenhorn that I was, I didn't always believe her position and, like her, would stop instead of moving forward. I would call her off point—usually to my chagrin—and if, for some reason, she ran through a covey or chased a wild flush, I would holler instead of picking her up and putting her back on point (the intelligent thing to do) as closely as I could from where she had made her mistake. I would learn these things, but because I was hot tempered, it took decades.

In time I have learned to move myself to point quietly and quickly, to take into account the strength and direction of the wind, to approach cover leaving tree trunks and other obstructions out of the quarry's angles of escape. I know on which side of a dog to walk, when to crowd a piece of cover, when to slow down, when to praise and when to scold, when to shoot and when not to. And it all began long ago and far away with Odia.

That dog's passion marked me more than my beloved Labrador, Spray, who until then had flushed and retrieved all the game I killed. Labs were the women one loved to talk to on car trips and pull under the blanket at ball games on cold nights, dogs whose devotions were equally divided between their master and the food they were fed. Bird dogs were the crazed bitches that kept you up all night, begging for more. The better the pointing dog, the greater its addiction to the opiate of wild scents.

To whisper the word "bird" into a pointer's ear is like turning the key of a Maserati. They are the performers of the dog world, high-stepping dancers reaching for cover, the acrobats. And the good ones are half a revolution off plumb.

There was something about Odia's primitive approach to finding game—her athleticism and fitness, the single-mindedness of her attention to specific fragrances—that drew me inexorably to the world of bird dogs.

Montana, Fall 1977

Today, I hunted the face of Sheep Mountain alone with my dogs. Rising to the west of the Yellowstone River, north of Livingston, Montana, Sheep Mountain is more of a high hill crowned with vertical rocks than a true mountain. The Shields Valley was not famous for birds, but grey partridge and sharptail grouse could, with a little resolve, be found there. The privately owned land was just steep enough to keep me from talking to the dogs during the ascent. Rain, my Labrador, followed me more or less at heel, while Becky, a young English setter from North Dakota, ran the slopes ahead. The wind picked up, as it usually does in the Shields Valley, before I reached elevation some distance above the grain fields in which the partridge fed each morning.

I took in the reassuring sights of stacked hay and green alfalfa pastures, the fields of harvested wheat, and the intermittent rectangles of harrowed black earth, small and checkered below me. The golden eyes of distant aspen groves watched us from across the divide. The Yellowstone River, protected here and there by knots of yellow cottonwoods, carved the valley below me. A late summer snow had gathered on the peaks of the Absaroka Mountain Range. The river was quick and bright and low.

As I had for almost all of my hunting life, I followed my dog. Becky, a little black-and-white English setter, was already a distance ahead of me. I watched her run the thin cover of the slope in front of us and wild flush a cluster of sharptail. Gathering wind under their wings, the grouse made short, powerful tacks across the hill, displaying the strength that marks them as the western falconer's game bird of choice.

Circuitous game trails led Becky up a coulee at the head of which she stopped, her feet solidly planted uphill in an expanse of pale mountain brome grass. The bitch held her head high, her inflexible eyes staring at the trunk of a century-old Juniper tree. The wind played on her coat's long, silky feathers. A covey of grey partridge hesitated before rising in a sunburst of insistent wings, treating us to a disharmony of gritty calls and single-minded haste. Rain retrieved dinner.

Becky was a two-year-old blooded princess, directly related to 1975 Grand National Grouse Champion Jetrain and Johnny Crockett, the last setter to win the National Bird Dog Championship in 1970. She was short-coupled and weighed thirty-six pounds. The calm brown eyes that gazed at me with devotion after dark would erupt out of her chiseled, spaniel head whenever she was in concert with birds. We loved each other and, in theory, should have had a long and lasting affair. However, within a year of owning her, I considered, in my angrier moments, burying a hatchet in her pretty skull.

An opportunity queen with the impeccable bloodlines and obsessive nature of her illustrious ancestors, Becky, I realized with no little resentment, was too good for me. Her opinions ran counter to my wishes, and my approach to training her stemmed from feelings of entitlement, instead of trust. The first time she ran out of my sight with all the joyful energy of adolescence, I yelled her back expecting what every other weekend hunter clamored for: a fully broken, one-year-old dog.

Miss Becky was a "door dog." If one was open, she was through it and gone, looking for birds. I could not control her any more than I could control any woman. She set about the task of hunting with the alacrity and single-mindedness that make great dogs and famous human beings. Left to herself, she was special, but in those days I didn't listen to anyone but myself. That was not only a mistake, but the height of conceit, as if I could order a dog's nose to where it belonged.

So instead of trying to understand her motives, I fought her. In the process, I not only gave up the pleasure of watching a beautiful creature committing to her instincts, I forfeited her trust. When she would curl up next to me, close-fitting as pillow, and exude a willingness to forgive me, I accepted her love until a new sun blessed her profound need to run and mine to direct.

I ended up giving Becky Train of Thought to a friend whose southern temperament accepted her eccentric behavior as normal. Over the years, they made a team that, because of the length of her nose and his talents with a shotgun, grew famous together, fixtures in the bean fields surrounding Point Clear, Alabama. They returned and hunted with me after I bought the farm in Tallahassee in 1990, and I immediately realized that what I had struggled so mightily to orchestrate was simple, graceful choreography to them.

After a while, I became invisible to Becky. Her attention was completely focused on my soft-spoken friend, who treated her as one would a child (which is what dogs are). The years passed quickly, and the girl turned into a lady. Then, one day, Becky was old, her lovely face tight to the bone. Their love affair lasted eleven years. When she was gone, my friend mourned as we who love dogs mourn, bone-deep, insulted by the finality of death.

The control I expected to have over my dogs stemmed from the same base feelings of propriety that have plagued my character for all the wrong reasons most of my life. Instead of accepting the complexities of training, the particulars of an individual dog, the required disappointments and setbacks, I expected perfection (it never happened) and the esteem of my peers.

As much as I loved my dogs, I was loud with them, turning what should have been a miracle of evolutionary good fortune into pointless commands—the opposite of the silence I have grown to cherish. Now, I willingly subordinate myself to the caprices of dogs and am quietly grateful to have spent a life following them through landscapes that few other men have known.

Canada, October 2000

As a beater on driven shoots in France, I had helped move thousands of game birds over gun lines, but I had never seen—and doubt that I will ever see again—anything equal to the natural concentration of grey partridge we moved that first morning outside of Assiniboia, Saskatchewan. To my surprise there were very few falcons working. My host Rod Annan explained that the fall migration of hawks would start shortly after we left and that the coveys would be thinned by the prairie falcons, peregrines, goshawks, and occasional transient gyrfalcons.

My mistake that morning was not only to put Heather, the yearling English cocker, on the ground, but also O. B., a six-year-old, black-and-tan male French Brittany that, as we hunted parallel to the first row of caragana plants, was embarrassed by a snowshoe rabbit, whom he chased barking for more than a mile. Rod, who didn't mind what I did, reacted to my antics—"O. B., get back here you mother f . . . . ."—with hilarity.

The open spaces of Canada would prove to be too tempting for the little French dog whose sobriquet stuck. But since I forgive my dogs their acts of disobedience, secretly wishing all the while I could get away with what they do, some years later in southern Idaho, I put the same dog down to hunt late in the day at the bottom of a steep hill filled with rose buds and partridge.

O. B. had hunted well for me in North Florida for years, perhaps because he was born in the woods, but whenever I took him west, the open landscape stretched his pace and damaged his already limited sense of being. He had been steady in the southern broom sage he couldn't see over, but out west, where the cover is thin, his idea of pointing was to raise his nose to the horizon and run after it.

I looked for O. B. for fifty minutes, begging after a while to a god I don't believe in to spare him. At dark, my heart was filled with visions of mountain lions. Soon after, however, the dog returned to the truck, having indulged in the kind of canine fantasy I, as a man, never got away with. He wiggled and rubbed against my leg, oblivious to my misgivings. Filthy and pleased with himself, he knew that, happy to see him, I wouldn't smack his stupid little face for scaring the shit out of me.

A few hours later in the comfort of the Airstream my dogs and I travel in each fall—and after a few glasses of wine—I talked to him mostly about obedience and gratitude (neither of which he displayed) and what I expected of him the next time he pretended to be lost. Petting his little head, I realized that the day would come when he would be gone and that my hand, which was familiar with every bone in his skull, would miss him as much as my heart. I commiserated with O. B. about the muscles in his hind legs, which reminded me of my arms, and how neither of us was the man he used to be and that the greying of his dark coat copied my own hair and that I understood too well the stiffness in his joints. I didn't mention our dicks.

The Farm (Tallahassee, Florida), December 2002

I woke that morning knowing it was time to call Greg Winter, my veterinarian friend with whom I chase quail and the man who would put Carnac to sleep.

In 1994, I wrote about a roan-colored French Brittany as the dog who would see me through my salad years, a stubborn, handsome little-man dog that I loved for his spirit and total acceptance of who he was. He was the first of a breed that suited my character and disposition.

Carnac would often range where I didn't want him to, he could be hard-headed when called off a false point, and he had no interest in hunting dead. He was all about finding coveys and holding them under his will until I found him.

At the mere suspicion of birds, Carnac would hunt cover until he was satisfied, no matter how long it took, or how hard I tried to change his mind (a means of discipline I gave up early in his third year). Flowing, roan-colored feathers fell from his flanks. When he was on point, they filtered the sun. His strength was his home beat and, as time passed, I used him as an advance scout in the farm's quail woods. As a young dog, he was my companion out west and in Michigan where, to be honest, he was almost always outdone by the larger, faster, rangier dogs owned by my companions. Coming up on birds second or third in line didn't bother him, though. His backing was impeccable, and he was where he wanted to be—in the field with me.

Carnac was a woman's dog. He loved them without prejudice, and it didn't matter to him what species they were. He was so horny I had to lock him away when we had mixed company for dinner.

One night, when Carnac was young and impetuous, I talked to him about his penchant for humping pretty women's legs. Back then, whenever my wife would leave the farm for a few days, I would, on my first night alone, cook myself hot Szechuan dry-fried beef and drink Bombay gin.

To the amusement of the dogs, it didn't take me long to dance around the room with a broom. One such night, I decided that I should have a come-to-Jesus talk with Carnac, who was feigning uninterest in my antics. I got down on all fours, level with his face, and offered my thoughts. The message he gave back was hard to misinterpret. After putting up with a few minutes of my besotted gibberish, he walked around me, wagged his roan-colored tail, and pissed on my leg.

When he was seven years old, he fractured his tibia lengthwise down the length of the bone. Over the next year, he went through three painful operations, the last ending with his elbow being fused. The little dog was tough, and although he dragged his front foot, he was game. I had plans to hunt him that fall. In August, though, a cancer was discovered in his lung. He was eight years old. I would watch him sometimes sitting outside, staring into space, rekindling memories through a nose a thousand times more discerning than mine.

One morning, I carried my friend down from my wife's room out to the grass knoll on which the house was built, a place he favored with a view over his domain. When Greg arrived with his assistant, Carnac recognized him and wagged his tail twice. That is the last and most poignant picture I have of him.

As a matter of self-preservation, I have always declined to look at loved ones after they are dead. Ever since I was very young, I have known that the image of death would replace all others and would be the picture of that person or animal I would carry to my grave. I refused to see my father at the morgue and, later, my mother in her bed—innocent and, according to my sister, lovely in the liberation that her passing had accorded her. I choose to remember those I love alive. The Labradors I owned as a young man were, when the time came, dropped off at the vet's (much to the disapproval of the attendants), allowing me to bolt, choked with grief, but steadfastly refusing the picture of death.

I didn't do that with Carnac. And now what I remember most of our years together are the two tail wags with which he greeted the man who would take his life.

It's a mistake I won't repeat.

Montana, October 2003

Today, I hunted behind Brigitte Bardot, a year-old French Brittany who had never pointed a grey partridge, with a fifteen-year-old boy who had never shot one. The bitch had fawn-colored freckles on either side of her nose; the boy had acne. B.B. would mature into the best pointing dog

I have ever owned; the boy would soon discover girls. They were both keen and lanky and naive.

A dozen women concealed behind flowing black skirts and white blouses moved with purpose from a cluster of cement block buildings to an aluminum Quonset hut through the immaculate courtyard of a 20,000-acre Hutterite colony in Central Montana. The women raised their round, pink, peasant faces to the encroachment of our SUV on their communal world and smiled. The knot of men standing at the Quonset were dressed in tight-fitting black jackets and pants, their faces shaded under the wide brim of black felt hats. Flocks of pigeons flew in tight formations above the silos, just as they had the last time I visited the colony a decade earlier. For once, time had waited for us.

That day we walked across great rolling expanses of wheat stubble planted up to the heels of arid buttes. There were folds in the hills interrupted by miles of barb-wire fencing, odd clusters of attentive mule deer, the white-ass fans of antelope, and an occasional silver silo overexposed by the sun. The partridge had fed earlier that morning and were now loitering in the stubble where the sighting was good and a dry insistent wind ruffled their feathers.

Brigitte had never hunted open country before, and when she spread out over what must have seemed strange, uninterrupted terrain, she glanced back often, like a coyote, fretful that we were not following her. In a rare stroke of luck, she sorted correctly through a scattering of choices attached to the wheat stubble. On her first cast, she stopped suddenly, unyielding, a youthful symbol of certainty.

The bitch found seven coveys that day, each time displaying more confidence, until her last effort was held a quarter of a mile away under the bonding properties of shadows falling. The young man walked up to his first challenge that morning stiff as a lead soldier, his new leather boots cruel, his canvas pants chafing, and his oversized jacket billowing. He shot into the covey rise (only he knows if he killed what he aimed at) and picked up his first partridge.

The moment reeled time backwards, decade by decade, and unexpectedly I was a young man in France again, looking at the warm body of my first partridge. To highlight the moment, the boy's father wiped a drop of blood off the partridge's beak and proudly applied it to his son's cheek.

The boy killed a second and third partridge behind Brigitte, who by mid-afternoon was mindful of what was expected of her. The early morning praises had become superfluous. All she sought was birds. I observed the young man smiling to himself when things were slow, his mind undoubtedly returning to such familiar grounds as school or the drive through burger joints in town. When he stood next to me or his father, he appeared bewildered. If Brigitte was in range he patted her head, a subtle acknowledgement of her role as his accomplice on a day he would remember as an old man.

Boys, like crows, follow the cadence of seasons without question. Driving back to Livingston that evening, I watched him staring at the sun angling off the waters of the Yellowstone River and realized that, because he lived in Montana, he had witnessed that particular light a hundred times each year, rich golden light moving across the current, a light most children in America will not see. Or maybe he was staring at the black pickup truck passing us. It was filled with girls, pretty faces glancing with interest in his direction.

In my dreams, my friends and I are always young. When I shave in front of the same mirror I have used for twenty years, I doubt it recognizes me. My suggestion to the boy that day was simple: avoid growing up at all costs. Forever, if possible.

The Farm (Tallahassee, Florida), April 2009

I have a new dog. His name is Louis and he is five months old. He flew over from France in a jet plane to be with his distant cousin Brigitte, who turned seven. He is handsome. The other dogs bully him but it won't last. He will be strong when they grow weak. Meanwhile, he eats everything he can get his face into. He runs into things, slips on carpets, pisses on the floor, destroys the furniture, and licks my face. Chances are he will be my last bird dog. I would give anything to be Louis.

I let O. B. go in May and I cried, as I always do. That afternoon, I took a long walk with Heather to get away, this time from sorrow. I don't understand where any of us go when we die. If I did, it wouldn't be so difficult.

Sometimes, though, when I gather little Louis' face close to mine, I ask, "Are you in there, O. B.?" He glances sheepishly away.

I often read W. S. Merwin's poems to my dogs—"Crow tried to be cormorant/drowned"—and by the perk of their ears and the look on their faces, I know they love the poems as I do, even if we don't always understand their meanings.

Sometimes, the sound of the words is enough.

Four Queens

Robert DeMott

". . . the so-called 'perfect' dogs are usually the product of after-hunt cocktail hours . . . created by hunters who let their imaginations run wild."

—Roy Strickland, *Common Sense Grouse and Woodcock Dog Training*

1. Good Dog, Bad Dog

I'm down on my stomach in a tangle of wild grape vine, greenbrier, winter fern, and staghorn sumac decked with blood red lanterns of fruit, my nose pressed into November leaf litter and woody detritus. I'm gulping deep breaths of the spot where a ruffed grouse flushed, but I smell only damp earth and moldy leaves. Two minutes earlier, as I was walking an old railroad bed in northwest Connecticut, my first bird dog, a sweet little tri-colored Llewellyn setter named Suzie, pointed a grouse a few feet below me. The bird rose and angled away, left, into my shot string, and crumpled thirty feet from where I'm standing.

I don't recall any other particulars of that day in 1958—not the weather, not the time of day, not the company I was with, not what I was wearing or ate for lunch, or the hour-long ride home—but that grey bird rising over Suzie's point remains as clearly etched as if it were an Eldridge Hardie painting. Before Suzie covered the downed bird I scrambled to its flush point. I was new at this wing shooting and pointing dog business,

(Photo by James DeMott)

Young Bob DeMott with English setter Suzie.

and not knowing any better, I figured maybe I'd smell what she smelled, but no soap, because all I got was a low-register dampness and earthy taint that gave away nothing. When I finally picked up the dead partridge it smelled like my mother's feather mop—dry, dusty, a bit acrid and ticklish to my nose. Nothing to get excited about, except to a bird dog. I praised Suzie to the skies, marveling more at her feat than mine. "Good girl! Good Suzie!" I looked at her in disbelief. Signs and wonders.

A lifetime of upland bird hunting kick-started that day not just with the flush of first success, but with a question—really a riddle or conundrum—that fifty years later I still have not answered and, given my entry into the twilight years, no doubt never will: how do bird dogs do what they do? Physiological differences between men and dogs aside (canine olfactory receptors are a thousand times more sensitive than those of humans, which is a fact not hard to understand given that a dog has more than 200 million olfactory receptors in its nose), it is a remarkable act to locate and pin a wild bird by scent alone.

Half a century later I never tire of watching a bird dog go about its nosey business. The single mindedness, the inexorable directedness, of a dog working a loose skein of scent back to its source is tonic to me. Contemporary cultural theorists frown on such single-minded behavior as being "overly determined," but in the grouse woods, where no one reads Michel Foucault or Jacques Derrida, it's exactly what you want. Nature naturing itself. The world reduced to the one vivid thing. The magnet and its metal filings.

Even though I eventually shot only a pitiful few grouse, some pheasants, and a handful of quail over Suzie, she was my first "great" dog candidate, because in those crucial impressionable years when I was between twelve and sixteen, she opened a door for me that has never closed. Her influence, as I see it, was profound. Although I did not realize it then, Suzie became the indelible model for the kind of dual-quality bird dog I would always favor—close-working and biddable in the field and thoroughly companionable around the house. Except for three others (Rosie, Babe, and Meadow) I did not always have that kind of exemplary dog. Nonetheless, whether or not you consider them "perfect," "great," or "best," all dogs are destined to break your heart: if they are bad they continually find ways to fuck up that crush you to the bone; if they are good they manage to break your heart by eventually dying (in my case always before their time) and leaving you disconsolate and inconsolable because you think they can never be replaced. The sad fact of existence for those of us who are not pro-dog men is that there are too damn many of the former and never enough of the latter.

★ ★ ★

There was a long hiatus between Suzie and my next bird dog. Life intervened, as it has a way of doing. I think it was poet Randall Jarrell who said that the way we miss life *is* life. Life became college, marriage, fatherhood, and graduate school, all squeezed into a concentrated period of eight years. Each stage was exponentially difficult and complex in its own way and deserving of significant absorption, which is why, though there was hunting during that era, especially with my uncle, Tony Ventrella, and his beagles (sometimes in rural Connecticut after cottontails, sometimes at our Vermont camps after varying hare and the occasional wild grouse), those pursuits were more random and casual than I would have liked.

So as soon as I got my first full-time teaching job—at Ohio University in 1969—and moved to rural, hilly southeastern Ohio and saw the reclaimed strip mines, the abandoned farms, the hills and hollows with their second and third growth forests, and silky dogwood and alder swales, I knew it would be difficult to live much longer without a bird dog. After several months of searching I found Spike, whose name came to symbolize everything about him. Think of the kid who got his driver's license when he was in junior high school while the rest of us were still peddling bicycles—that was Spike. Spike was an eighty-pound white-and-tan Elhew English pointer who had that square jaw, blocky head, barrel-sized chest, and chiseled shape that has come to define the descendents of Robert Wahle's in-your-face breeding program. I bought Spike, who looked like a buzz-cut Marine drill sergeant, from a local field trialer of some repute, whose impressive shelf of trophies and ribbons testified to his expertise.

According to my uncle's tutelage, I should have been wary of Spike's field trial background and the way a dog out of such breeding is the last thing a foot hunter needs. But caution went out the window when I rubbed my hand over his rippling shoulder blades and felt a layer of steel cord under his skin. His owner planted a few pigeons in his mowed back meadow, and I watched Spike methodically nail each one in what looked like automatonic perfection. Here, I thought, was a dog to believe in, and I laid down my cash on the spot.

In those days I had an old knock-about Chevy Suburban that was at least twice the size of our family car and capacious enough on the inside to accommodate an inflated rubber fishing raft. It was the heaviest, longest, tallest vehicle I have ever owned, and the first thing Spike did when I brought him home was to mount this monstrosity and screw the right front wheel until his dick was sore. When he ejaculated, sperm hit the side view mirrors three feet away. It was an act, I came to realize, that defined Spike's attitude toward the world—sheer recklessness and outlaw abandon. Except for his coloration, he could as easily have been descended from Lion, the great bear-hunting mongrel in William Faulkner's novella, "The Bear." Both had a complete disregard for social niceties or effete notions of companionability.

"When that kind of a dog finally nails a bird, it will be such a beautiful point you'll never forget it," my former OU colleague and dog training guru Randy Lawrence told me a few years ago in another connection. Spike was the first in an on-again off-again series of more or less unmanageable grouse dogs I've owned about which no truer words were ever spoken. Once in two hunting seasons, Spike had an exceptional day when all the fickle grouse gods smiled in unison. It wasn't that I limited out that day and also put my hunting buddies on birds. We could just as easily have missed all our shots, and Spike's performance would still have moved us to awe.

In a rugged near-to-home covert called The Wildwoods, Spike for once did everything a foot hunting grouser expects of his dog—work close, obey commands, and nail the birds cold with staunch points. According to my hunting diary it was a banner day and made me think Spike had just read a dog-training book and was following its precepts point by point. He was flawless, even holding rock solid on a bird at the top of a windy ridge that took me five minutes of vertical climbing to reach. He could have been the poster boy for a dog food advertisement: shoulders squared, body slightly turned, head lowered a little below the plane of his spine, eyes like lasers riveted on the sniffed but as yet unseen bird, tail cocked straight up like an exclamation point, and that patented look of intensity that is the pointer's signature, its stock in trade. Finally, I gloated to my pals, he'd turned a corner, and from now on our hunt life together would become the success I had long envisioned. I could have kissed his ass I was so happy.

That such a day happened only once in two years, however, came to be more significant than the shining nature of his momentary achievement. After several more months of having my heart busted—during which time Spike developed a penchant for rigidly pointing treed opossums for hours on end, then escalated toward humping porcupines (with predicable results) on our annual Vermont trip, I gave the horny bastard to one of my graduate students, an avid hunter named John Paul Montgomery, who, newly minted Ph.D. in hand, was returning to his native Tennessee to teach, and who promised me that, by putting Spike on plenty of local quail, he'd by God "get his ass straightened around." The last I heard, Spike had killed a neighbor's chickens and the farmer threatened a lawsuit unless John Paul put the rogue down. I wasn't surprised. From the first, as Aaron Parrett sings, Spike "had the graveyard in his eyes."

2. Brag Dogs

For many of us, life is too often about the interregnums, the long, silent stretches filled by bonehead dogs we keep cycling through as we look for the next king or queen of our heart, what Georgia novelist Vereen Bell called a "brag dog." With Spike gone I entered a hodge-podge period in the next seven years and burned through another English pointer (Whitey, who turned out to be deaf and occasioned a court case), three Brittany spaniels (Coco, Mardi, and Muffin), and a Springer spaniel (Skip, who besides bumping every bird he worked, adamantly refused to retrieve a woodcock or grouse). Not one of them rang my bell, though Mardi, who was a passably workaholic little dog and apparently had a brain slightly larger than all the other misfits together, came closest and gave me some decent days on grouse. "Mardi worked well," a cryptic note in one of my hunting diaries says. Apparently, praise meted out in teaspoons was her portion in life.

Gradually, I hooked up with a local hunter named Bill Perine who, though he had a dashing young pointer when I first met him, actually preferred to hunt without a dog. Known locally as "Brush Hunter," Bill was regarded as one of the premier grouse hunters in the southeastern quadrant of Ohio. He regularly shot seventy-five or eighty partridge a year, an unheard of tally for the secondary range population in our part of the Midwest. Dog or no dog, Bill was the best wing shot I have ever seen, and he was equally adept at bagging every manner of wild game. (Years later, bored with shotguns, he turned to bow hunting pheasants on the wing, at which he was remarkably successful.)

I was hot to trot myself, eager to expand my range of outdoor experience, and got swept up in the rough shooting fever. Suddenly, a pointing breed seemed a bit too limited for my needs, and I began shifting my desire to a retrieving type (enter Skip) whose versatility I thought might fit my changing pursuits (exit Skip). I also started buying and trading side-by-sides, over-and-unders, and even auto loaders with hideous twenty-inch barrels (useful for hiding under a raincoat if you were planning to rob a convenience store), all in an effort to find the perfect short-swinging upland scatter gun for our exceptionally gnarly cover; began experimenting with various gun powders and religiously loading my own shells to achieve the fastest foot-per-second velocity possible; and with Perine and Company (his colleagues at the technical college where he taught, all of them hardcore outdoorsmen), frequently hunted from dawn until dark.

During the third and fourth weeks of October, when grouse and duck seasons were open and the woodcock migration was ratcheting up, I routinely left home at 4:00 AM to meet the crew at a coveted slough, where we would have fast action on wood ducks for a couple of hours, then start off on a woodcock/grouse road trip that would take us to half a dozen prime coverts miles away in Jackson and Vinton Counties. We'd end up back at the Mineral duck marsh until the end of legal shooting time. Fridays and Saturdays went on like that for several years and while they broadened life in one direction, they narrowed it in another as my marriage began to unravel. I should not have been surprised: my journals from 1975-1980 record an average of sixty-four hunting trips a year. Whether I was causing problems anew or escaping from an already deteriorating situation was never quite clear to the parties involved, though both sides were aided and abetted by indiscretions and blunders, as well. Stupidity reigned and one looked for stability where one could.

Enter Katie, a savvy field-bred, honey-colored golden retriever that belonged to a member of Perine's hunting posse. I popped away at many birds over Katie, and when her owner, Dave Enterline, promised me a pup out of a future litter, I leapt at the chance. When the time came two years later, I brought home Rosie who, like her mother, proved to be a crack field dog, and even then struck me as smarter than some of my freshman students. I bagged my first grouse with her on a cold day in mid-January 1983, when she was only seven months old. The grouse, which Rosie tracked fifty yards through a couple of inches of fresh snow, then flushed out of a blackberry thicket, was too big for her to pick up, and her struggle to retrieve it was comical, but her determination showed even then, and it would remain undiminished for the next eleven years.

So would her quirks—I quit hunting ducks with her because she adamantly refused to retrieve or pick up a woodie. Upland birds were her forté, and she used to amuse my bird-hunting pals and my string of new girlfriends by pointing woodcock, though where and how she came by that delightful weirdness, I never knew. She was a mild-mannered and tractable companion, but twice I had to chase her down when circuits blew and she went on the offensive. Once she attacked a woodchuck, which, like Thoreau, she must have wanted to eat raw. The other time all her biddable training went out the door like a scalded pig when she honed in on some chickens in a mown field near one of my woodcock spots. I screamed, I yelled, I cajoled, I pleaded, but she gave me the finger and dove into the flock, emerging from a haze of drifting white feathers with a fat hen in her mouth. The man who owned the birds witnessed the whole sorry debacle from his front porch. Fortunately, he was getting ready to butcher a chicken for dinner, so Rosie's killer antics saved him the work of dispatching the bird. I gave him ten bucks anyway and went on to hunt woodcock, relieved that Spike's fate would not be hers. "You lucky bastard," was all I could mutter.

Many bird hunters have an informal way of naming their coverts, not by registered landmarks or official plat maps, but by a wing-and-a-prayer kind of nomenclature borne out of direct experience. When something unusual happens at a particular spot, its moment becomes an identifiable part of the place and time. Cultural critics are finally catching on to the fact that region, place, and locale form us as deeply as race, gender, and ethnicity. Bird hunters have known that for eons: geography and environment joined with intimate sporting experience creates a specialized site of personal memory. A reliable piece of grouse cover is as much a physical place as it is a state of mind. Rosie was about eighteen months old when the "Gift Covert" got its name.

It was one of those leaden December afternoons when the sky's so low it's a wall shoved in your face. In a few days I'd be turning my house over to a renter, driving to Connecticut for a family Christmas, then moving myself to northern California where I'd accepted a two-year visiting professorship. It was a plum gig—teaching American literature and directing a research center—but I was anxious about the dislocation that I feared was coming. Tiny rural Athens, Ohio, where I could be in grouse cover fifteen minutes from my door, was a far cry from urban San Jose, the thirteenth largest city in the United States. The apartment I had rented wasn't pet friendly, so I'd be dogless. I might as well have been sent to Hell.

I was hunting Arrow Farm, one of my favorite close-in places. I wanted to imbibe everything I could of its terrain because that week would be my last stab at grouse for twenty-five months—the longest layoff in forty years of continuous bird hunting. Rod Lyndon was with me, as he often was in those days, on welfare most of the time I knew him then, and undoubtedly the worst drunk I've ever known. He was also extremely talented—mathematician, fly fisherman, cabinetmaker—the kind of person who could achieve anything if only he wasn't dysfunctional enough not to. People warned me Rod was an odd choice for a hunting companion, but he was a true-blue lover of working dogs, and bird hunting was one of the few things that kept his boozing at bay. We hunted together for a decade and a half without an untoward incident, and until our parting a few years before he died, it was just about the only endeavor during which he was responsible and trustworthy.

We'd been running Rosie a couple of hours in a cold rain without success and had turned west along the last thicketed bank, heading toward my truck. Rain kept falling, light kept draining out of the sky, and it felt as though it might snow any minute. Within fifty yards of the truck Rosie got birdy in a small hollow choked with autumn olive and a clutch of four grouse. Three broke left past Rod and were gone before he could shoot; a single flushed right, headed straight over the brow of the hill, past an abandoned farm house that looked like a setting for a slasher movie. I could hardly see the bird in the deepening gloom, and when Rod heard me shoot, he yelled to see if I'd gotten it. "No way!" I swung toward Rod and we started hiking after the three other escapees when Rosie, who had gone over the hill, returned with the single, stone dead. Rod and I stood around shaking our heads, lighting cigarettes, looking up at the sky, then down at our boots. "What a fucking great dog," he said. It wasn't booze talking.

Back at the truck, I ogled the bird—an adult male with a chocolate-colored ruff and chocolate tail band. Of all our Appalachian red-phase

ruffed grouse, those with brown (rather than the usual black) accents
are rarest, and come to hand once every three or four years. Opening its
crop was like peering into a secret cache of treasure. It was stuffed with
fruit of American bittersweet vine, a favored winter food for southern
Ohio grouse. Arrow Farm had some stunning stands of it, twined here
and there well up the trunks and branches of chokecherry and hawthorn
trees. I'd often picked low-hanging sprigs of it as a table decoration for
my game dinners. In just the right light—by dusk in the woods or by
candlelight around the table—the small orange berry clusters seem to
glow. I plucked the grouse on the spot—it had one 20-gauge #7 1/2
pellet in its head.

I handed the unzipped bird to Rod—if he got too crocked to
remember to cook it that night, his companion, Sue, would roast the
bird for both of them. (Rosie would be boarding with Sue when I left
town.) Unexpectedly, Rod countered with a gift of his own, drawing
from his canvas hunting bag a carefully wrapped Christmas present,
which he handed to me. The only other thing that kept Rod off hooch
was his woodworking and cabinet making. He'd long ago given it up as
a possible commercial venture, but when time, sobriety, and inclination
allowed, he turned out small pieces.

Rosie was the only dog I ever owned who could open a wrapped
Christmas present without ruining its contents, and she fell to when I
put the package on the floor later that evening. What emerged from the
wrapping and bows, with a little tweaking from me, was an exquisite
cherry-wood Shaker-style box with a dovetailed sliding top. Its unadorned
simplicity, minimalist lines, and seamlessly joined corners took my breath
away. I pasted one grouse tail feather in my hunting diary and put a
second one in the box with a small sheet of paper smeared with Rosie's
muddy footprint and a sprig of bittersweet. Rod's gift, which I still have,
seemed like the ideal place to sequester valuables.

In more than a decade of hunting with Rosie, she astonished me
so many times her performances became almost routine. I saw her find
other grouse I didn't even know I or a companion had hit, retrieve
downed woodcock from the middle of flooded Raccoon Creek, track
running grouse 100 yards, and nab wounded birds that otherwise would
have been lost forever tucked up under sycamore roots or limestone
outcroppings. She started to gain a word-of-mouth reputation; now and

then I hosted bird hunters—friends of friends—who drove over from Cincinnati or down from Cleveland to chase grouse with us. When she died of liver cancer in February 1994, two weeks shy of the end of grouse season, it left a hole in my heart that I thought could never be filled.

★ ★ ★

Sometimes the best things spring from the most inauspicious beginnings. Five months later I looked out my study window to see a grouse, which flew out of the woodlot behind my house, strutting its stuff on my walkway. My new dog, a slightly built eighteen-month-old, mostly white English setter I had gotten a few days earlier, was tied out in the back yard. The grouse sashayed within three feet of Babe, who showed not one iota of interest. No curiosity, no raised ears, no flash point, no chase, nothing, nada. At a hundred bucks, she was a bargain—a mercy purchase, runty last-of-a-litter that had to be sold because the owner—a friend of a friend—was headed to a place where she and her husband would not be able to keep all their dogs. I had hunted once with Babe's sire, so I knew the genes were there. But as I watched Babe ignore this gift grouse I was sure I had blown my money on a dud.

I placed Babe for a month with Randy Lawrence, who put a foundation of voice commands and pigeon work under her. As soon as woodcock season opened in September, I had Babe out every spare minute on as many resident, then migrant, woodcock as I could. To say that progress was slow is an understatement. She was such a timid little soul that, during the first few weeks when a woodcock or grouse flushed, she would retreat behind me and cower. Well meaning observers (Rod among them) urged me to get rid of her—"She'll never amount to anything," they said. I worked hard at Babe's wild bird training, even though she ran past sitting birds and bumped others or backed off a point often enough that I began to think those voices were correct. "Maddening," "frustrating," "perplexing," I scrawled in my hunting diary.

But when Babe screwed up, I patiently followed Roy Strickland/ Randy Lawrence protocols (no harsh methods, no electronic collar)—I spoke to her quietly, whistled softly, handled her gently, set her up on point again, and whoa-ed her firmly. Repetition is everything with dogs, especially setters who habitually come along more slowly than pointers.

I was fortunate enough to have a new cadre of hunting companions—Mike McCollister, Lars Lutton, and Jaimie Roederer—who bought in to my commitment to Babe's slow-hand education, and on many trips they took care of shooting while I took care of Babe's check cord. By mid-November, when I had worked her on nearly 100 different woodcock, she finally put together a string of a half dozen solid finds and points that signaled, faintly anyway, the possibility of future success.

Handling woodcock was one thing; handling grouse was another. Babe had been inconsistent on the latter, so I was skeptical that she would be able to make the leap. After the woodcock migration was over, I hunted her a dozen times with intermittent success. Then it happened. The student in the last row suddenly caught on to calculus. On the last day of December 1994, everything fell into place. Babe nailed a running grouse in a blowdown and held the point while I got into position. I dropped the bird going straight away and she fetched it handily.

The whole moment was as simple—or as complex—as that. After thirty trips and three and a half months of reinventing the wheel daily, she made it seem effortless. "Atta girl," "Good Babe!"—I squealed on and on, praising her lavishly, petting her up, feeding her snacks, waving the grouse in her face so she wouldn't forget what we were after. Who can say for certain what sets a bird dog flowing? Somewhere inside her a light clicked on, a circuit closed, a spark ignited. In the remaining two months, we killed another dozen grouse over her points.

Babe wasn't an imposing-looking animal. She was not a stylishly long-limbed or long-feathered setter. Sometimes her tail was a glorious flag; other times it barely made half mast. She did not have a fluid gait but a choppy, ambling run. She did not quarter naturally, but she divined early on that zigzag hunting the heaviest cover was the way to go. In athletic trim she weighed only about thirty-eight pounds (roughly half the size of the late, lamented Spike), but she had incalculable stamina and endurance. From the time her bell-collar went on until it came off three, four, five hours later, she was all business, and she put my lazy ass to shame. She had no quit in her and if I took a break, she refused to recline, but stood up the whole time as if poised for flight herself. Entreaties to "lighten up," or "put a lid on it" went unheeded. She almost always hunted within ear or eye shot, and when she did make a bigger loop to find a bird, she often held her grouse—the wildest, wariest of all upland birds—for seven or eight minutes until I trotted up to her, ready to shoot. "Babe was spectacular today," I noted in my journal on the last day of the 1998 season.

More than anything else she had a tender sensibility, perhaps born of her early timidity. She would never charge a grouse, no matter what the provocation or seduction. If she was out ahead and got a suspicion of scent, she waited for me to come abreast before she pushed on. And when she was in her work-a-bird zone, she moved with such purposeful patience and deliberation that it looked like she was "walking on soft-boiled eggs," in Leadbelly's immortal words. She was so adept at her approach that the birds were almost always within a few feet of her nose, so very early in our partnership I changed chokes in my over-under to Skeet and Improved Cylinder because my shots were too close to require tighter patterns.

When Babe had her mojo working, she was dialed in to her destiny in a way I had never seen before. She had that mysterious quality borne in the blood—an indefinable element—that can't be taught, bought, manufactured, duplicated, but only witnessed, praised, and honored. Once, after a grouse flushed off her point through cover too thick to see the bird much less mount a gun, she followed it fifty yards and pointed it again. When I reached her she was frozen in classic mode—blood-tipped, brush-beaten tail high, right front leg crooked—but her head was craned upward. I followed the angle of her nose and saw the grouse perched twenty feet up on the limb of a chokecherry. It was a special moment made even more special by the grouse itself—when it came to hand, it turned out to be another of those rare chocolate-accented birds I admire so much, and I gave thanks twice over. How Babe knew to tip me off, or how at other times she stood her ground staunchly for a second and third woodcock or grouse after the first had already flushed, never ceased to amaze me. That she never ran deer or rabbits or messed around with turkeys was icing on the cake. I know I sinned against her by frequently taking her for granted, or praising her so immodestly that her ears must have burned. She spoiled me silly.

Babe's abilities moved my hunt companions, too, and taught us more about bird hunting than we deserved to know. She's the only dog I've owned that inspired an oil painting and a poem. My lifelong friend,

John Mitchell, frequent beneficiary of Babe's dexterous points, called her "a heart-borne arrow stuck into a mix/Of shadows. . . . Her white coat urging forward winter. . . ." She was the chief actress in so many wonderful moments of doggy derring-do that I can never recount them all, though my journals from her era are chock-full of the particulars, including photographs, in nearly every one of which she looks utterly bored and nonchalant. I don't think the end product—the woodcock or grouse in hand—meant much to her, but the process, the hunt itself, was everything. Hoovering every bird in the woods was a matter of pride to her. Watching her work was endlessly exhilarating: the magnet and its metal filings, over and over and over.

3. Her Royal Highness

Aside from varied physical skills, mental attentiveness, sensory impressions, and a storehouse of stories picked up in a lifetime of hunting, the most important thing I've acquired is that the definition of "great dog" or "best dog" varies and changes over time. Factors that make a brag dog are highly subjective and personal, and they change inevitably as time passes and as our requirements, expectations, habits, and habitats evolve. When Babe died in late February 2002, she had locked up on nearly 400 live grouse points. This was a startling number of productives in her way-too-short eight seasons, considering that the Ohio grouse population steadily and precipitously declined after 1983, its peak year according to the Ohio Department of Natural Resources (which has done relatively little to stop the free fall into oblivion, preferring instead to put its efforts and resources into managing deer and turkey herds, which now overrun most of my coverts).

When I got over my extended bout of weeping and blubbering about Babe's demise, I entered another try-out period, and I blew through several candidates before I hit on Jen, a leggy orange Belton Llewellyn setter out of fabled field champion Tekoa Mountain Sunrise. After my experience with Spike, I should have known better, but I was desperate to fill Babe's paws ASAP, get back in the game, and plug the hole her absence made.

Jen, perversely inconsistent, took up almost two years of time, money, and patience developing her devious specialty, which was to act nice and buddy-buddy by hunting close and checking in for the first ten to fifteen minutes, then, at the outer edge of a cast, quietly disappearing over a ridge to bust flocks of wild turkeys two, sometimes three, hollows away. On successive trips over a period of two weeks in late 2003, Jen's marathon bust-outs grew longer and longer until she was AWOL more than three hours at a time. I put her on waivers with my go-to guy Randy Lawrence, and in early 2004 drove over to Terra Alta, West Virginia, to pick up a seventeen-month-old tri-colored Ryman-style English setter from Preston Miller's Ruffwood Kennels. Meadow, regal from the get-go, got hold of my heart in no time flat.

When Meadow came aboard, the grouse population in southeast Ohio had long ago bottomed out. Numbers don't always mean much, but they provide context and perspective. I shot my X-hundreth in early 2002 during Babe's last days; since then I have managed a meager two dozen more, almost all of them over Meadow as well as occasionally my friend Dana Johnson's dogs. Quail were wiped out by a severe winter three decades ago and have never rebounded in huntable numbers in Athens County. If it weren't for woodcock in this part of the state, there would be little for a bird dogger to chase.

So dreams of an endless procession of staunch points on gangs of wild birds are just that—dreams, reflections, memories. According to the 2009 Ohio DNR survey, the range-wide flush rate for ruffed grouse is 0.38 per hour, which is to say that something close to three hours of hunting are needed to flush the equivalent of one whole grouse. To put it another way, thirty-three hours of hunting are required for each bird bagged. In the past seven years I've averaged thirty trips afield each season, about half of what I did as a younger hothead three decades ago. The dog works harder for less, and though I worry that she will get discouraged and throw in the towel, the truth is Meadow seems not to mind. Perhaps, like me, Meadow accepts the gambit as a test of character, though even having said that I know it isn't quite true. Moral high ground aside, neither of us can let go of ingrained habits. In such diminished times, perhaps nostalgia about the good old days is our inevitable portion, but I still hold out for something more palpable—if not the bird in the bag, then certainly the aerobic exercise we get in this unglaciated part of the state that does us both good. Better to say that ruffed grouse have become a trophy species here, an improbable challenge like fly fishing for permit or plug casting for muskies. If my traditional game dinners occur less frequently than they once did, the rarity of the game birds makes them even more delectable.

Meadow hasn't got the exceptional nose or extreme prey drive Babe and Rosie had, but she's solid on woodcock and the occasional planted quail or chukar at a local game preserve. She's dependable on grouse, too, though she isn't able to exercise her skills often enough in our home covers, which seem in recent years to be populated with extremely nervous, flighty survivor partridge that often won't hold for more than a nanosecond. Whatever the quarry, Meadow stands her ground at the flush, but no amount of gentle correction has been able to curtail her breaking at the shot. The good news is that she covers downed birds like a sweat, and feels it is her right to give them a parting love bite. She reliably finds winged or dead birds in challenging cover, but will retrieve them only a few feet, if that, before letting go. None of Meadow's habitual quirks and tics matter to me. The pleasure I derive from watching her work and move in the woods even when we come home empty handed is—for reasons I don't fully understand—more fulfilling and joyous than it was with superstar Babe. Perhaps it is because Meadow takes the crown as having the most queenly personality of any dog I've owned. When she arches her eyebrows in a dead-on impersonation of Mr. Spock, she borders on the imperious, and there are times when I wonder who is the real boss, who owns whom?

My partner, Kate, and I have young grandchildren—five on her side, one on mine—and now my late-life definition of a great dog, a best dog, is one who comes in from a hard hunt, having given an honorable account of herself, stands still for a thorough de-burring, then lies down on the sofa or in front of the fireplace next to our other dog, an aged Keeshond, and does not raise a hackle when one- and two-year-olds climb all over her, tweak her ears, and pull her tail. Maybe the profoundest mystery after all is how bird dogs insinuate themselves so deeply into our hearts and lives. Maybe the greatest question is why—in spite of all we know otherwise—we go on needing them so much?

Bird Dog Ben

Clyde Edgerton

In 1971, I separated from the Air Force after my five years of duty and rented a small apartment in Chapel Hill, North Carolina, near where I grew up. My bird dog Ben had died the year before while I was away. Soon I was teaching high school. One day I promised a group of my students all the pizza they could eat if they'd help me move an old upright piano from its home (up two flights of stairs in an apartment across town) into the back of my pickup truck, back across town, and into my place. Thirteen students volunteered. We got the piano moved into my first-floor apartment, ate pizza, and within the next few weeks I started writing songs. The first song with words was about Ben, and the first verse went like this:

Bird dog Bell had some puppies, I think she had ten.
The one I chose was a hotshot—I named him Ben

★ ★ ★

Young Clyde Edgerton & Bird Dog Ben. *(Courtesy of Clyde Edgerton)*

I've owned *one main* dog in my life—Ben, a liver-and-white English pointer. (For some reason the adult bird dog owners I knew when I was growing up—friends of my father and Uncle Bob—when speaking of a bird dog's color, always used the word "liver" instead of "brown." But of course they would never say, "Hey, there's a liver baseball glove," or "She's one fine woman—tall, laughs a lot, liver hair.")

I owned Ben over his ten-year life span, from the time I was sixteen in 1960 until I turned twenty-six in 1970.

* * *

My first pet was a black cat named Inky who one afternoon got run over, but not quite killed. I was in the front yard when it happened. My mother took it upon herself to finish Inky off with a baseball bat—as a good deed. I was six. This event marks a significant milestone in my life for it's the day I learned that when things die, they stay dead. Next came several dogs in succession—Sergeant, Bullet, Dusty. Little mixed-breed dogs, called "sooners." Sooner be one thing as another. We never actually bought any animals—never a need.

It just occurred to me that you might think my mother killed them all, but she didn't. That I know of.

★ ★ ★

When I was growing up, my father always had bird dogs. The two he had the longest, from when I was a toddler until I was eight or ten, were English pointers, Nick and Sam. Nick was black and white, and Sam was liver and white.

My father, a farmer turned insurance salesman, was—as I knew him—a relatively passive man, not much of a joiner. He went to church but never prayed aloud—in a church where many people did—and though there might have been empty seats in the church sanctuary during a service, he always sat against the back wall in a cane-bottom chair. (My mother sang in the choir.) He read no books, only the newspaper. And I'm not sure how *much* of the newspaper—he *would* have read most anything about baseball, for he loved baseball. And he loved quail hunting. Those seemed to me to be his only two passions. Well, he loved to eat, too. Especially Mama's good cooking. Mama liked to cook while looking out the kitchen window for badly wounded cats.

My father started smoking cigarettes when he was twelve and quit when he was sixty-two, but not before emphysema had started its cruel march to the sea. He lived fifteen more years but didn't have the breath to do much hunting during his later life.

On those occasions I was home on leave from the Air Force in the winter, my father would ride with me out to the woods of his boyhood home for a quail hunt. That farm, more than 100 acres, was still in the family then, intact, and was usually home to several coveys of quail. Because he didn't have the breath to walk much, Daddy would sit in the car and wait for me to come back in with Ben after the hunt. Then we'd talk about the hunt—and about Ben, who had turned out to be, with minimal training, an exceptionally good bird dog.

My father's passion for hunting and baseball more than made up for his passivity in my eyes. And he taught me all he knew about both. What if he'd been interested only in literature, politics, religion, or other abstraction-studded endeavors? In college and after, I stumbled onto all the abstractions I'll ever need, but without him, I would have missed the finer points of baseball and quail hunting, perhaps missed them altogether. And I would have missed out on bird dog Ben.

* * *

Nick and Sam, those dogs my father owned the longest, and that I grew up around, were family. They weren't brothers or uncles, of course. But they somehow seemed more *important* than my pets—Inky, Sergeant, etc. For one thing they had a job. Hunting. And they had clear, adult personalities. Nick was cool, distant, proud—not easy to know. Sam was warm, friendly, the type to walk up, throw an arm around your shoulder, and say, "Hey, man, what's up?" Or that's how it seemed to me way back then.

Early on, I got an idea of how bird dogs should be treated. To this day, I hold on to the rules, prejudices, and guidelines I learned from my father and mother about dogs, especially bird dogs:

- Feed your dogs a combo of table scraps and cheap dog food mixed together. Leftover chicken bones are fine. Mix the scraps with dry dog food and water and serve up. Feed them once a day, at evening—after they've been let out of their pen to run around a while.
- Dogs should have good manners. They must come when called— no hesitations. No leash is necessary. They should never jump up on a person. (A few sharp knee kicks, or a short section of garden hose to the nose should solve that bothersome problem).
- If you don't have time or knowledge to train your dogs yourself, then perhaps your priorities are jumbled.

- Dogs should stay out of the house. Bird dogs, anyway.
- Dogs should be trained not to chase chickens.

★ ★ ★

I owned a shotgun when I was twelve. That family custom seems out of date these days—in my academic circles anyway. If I gave my son a shotgun on his twelfth birthday, somebody would call Social Services. If my mother were alive, somebody would have already called because of some neighborhood cat situation.

★ ★ ★

We had a few bird dogs after Nick and Sam, and by the time I was sixteen, Queen was our bird dog—the only one. She was sired to a dog belonging to a friend of my father's and on a snowy day, February 29, 1960, ten pups were born to Queen there in the doghouse in the backyard pen. I had first choice and I chose the biggest one, a liver-and-white big-footed prize.

I remember a few more of the lines from that song I wrote about Ben. I changed his mother's name from Queen to Bell because Bell sounded better than Queen. I remember:

For five long years we hunted many a field and hill, what a thrill.

Yes, the song didn't win any awards.

During my last two years of high school (1960–1962) my father and I trained Ben. Our methods had been passed down from father to son, uncle to nephew, for generations—among people who hunted in order to put food on the table and money in the bank. Around the turn of the century my Great Uncle Alfred sold bundles of quail—tied around the necks—for a quarter a bundle in Raleigh, North Carolina.

I gathered from my father and also from my Uncle Bob, who lived and hunted quail near Ocala, Florida, that it's important to hunt a young untrained dog with an older one, and an early task is to train the newcomer not to rush headlong into a grounded covey of quail, but to rather hold the point, giving in to that powerful bird dog instinct to stalk quietly and very slowly—then to freeze, never pouncing.

For puppy Ben—while teaching him to point like Uncle Bob and Daddy showed me—I'd tie a small ball of newspaper onto the end of a string that hung from a fishing pole. Then I'd sling it out in front of him. He would charge it. I'd jerk it into the air before he reached it, drop it elsewhere. He'd charge it again but perhaps hesitate just a second before getting to it. I'd lift it, fling it out again, and he'd drop into a beautiful point for maybe three seconds and then he'd charge the paper. Within a few days, little Ben, only weeks old, was holding a picture perfect point for a long time. The instinct to stalk prey and freeze is so strong that in some bird dogs this training is relatively easy, but in others it's not. Ben was easy. In fact, Ben was already coming into what would be his eventual person-like qualities. He was smart, enthusiastic, obedient, and *brotherly*.

In the field, Uncle Bob's technique was to tie a long rope around a young dog's neck. When the pup charged a covey pointed by another dog as he invariably would, Uncle Bob let out rope, the dog picked up speed, and then just as the rope gave out, Uncle Bob jerked on it—a shocking discouragement for running into a covey of quail. Several of these episodes would normally teach a smart dog proper pointing technique.

Ben learned everything naturally and easily—honoring (or "backing") another dog's point, retrieving, circling a field with nose to ground, winding, hunting close in thick woods, and farther out in thin woods.

Because my mother, father, and I spent time in Florida at my uncle's home each winter during hunting season, Ben learned the ropes there and also in North Carolina, where he and I often hunted alone, most often across the rolling hills and old fields of my father's boyhood home. Here's the full process for hunting quail as I knew it back in the 1960s:

I'd put on my boots, briar-proof hunting pants, and a hunting jacket, get my shotgun and shells. I'd let Ben out of his pen in the back yard and after he ran around a few minutes, I'd order him into the car trunk, then lower the trunk lid, and tie it so it would neither close nor pop open. I'd drive to "the farm" or another suitable hunting place, let Ben out, load my gun, place the safety switch on, and start walking on a general route I knew if I'd hunted that place before. Ben would gallop ahead with his nose lowered. He knew exactly what he was hunting for, and this process, now in fields and woods, held a pleasing tension and suspense.

If it were relatively late in the afternoon, the birds would likely be feeding in a field of wild lespedeza or perhaps in a patch of soybeans. If I was lucky, I'd come around a bend in a footpath and see Ben pointed in a field, as still as a statue—you've seen pictures, at least. I'd walk up behind him, talking to him softly, "Whoa, boy. Easy." I'd walk on past him, kicking my feet in the grass and weeds. My heart would be pounding, and on cold days my eyes would water from excitement. A covey of eight to fifteen quail would explode from the earth in front of me. I'd pick one with my eyes, pull the gun to my shoulder and shoot, swing to another and shoot, and by then the birds would be out of range. I'd watch where they scattered to, as best I could. If one of the two (or in rare cases, both) quail had dropped, I'd call to Ben, "Dead bird, Ben. Dead bird." He'd crisscross in front of me, nose to the ground, find and pick up the dead bird, and bring it to me.

Next, I'd start walking toward where the singles scattered into the woods. They often went for thick cover—a swamp or thick grove of small pines. "Hunt close, Ben." He'd stay close, and we'd hope to come upon a single or two, or maybe three, with him freezing within a few feet of the bird, so that I could, heart thumping wildly again, kick it up and shoot. Approaching Ben on a point was intensely satisfying. We'd likely be alone and he was holding perfectly, waiting for me. We were working together with unspoken expectations. After an episode like this, I'd realize anew that I needed no human being with me on a bird hunt.

And did Ben love his job. One day I was in the back yard, changing the oil in my car. The hood was up. I let Ben out of his pen, he saw the open hood, and thinking it was hunting time, jumped up on the engine, realized his mistake, and hopped back down.

* * *

Around home were neighboring farms with chickens roaming free. When Ben and I crossed a yard or field near a farm, he'd show an inclination to go for a chicken. After all, what's a chicken but a giant quail that you can catch? The first few times he chased a chicken I beat his ass with a switch, and he learned not to chase chickens. Same with rabbits. After a few training sessions, he'd walk through a yard of chickens, and he knew to stick close to me, not wandering at all.

Don't chase those chickens, they ain't what you're hunting for.

Once I shot a bird that, only wounded, ran into a large hole near a big oak tree root. (Where was Mama when I needed her?) Ben ran to the hole, sniffed, and then completely disappeared into the opening. I looked in and couldn't see him. I called his name. Silence. Suddenly he emerged from the hole with the bird in his mouth. Another time, late in his life, on a Florida hunt with several of Uncle Bob's seasoned dogs, he found eight of the twelve coveys found in that single day. Given the strong talents of the other dogs, this was the equivalent of several holes-in-one, a couple of grand slams—all in one day. I was proud of him, often talked about him to friends, girlfriends, anybody with whom I discussed home. Where I was known, Ben was known. I loved to show him off. Uncle Bob would say, "Where's that barrel-chested, handsome bastard?"

★ ★ ★

When I left home for the Air Force in 1966, my parents and six-year-old Ben moved to a house without a dog pen out back. Ben took up with a little black dog in the neighborhood named Skip. I heard about Ben through mother's letters, got lots of pictures, hunted with him when I was home on leave, and also allowed a neighbor to hunt with him.

Mama and Daddy each loved Ben as much as I did. He became more of a pet than a hunting dog in his last days, sort of a substitute son even, in an odd way, while their real son was away at war.

"Bird Dog Ben," ends like this (slow and lazy tempo):

I had to go away and stay for several years.

When I got back, this is what they told me, I couldn't believe my ears.

(The tempo picks up)

Bird dog Ben got lonesome and started to chase them chickens.

Farmer John got mad, I'll shoot that dog, he said.

Bird dog Ben got too close to Farmer John's back porch.

Farmer John shot him dead.

(Slow and lazy again)

A difficult question I'd like to ask you if I can,

Which is worse—a chicken chasing dog, or a bird dog shooting man?

I was stationed in Thailand when—in a letter from my parents—I got the news of Ben's death. They didn't tell me who'd shot him, but they let me know there was no argument against the shooting—he'd been shot in somebody's chicken pen. Skip was dead, too. I sort of wanted to know who'd done it, but never asked. Having recently, in 2009, had a chicken killed by a dog, I kind of understand. Mama understood, I'm sure.

The Dog I Belonged To

Ron Ellis

My life with bird dogs began unexpectedly in October 1976 while on a weekend trip to visit friends in Columbus, Ohio. At the breakfast table that Sunday morning, I saw an ad (I have it still) in the *Columbus Dispatch*: "BRITTANY SPANIELS—AKC, liver and white, orange and white, out of top southern Ohio gun dogs. $100." My wife and I had recently moved into an apartment where the owner said we could have pets, so we had started to search for a bird dog—one that could be both a field dog and a companion at home. From my readings, and from what I had heard from experienced bird hunters, the Brittany spaniel could be such a dog. Since both Debbie and I were anxious to have our first look at a Brittany pup, we called the breeder and arranged to see the puppies that afternoon.

The little orange-and-white pup growling and gnawing at her litter mates, her stubby tail already erect and twitching like a seasoned bird dog, got our attention from the very beginning. Debbie favored her and thought we should pick her, but I wanted to know more about the

(Photo by Joe Munson, courtesy of Debbie Ellis)

Ron Ellis & Lady, his Brittany Spaniel.

pedigree and to look over the litter some more before making a decision. While we played with the pups, the breeder told us that both the sire and the dam were from a well-respected kennel near Athens, Ohio, one known for producing close-working, affectionate gun dogs. By then I had hunted grouse and woodcock behind enough pointing dogs to know I wanted a small, close-working dog, preferably a female. Over the years, I had watched a number of hunters struggle to train their dogs to hunt close, beginning in boyhood on a quail hunt with a friend of my father's, who yelled at his English setter the entire day and nearly blew the pea out of his Acme Thunderer as he tried, unsuccessfully, to keep the dog from becoming "a speck on the horizon." So I knew right from the get-go I wanted to avoid such a dog.

What I wanted most at that moment was to know more about the pedigree, so the breeder put the pups back in the kennel, and we went to look at the papers. As we walked toward the house, I remember turning and seeing that same sweet pup plop her butt down at the kennel gate, point her soft muzzle skyward, and let out a mournful howl. And then she began to whimper, cry, and jump against the gate, and, well, that pretty much did it. We went back to talk to her, letting her hang on the wire, chew on our fingers, and take immediate possession of our hearts. There are some things papers can't tell you about a dog, so we skipped those, paid the breeder the $100, and took our new pup home to Kentucky.

We named her Lady—her official AKC-registered name would be "Ellis' Lady of Autumn"—but we soon learned she was anything but a lady. We tried keeping her out on the back porch in a custom-made dog house, but she howled most of every night and cried a lot while we were at work, or so the neighbors told us when we pulled into the driveway each evening. Soon, she owned our living room couch, slept in our bed, and rode up front with us in the new Buick hatchback. Her training, and mine, came along just fine: she learned the meaning of "come," "sit," and "whoa," and I learned she would sometimes obey those commands, or ignore them, as it suited her mood. At times it was difficult to know just who was training whom. Soon, it was clear I had much to learn about being owned by a bird dog.

Lady quickly adjusted to the loud noises I made by clapping aluminum dog dishes together at feeding time, and gunfire never frightened her, as she associated it from the beginning, I suppose, with the mysterious bird scent she was always pursuing. Back then we hunted grouse nearly every weekend, from the season opener in early October to the last day of February, and found quite a few grouse and woodcock on our hunts in southern Ohio and northeastern Kentucky, so Lady was exposed to lots of wild birds as opposed to planted quail. She knew more instinctively about all of this training than I knew from reading a pile of books on how to produce the "perfect grouse dog." Lady had great bird sense and was bold and energetic, and incredibly mischievous, which endeared her to me, of course, but also got her into some amazing predicaments over the years.

The summer before her first full hunting season, while exercising in a woodlot near our apartment, she was sprayed in the face by a skunk, which necessitated a tomato-juice bath followed by an extended stay in the custom-made dog house on the back porch. A few weeks after the encounter with the skunk, she knocked herself silly running into a telephone pole while chasing after me in the back yard. The following year she found herself caught in a leg-hold trap and when Bill, my oldest friend and hunting partner, and I attempted to free her, she snapped and growled and tried to eat us. Eventually, we slipped her head into the arm of my hunting coat and wedged open the trap. Later that same year, she nearly died after being poisoned, apparently by some tainted meat she had snatched from an illegal trap. She would have died if the vet hadn't thought to try an old remedy that relied on buttermilk to cure the stomach problem that threatened her life.

On our first grouse hunting trip to Wisconsin, she had her second run-in with a porcupine—the first encounter was during a camping trip to southern New York the year before—which resulted in emergency surgery some two weeks after we had returned home to remove a single quill that had gone undetected and migrated into her nose.

And then there was that hot October day when she dove into an uncovered well while we were hunting grouse on an abandoned farm in southern Ohio. Bill and Gary, another friend and hunting partner, were with me that day, so they graciously offered to lower me headfirst into the well, saying, "Well, she's your dog." When they lowered me into the hole I could see Lady swimming around in tight circles, already showing signs of fatigue. While being dangled down into the well, I managed to snatch Lady by her collar the third time she swam by me. Bill and Gary hauled us back up into the daylight and as I examined Lady for any damage, unbelievable as it may seem, Bill's Brittany, Smitty, blasted over the mound that hid the still-open well from view and dove headfirst down the hole. We couldn't believe our eyes, but it helped explain how Lady had made that same plunge. Once again, Bill and Gary offered to lower me into the darkness, this time with, "Well, you're already wet." So down I went, managing to rescue Smitty the first time he swam by me. Amazingly, both dogs escaped their dives without injury, so we leashed them and let them rest in the shade while we gathered logs to cover the well. As we worked, I remembered that Ivan Turgenev wrote, "Hunting with a gun and a dog is a delight in itself . . . ."

Most of our hunts over the years actually occurred without incident, and I often counted myself lucky to have stumbled onto such a wonderful dog to partner with in loving wild birds and the beautiful places they called home. My worries about having a dog that preferred to hunt the "far country" were put aside (most of the time), since Lady seemed to favor hunting close, steadily casting out in front, running her familiar figure-eight pattern. Because of this looping search-pattern she favored—she taught herself to do this without any help from me, which is why it was probably so effective—grouse often froze in their tracks on her return casts. This, of course, made for some memorable points and provided me with some great shots, many of which, I must admit, I missed. Since this was in the early years when we were still learning to play the game of grouse, we tolerated each other's weaknesses, whether it was my poor wing-shooting or Lady occasionally busting through birds.

But mixed in with those hunts when we seemed to stumble about and make every mistake listed in the dog-training books were some halcyon days when Lady and I seemed bathed in a special magic, and we created a few memories that I could summon later in life when my hunting would likely be confined to an armchair. These were hunts that, in the words of Dana Lamb, "it's safe to say we never will forget."

One such hunt occurred in January 1978 at the end of Lady's first full hunting season and after a blizzard had covered the region with record-breaking amounts of snow and bitterly cold temperatures. For a good while the roads were open only to emergency vehicles, but as soon as they reopened, Bill and I went after grouse in southern Ohio, along with Jim, our newfound friend and hunting partner, who was even more addicted than we were to Brittany spaniels and the whirr of grouse wings.

On the first day out, I found myself searching for Lady in thick cover—she was so full of pent-up energy that she had surrendered to the siren-call of the horizon shortly after we had entered the woods—and in doing so, I stepped into a drift that buried me to the top of my chaps. When I finally swam out of the drift, I struggled uphill to have a look at the cover along an old logging road, which long ago had been converted to a beautiful tangle of birdy looking honeysuckle and wild grape vines. I found Lady there, standing still as a statue along the edge of the road, her butt sticking out one side of a honeysuckle thicket, her head poking out the other, pointing toward a small clearing. If I expected to have any chance at a shot, I knew I needed to be as close to that clearing as possible, and I had to get there quickly.

With the snow averaging better than eighteen inches on that hillside, the trip was more lunge than creep. Lady never moved as I approached. With her eyes nearly bulging out of her head, she never so much as glanced at me, which, she had taught me early on, meant the bird was probably right under her nose. I took a deep breath, checked the safety and my grip on the new gun—my first double, a used Spanish side-by-side in 20-gauge—and eased past her point.

The grouse went straight out from me, close enough that I felt a backwash of snow-spray against my face. The bird seemed to hang out there in midair for a moment, the reddish hue of its tailfan appearing enameled in the sunlight, before heading for a narrow opening in the snow-covered vines. I was aware of the gun coming up, the bird floating above the barrels, and snow crystals spraying around the grouse as it tumbled. At the sound of the shot, a second grouse flushed off to my right and I missed it just as cleanly as I had taken the first bird. I broke open the gun and tried to pull the empties from the barrels—the little double was equipped only with extractors—but the faded red paper shells I had bought the previous summer at a garage sale were swollen and difficult to remove. And so there was no way I was prepared to shoot at the next four birds that came up out of the cover. In the distance, Bill and Jim hollered for me to say which way the birds had flown. I yelled the best directions I could manage and then stood there in the honeysuckle and pictured again that first bird rising and disappearing in the shower of snow crystals.

I found the bird not forty yards down the hill, lying with its wings spread, head turned to the right and its eye closed, looking as if it were sleeping, with only a drop of cardinal-bright blood on the snow to betray that image. I picked it up and smoothed its feathers before holding it out for Lady to nuzzle, and then I sat down on a log, draped the grouse across my thigh, and lit a cigar.

As I sat and smoked and praised Lady, I admired the handsome russet bird and thought about how much I needed the lovely wild places where grouse could be found. I thought, too, about how Lady's passion equaled mine for these "old brown birds," which is how one old Kentucky farmer described the grouse that lived in the hollow behind his tobacco barn, as I stood talking with him and asking for permission to hunt his farm with my new dog. I marveled, too, at Lady's tenacity in the grouse woods and how she had already taught me to never give up on a hunt, to move endlessly toward new cover, to the top of the next ridge and beyond, even when my lungs and legs burned and screamed for rest. Because of her dedication to the hunt and to me, I always managed to find the energy I needed to follow her little twitching tail and bouncing butt as she searched endlessly for the ribbons of scent that controlled her every move on this earth. And when she pointed, after working a bird long and hard, I prayed that I'd make the shot so she could find all that scent piled up in one place on the forest floor. She hunted her heart out for me, always, throughout all of our years together, with the meager expectation at day's end that she could remain close to me, maybe even sleep curled-up on the car seat beside me on the long ride home. And I tried never to disappoint her.

Lady grew anxious just sitting there and wanted to move on, so I packed my musings and folded the bird's wings against its still-warm body, before placing it into my vest. I called Lady to me and when she jumped up, I put my arms around her neck and felt again the excitement in the shared wild beating of our hearts, an excitement that never diminished in the more than fourteen years I belonged to her.

In memory, of course, Lady seems almost perfect, except for her undeniably hard mouth—she once denuded a fluttering grouse in just seconds after it crashed into a hillside less than fifty yards from where I had shot it, before either Jim or I could get there on a dead run. And though my skills at "shooting flying" needed improvement to the very end of our time together, no one ever tried harder to find and shoot birds for her, nor was anyone more dedicated in searching with her through autumn's colors to find the wild birds that made our hearts drum so fast and true. I'm certain no one could have loved her more, except possibly for Debbie, who stood with me that December afternoon as I placed Lady in the earth, along with the tailfan from the first grouse I ever shot over one of her points, her woodcock bell and faded orange collar, and a handful of spent shells loaded with memories, and then cried with me for what seemed like an eternity.

Hunting Without a Dog

Scott Ely

In the mid–seventies, I took a job teaching English at a small community college in northern Alabama. Professorial positions were scarce then, and I'd further limited myself by applying only to schools in rural areas, where the bird hunting was likely to be good. Sand Mountain is a plateau near the Tennessee line where the plantation system was never used, the soil being too poor. The land was broken up into small farms whose owners grew corn and beans and made whiskey in stills hidden in remote coves. Their sons had just started growing marijuana, a more profitable crop. It was still an isolated place where snake-handlers could practice their quirky brand of religion in peace. But the bird hunting on Sand Mountain turned out to be only fair.

I remember complaining about the hunting to the president of the college, who had once been a hunter of sorts. I suppose just about every boy who grew up in rural Alabama during the thirties and forties was a hunter at one time or another.

(Courtesy of Scott Ely)

Scott Ely with his Portugese water dogs.

"When I was a boy, there were so many quail you didn't even need a dog," he told me.

He went on to explain how late in the afternoon he'd wander out into the pea patch behind the farmhouse where he always found a covey.

And after he shot the covey rise and walked up a couple of singles, he'd go find the covey that hung out at the edge of the cornfield down by the creek.

"So if you started in the morning how many coveys could you find?" I asked. "I mean without a dog."

"As many as you felt like walking up," he said.

★ ★ ★

I still quail hunt, now in South Carolina. Last year was the end of quail hunting for my Brittany Patti, who has heart problems and arthritis and is going blind. We'll hunt my friend Dick Morris' Brittany this year, mostly on the Sandhills National Wildlife Refuge and the Sandhills State Forest. Both look like picture postcards of quail hunting country, park-like expanses of long leaf pines with an understory of clumps of wiregrass and evergreen shrubs. It's managed for quail both by burning the undergrowth and by planting food plots.

But there are very few coveys to be found. We shoot only covey rises because the singles escape to the swamp where it's difficult to hunt them in that dense tangle of shrubs, vines, and cane. It's impossible to walk, much less mount a gun when a single flushes. On warm days it's best not to go in there at all because we'd have a better chance of harvesting a few water moccasins than a quail. I've shot at a few singles from a sitting or kneeling position and have yet to hit one. The only result has been a few leaves floating down from the passage of the shot pattern and disappointed dogs running wildly about in the tangle.

Everyone has theories about why there are so few birds, but it's probably just hunting pressure. Once a farmer in Mississippi told me the decline of the quail population was the result of the sonic booms from the National Guard fighter aircraft cracking the quail eggs. That would be a simple solution; just ask those hot pilots to ease off a little. No need to worry about coons, hawks, possums, foxes, coyotes, or feral cats—the usual suspects.

But back to hunting *with* a dog. I've owned only Brittanies until last year, when I acquired a Portuguese water dog. My wife Susan was against getting another Brittany. She wanted a dog that didn't shed. Xanti will retrieve doves and go on quail hunts. I wonder if he will ever point and won't be surprised if he does. If I had been living in South Carolina seventy or eighty years ago, I might have shot a lot of birds hunting without a dog, but the hunting would just not have been the same.

Dick likes to say that he wouldn't mind being reincarnated as a young bird dog. I recall my first Brittany, Gill, barely a year old, retrieving a duck from a pond. I was bird hunting, and late that afternoon a flight of mallards came in to a little pond at the end of a cut cornfield. I crouched in a patch of head-high weeds with Gill beside me. When I put my hand on his back to make sure he stayed still, he was trembling with excitement. The ducks, four or five of them, circled once, then twice, then three times, and finally cupped their wings and came in to the pond. I don't recall the shot I made on the duck, but I do remember Gill launching himself off the dam and swimming out to retrieve the bird. I can still call up the image of him in mid-air, hanging suspended over the pond. I wish he could hang there forever and I could gaze at him. I'm not much of a dog trainer. Gill was simply a natural retriever. That was the first duck he ever saw shot. He knew what to do.

Gill was the first dog I ever owned who lived in the house. My mother was against animals in the house, and the two non-hunting dogs I owned as a child, a collie and a boxer, slept in the garage. Gill was a liver-and-white Brittany I'd bought from an Ole Miss administrator who hunted quail on horseback. Gill slept in the bed with my ex-wife and me. He went everywhere with me, riding in the front seat of my Volkswagen. When I picked my wife up from her chemistry class, I'd let Gill out of the car and he'd make a frantic circle through a large grove of oaks, sending every single squirrel into the safety of the trees. Occasionally he caught one and I'd take it home to eat, a squirrel grown fat on mast provided by the state of Mississippi.

And there was Avery, the magnificent handsome Brittany Susan rescued from the pound. His picture appeared in the newspaper as the dog of the week. Avery was orange and white with long silky hair grown to beautiful feathers on his legs. Susan tells the story that I was not very enthusiastic about his arrival. We had recently bought Patti as a puppy from a man who used Brittanies to hunt grouse in the Carolina Mountains. I deliberately selected a mostly liver-colored puppy so she'd be camouflaged for dove hunting. Actually Patti's name is Paté, her dark liver color reminding my wife of some good meals involving ducks in France. But it was not really a name I could call out in a South Carolina dove field, not unless I wanted to listen to my fellow hunters' gibes.

When Avery appeared we were spending several months in France every year, and I guess I thought two dogs would be too much for our house sitter to handle. Or maybe I was just in a bad mood that day, possibly irritated by a problem with the computer. That's the story Susan tells. I did complain mightily, but I was petting Avery at the same time. When she suggested that she would find him another home, I found myself suddenly adamant about his staying.

A few weeks later I watched Avery point a covey down in the Sandhills, undoubtedly the first covey he'd ever smelled. The story my wife got from the pound about Avery was that he was the pet of an elderly couple who died within a few months of each other, their kin too lazy to take the trouble of finding Avery a home. It would've been easy. Avery was the perfect dog. He was obedient and calm. Other dogs respected him at first sight. Even those big labs at my dove club never growled at him or tried to assert dominance. They recognized him as a sort of prince of dogs and gave him the respect he deserved.

But back to Avery's first point. It was in one of those glade-like places among the long-leaf pines, and the birds were in a patch of some sort of knee-high evergreen shrub whose name I always mean to look up but never have. Every fall when the season opens I find the dried leaves of the shrub, which I have dropped into my game bag, intending to identify them later at home with the help of a tree and shrub guide.

Avery pointed and Patti backed and I stepped into the patch of shrubs to flush the covey. I brought down one bird and watched the singles sail off to the safety of the swamp. I could find that spot easily, although I suppose those shrubs have grown taller by now. I wonder sometimes if Patti remembers that covey rise. There's a chance she does because there have been so few of them.

The first time I ever saw a dog point a covey was in Mississippi. That dog was Gill. I was hunting on federal land next to Sardis Lake, one of those lakes built by the Tennessee Valley Authority. Once, the land had been farmed. The only signs of human activity remaining were an old stone water trough and pieces of a still, dynamited by federal agents. That was when coveys were holding for a dog in fields of broom sedge. I can recall standing beside Gill, who was locked on point, and watching his eyes move as his nose tracked the location of a bird at my feet. I took a step and the covey exploded out of the grass and—like so many times—I shot too soon, before the birds were far enough away for the pattern to be effective. I watched the birds sail off a few hundred yards to land in the honeysuckle. At least then it was possible to hunt the singles.

On that day of Gill's first point, halfway across a broom-sedge field, he abruptly changed direction, his nose high in the air, and trotted in a perfectly straight line to a clump of honeysuckle at the edge of the field and went on point. I flushed the covey and didn't hit a single bird. I did better on the singles, which Gill found scattered about beside the creek on the other side of the field. It was an overcast day, I recall, with a fine mist in the air. I remember the smell of the wet leaves and their mushy feel under my boots. I put two birds into one of the big pockets of my army field jacket. It had been only a year since I'd returned from Vietnam. Maybe it was the shotgun in my hands or the smell of my fatigue jacket, but I recall pausing for a moment while Gill drank from the creek and suddenly being borne back to one of those night ambushes in Vietnam.

But it wasn't a bad memory. I recall wishing I were hunting ducks, not people, as I sat with my squad in a stand of bamboo at dusk, waiting to move into our ambush position. It was unwise to walk at dusk because it was hard to see. We'd have made excellent targets, silhouetted against the dying glow from the sky over the mountains. Often ducks flew in low overhead, on their way to roost in the paddy fields. I carried a shotgun, a Winchester Model 12 with a short barrel, but it was loaded with buckshot for people, not ducks, and besides we were trying to be very quiet.

As I sat there on those fear-filled evenings, waiting for my eyes to adjust to the falling darkness, I sometimes imagined having a dog by my side and my Browning automatic in my hand loaded with 4s or 6s. I'd even have been willing to call a truce and shoot ducks with the North Vietnamese soldiers. We could uncrimp the buckshot shells and cut the shot up into small pieces and recrimp them. I wonder if their army issued them shotguns. I wonder if we could have found a Lab someplace, maybe one of those dogs the army had trained to sniff out ambushes.

I hunted the land by the lake many times. One day I spent a few hours in the car with Gill, waiting for the rain to stop. I finished off a bag of boiled peanuts and then took up a collection of Wallace Stevens' poetry. It was a good day to think about Stevens basking in Florida sunshine in the middle of January. I wonder if he ever hunted quail like Marjorie Kinnan Rawlings did? I doubt it. He was a man who lived mostly in his mind. The rain finally let up. We hunted up through the woods to the water trough where Gill always got hot; but I never, during all the years I hunted that place, found a covey there. We were hunting the broom-sedge fields when dark, thick clouds moved in again. The thunder boomed and the lightning flashed. Ever the optimist, I thought I could see lighter sky over the lake and hoped it would clear. But Gill had more sense than I. As the rain came driving down and claps of thunder rolled through the woods, Gill stopped and looked back at me as if to question my sanity. We returned to the car and gave it up for the day.

★ ★ ★

I can recall Gill competing for sleeping space with my four-year-old daughter in the back seat of my Volkswagen. Because there wasn't quite room enough for both of them, they ended up entwined with each other. He never growled at her, even when she was sleeping hard, one hand tugging at his ear. That's one reason I like Brittanies. They're patient with children.

Arrian, who lived in the first century A.D., tells us in his manual on hunting that it is best that dogs sleep with humans, that they "find pleasure in human skin." Our dogs don't regularly sleep in the bed with us except during thunderstorms when Patti is frightened by the boom of the thunder or maybe the flash of the lightning. But she isn't bothered at all by the gunfire, even at a dove hunt, when I'm thankful for the noise-canceling ear protectors I'm wearing.

Patti was a great comfort to me when I was doing chemo. I was being treated for lymphoma, the result of exposure to Agent Orange during my year as an infantryman. I also had Agent Orange-induced prostate cancer and leukemia, the former treatable by surgery and latter not treatable but not likely to kill me for a long time. It was the lymphoma that might keep me from ever hunting again. Sometimes she'd sleep at my feet on the sofa or lie on the floor beside me, and I'd rub her belly until I dozed off. I became sort of like a dog. There were days when I spent most of my time asleep, only waking to eat. Some hospitals allow dogs into rooms of patients who are going to die. I read somewhere that the writer Corey Ford died lying in his hospital bed not long after he had wrapped his arms around the neck of his favorite setter. Patti seemed to know that something was wrong with me. I sometimes wondered if she could smell those toxic chemicals circulating through my system.

I'd lie on the sofa and think about my friend Dick, who was hunting down in the Sandhills. It was the last month of bird season. He'd call and tell me where he was going to hunt, and I'd imagine hunting a particular spot with Patti. Occasionally I'd imagine having some success with singles in the swamp. I'd dream of us moving among those cypresses and gums, maybe even breaking a thin film of ice on a patch of the standing water and finding one or two singles in a thicket of briars. I shot a few imaginary doubles on some of those winter afternoons I spent on the sofa with Patti curled up at my feet. I'd feel the weight of the birds in my game bag as Patti and I walked out of the swamp at dusk, setting a course for the road with the compass I always carry. I'd gotten turned around before in the swamp at night and it's not much fun.

We've recently banned dogs from sofas because my wife Susan has had one reupholstered, and we've ordered an expensive leather one. Patti won't be sneaking up on one very often because of her arthritis. When we imposed the ban, I reminded Susan of how the Russian writer Turgenev, a bird hunter, who was living in France at the time, yearned to return to his country house in Russia. He spoke of "setters jumping over sofas." I can't recall if he mentioned that he wanted to go home to Russia to hunt. He was a man who liked to roam about the countryside with dogs. His stories are filled with them. He was not a fan of those English-style hunts in which birds are driven by beaters toward a line of hunters.

Obviously, sofa-jumping dogs seem more romantic to me than to Susan. Xanti would like to be a sofa-jumping dog. And if I have to do chemo again, the ban will be lifted and both dogs will be welcome to curl up with me if they wish. We'll all lie there and dream of covey rises in the Sandhills.

★ ★ ★

When dove season opened this year, I realized that I was going to have to go out without a dog. I hunt near Aiken, South Carolina, and the opening day forecast was for temperatures in the high nineties. Patti was going to have to wait for better conditions if she got to go at all. Xanti needed more training. I had taken him toward the end of the season last year, and he'd done well, but I thought it would be prudent to work on his retrieving. As I've admitted, I'm not a very good trainer. Patti always retrieved well, but I did have a few problems with her. One year she went out to retrieve the first dove I shot and picked it up and turned to face me, a contemplative, satisfied expression on her face, and sat down and ate it: feathers, feet, beak, the whole thing. I put her on a lead and didn't let her retrieve the next three birds I shot and had no more problems with her. Xanti had already demonstrated that, when I threw the tennis ball in the yard and gave him the command "fetch," he would sometimes want to play chase instead of bringing it back to me.

For the last few years South Carolina has suffered from a drought. Jerry Allen, the founder of my dove club, had to plant sunflowers three times this year. Not as much corn survived, which allowed for more pigweed and Johnson grass to grow up. So in places in the fields doves are hard to find. Last year a dog was bitten by a rattlesnake. The Lab survived. Even if the dogs came with me, I would hesitate before sending them into one of those tangles. I wouldn't worry about the middle of the field so much. But on the edges where the field merges with the pines, I'd be concerned.

On my first hunt this year I was glad I didn't carry Patti with me because it was brutally hot. Most of the hunters in my club drive ATVs, but I carry an ice chest and at least a gallon of water for the dogs on a collapsible cart designed to transport a deer. There are plenty of dogs at the hunt: Labs, a couple of golden retrievers, and of course, since it is South Carolina, Boykin spaniels. When a dog is sent out to retrieve, it leaves a trail of dust. It hasn't rained for weeks. I sit by myself on the ice chest. Usually Patti sits panting in the shadow cast by my body unless we're lucky enough to draw the pear tree stand or one of the Chinaberry tree stands. It turns out to be only a fair hunt for me. I lose two birds in a stand of Johnson grass, although I spend a long time looking for them. Finally I give up, thankful that I haven't stepped on a snake. I miss the company of the dogs, particularly Patti.

Then a cold front comes through, and instead of the usual nineties, the predicted high will be in the low seventies. I decide to take both dogs. We draw for numbered stands and move four numbers away, at the sound of Jerry's air horn, three or four times, to another stand. That way no one gets to have a hot spot for the whole afternoon. But I'm worried about how all that walking will affect Patti. I plan on taking my time. Susan and I also discuss what I'll do if Patti has a heart attack and dies in the field. We decide I'll bury her there. It will be easy to dig a grave in the sandy soil. I carry along a shovel to do the job. It's a place she loves. I wouldn't mind being buried there myself, but there's probably a law against it. When I arrive at the clubhouse, I ask Jerry if it's all right to bury her in his field, and he says he has no objections. I hope nothing happens to Patti. If it does, it's going to be a hard afternoon.

The dogs are ecstatic when they figure out that I'm going to take them. Patti has some trouble climbing into the back seat of my SUV. She is wheezing and breathing heavily, but lately that's been the norm for her. She curls up on the seat and Xanti as usual sits next to the window, his forepaw on the armrest. We go out of town and head south on the interstate.

In Columbia I go through a barbecue drive-through. Last year the girl who worked the window would always give the dogs a hush puppy. But today it is a new girl at the window, who shows no interest in the dogs. I order a barbecue sandwich, onion rings, and some banana pudding. Patti is sitting up and looking toward the window, but I know that she can't see much. I thought Xanti might remember those hush puppies, but he doesn't show any sign of expecting something. Probably it's because of the new girl.

We arrive at the clubhouse. When I unload Patti from the car, she is wheezing. It makes me think of the asthma I suffered from as a child. I recall reading in Seneca that the ancients called that affliction "rehearsing death." Some nights she wakes me up, and I reach out to pet her until her breathing returns to normal. I can't decide if I'd rather watch her die or wake to find her dead on her dog bed. I pour her a bowl full of water and she drinks most of it. I'm eager to find her a spot in the shade. She lies down in the grass in the shade thrown by the truck, while I sit on the tailgate and eat my barbecue sandwich, some of which I share with Patti. Xanti is off visiting other dogs. Before long he wanders back for a drink of water and the last of my sandwich and lies down next to Patti. I'm saving the banana pudding for after the hunt.

Xanti has no idea Patti is ailing. If I have to bury her in the field, I expect him to sniff at her before I lower her into the grave. Surely he will understand then. And it's then that I realize how much I would like her to live for another four or five years. But that is just the emotion of the moment. I don't want her to be uncomfortable. My neighbor's Lab made it to seventeen years, and I don't think the last couple of years were pleasant for her. I'm also thinking about myself. I'm not going to be one of those people who presses his oncologist to give treatments that will do no good. I have an ex-oncologist friend who retired from his practice because of those irrational demands from his patients. He now works for hospice, helping the terminally ill slide out of life as gracefully as possible. One afternoon, as we were walking to our court at the tennis club, he told me he had just left a patient with congestive heart failure who was sleeping peacefully and was not going to wake up.

After we draw, we drive to the field. It's located next to a church, one of those little country churches, and we park on the grass under some big pines. The club makes a donation to the church every year in return for parking privileges. I give Patti more water to drink and we linger in the shade. Xanti decides he is afraid of the deer carrier when I take it out of the back of the truck. I think it's the rattle of the metal parts that scares him. But it's pretty easy to calm him down. I just hope he doesn't become gun shy. Patti has lain down in the shade, and I check to make sure she is not lying on top of a fire ant mound.

Once she stops panting, I load the ice chest onto the carrier and start for the field, which is only a few yards away across the road to the church. The other members are already on their stands. Patti walks into the ditch before I can stop her. She's momentarily confused but gets out easily when I call her to heel. We go across the road and into the field, making our way slowly to the stand, which fortunately is in the shade of a Chinaberry tree. Patti has a hard time keeping up, and we stop several times and wait for her. Finally we reach the tree. I give her another drink of water; she begins to dig a hole. I sit down on the ice chest with Xanti beside me. When some shooting starts up from the other side of the field, his ears perk up. I'm happy he's not showing any signs of being gun shy. Patti concentrates on her digging. I do hope that she enjoys something of the day.

A few birds fly over, but they're so high that Xanti doesn't notice them. Patti still lies panting in her hole. I think about packing up and going home. Letting her die out in the field had seemed like a good idea, but now I'm not so sure. After a while I'm almost glad that I'm not getting any shooting because now Patti has stopped panting and seems comfortable. Xanti lies down too. After two hours sitting there, I've only heard a few shots.

One of the things I always liked about having Patti hunt with me was sharing the excitement of the hunt with her. She'd notice me crouch low when a bird headed my way. She'd follow my eyes and locate the bird. She'd react to the click when I took off the safety. When I mounted the gun, she'd follow the direction of the barrel, anticipating a retrieve. Now she can't even see the gun. I recall one long retrieve she made when she was still a puppy. I shot at a high bird I probably should have left alone. The bird flew on, but then we both watched it drop at least 200 yards way. I told her to "fetch" and she darted across the field, found the bird, and brought it back to me. Her tail was wagging furiously, her whole body trembling with joy.

When Jerry blows the air horn at 3:00 PM, we pack up and move to the next stand, which is about 100 yards away. Patti has a hard time, and I stop in the shade of a Chinaberry tree to let her rest. We reach the stand, which has only a little shade. When I take a seat on the ice chest, she lies down in the shadow cast by my body. Xanti works hard at digging a hole under a low bush. As the shooting begins to pick up, I see that the birds are flying a pattern at the upper end of the field. I take out my map of the field and calculate that we will be on a stand near their flight path at the last move that comes at 5:00 PM. I don't expect even to get a shot at my present stand. When the horn blows again at 4:00 PM, I'm proved right. I've spent my time petting Patti and giving her drinks of cold water from the plastic jug in the ice chest. I think about eating the banana pudding but decide to save it for the end of the day, as I'd intended.

Instead of going to the next stand, which is in the opposite direction of our final stand and at least 200 yards away, I find an unoccupied one close by, under a Chinaberry tree. There's plenty of shade. We slowly make our way to it. When we arrive, Patti immediately digs another hole. I take a handful of ice out of the chest and let her lick it. I rub some on her belly, which she seems to enjoy. Now the shooting at the other end of the field really begins to pick up. I expect people are working deep into their limits. We've decided to limit ourselves to twelve birds instead of the legal limit of fifteen in order to stretch out the shooting over the three seasons allowed in South Carolina. Xanti is interested. He looks intently toward the far end of the field. A few stray doves fly by, but none close enough for me to be certain I'll make the shot. I want to be sure Xanti associates the sound of the gun with a bird falling out of the sky.

But I never get that shot. Finally the horn blows for the last move. Jerry will let us hunt until six. We want to give the birds a chance to come in and feed before they go to roost. Patti is moving very slowly, but at least she's not wheezing. I hope that's a sign she's not going to die today. I reach the stand and set up the ice chest in the shade. The doves are coming from the West, from the field across the highway, flying out of the setting sun. The shooting is almost continuous now. Unfortunately, the stands are three or four deep between me and the highway. My fellow club members are dead shots, and very few doves manage to make it to the area around my stand. If I call Jerry on my cell phone, he'll try to move me to a better stand. But I don't want Patti to do any more walking. We're close to the truck, no more than 200 yards.

I spend that hour watching other hunters shoot. Xanti gets bored and digs a hole. Patti lies at my feet and licks a pile of ice cubes. I imagine her sound asleep, curled up on the back seat as we drive north on the interstate toward home. I hope that someone will knock down a dove near my stand and Xanti will have the opportunity to retrieve it, but that never happens.

Finally it's 6:00 PM, and Jerry blows the horn. I haven't fired my little 20-gauge Browning over-and-under. But Patti is not wheezing, and I'm thankful for that. We start back to the truck. We take our time. I stop twice to give Patti a drink of water. Finally we reach the truck, and she lies down in the shade. She's wheezing again. Now I'm mad at myself for bringing her. I give her more water to drink and some ice cubes to lick. I roll her over and pour some water on her belly, checking to see if any fire ants have gotten on her. But she is free of them. Then to my surprise she begins to roll about in the grass as if she were a puppy. Xanti tries to play with her, but one growl from her lets him know she is not interested.

When I load her into the truck, she gets in without too much difficulty. I turn the air-conditioning up as high as it will go and direct the vents toward her. She turns her head in the direction of the cold air and enjoys it blowing on her face. Xanti curls up on the seat. I load up the deer carrier and my gun and the bag I use to carry shells. Then I take the banana pudding out of the ice chest and eat it slowly. When I finish, I give Susan a call and tell her that Patti is all right.

We drive toward the interstate. Home is two hours away. The sun is slipping behind the trees. Now and then doves fly across the highway on their way to roost. As a young dog, Patti liked to ride in the front seat and every time she saw a bird of any kind—dove, vulture, or blue jay— she'd follow its flight. I know that this has been her last hunt. Darkness overtakes us north of Columbia. Both dogs are asleep and I'm listening to Mozart. Patti begins to whimper. She's dreaming, perhaps of something frightening. I try to stretch out my arm to pet her, but she's too far away. But then I decide it's all right, the whimper a joyous sound. I hope she's dreaming of a covey rise. I imagine that we follow the singles into the swamp, and there in the gathering darkness she goes on point and I slip through the briars and vines, and in a little open space I flush the covey and shoot a double. She retrieves the birds and presses them, still warm, into my hand. Now it is completely dark in our dream swamp. I take a compass bearing, and with Patti at my side, we pick our way through the thick tangle toward the open darkness of the big pines.

Almost Out of Season

Peter A. Fritzell

Fortuitous is often confused with *fortunate*. What is
fortuitous happens by chance or accident or without
plan; *fortunate* and *lucky* are not thus restricted in
meaning. What is *fortuitous* can also be *fortunate* or
lucky, but to employ *fortuitous* in the sense of those
terms, without clear indication in the context of the
operation of chance or accident, is loose usage.

The American Heritage Dictionary

There is much fortuitous in the hunting of ruffed grouse, and more
yet, along with a good measure of reflective indecision, in the aging
considerations of a northern January hunt, beyond the turn of a low-bird
year, and approaching the very end of the season—when temperatures
haven't been above twenty degrees for five overcast days, and the last
day of sun you can recall was colder than a witch's . . . or a well-digger's
. . . when you haven't been afield for ten days, and the dog has taken to
thrusting a squeaky toy at you during the evening news—and you no
longer have the élan you had in your late fifties, and working up the fire
has come to be more and more a matter of positioning yet another piece
of split maple or yellow birch.

Peter A. Fritzell & Brittany spaniel Jessie.

In the early evening of a Wisconsin January, there are many good reasons not to think of one final, season's-ending hunt, and to resign yourself to living out the winter on memories while you try to concentrate on some televised *Wheel of Fortune*.

There is much fortuitous, as well, and a good deal of the fortunate in your relationship with the particular bird dog—the fifth in a thirty-five-year series of Brittanies—"Jessie" by name, "Jess" for short, large for her kind, and largely white—who, having given up on the squeaky toy, is now curled on her bed in the corner by the fireplace, her sleep troubled (or comforted?) by residual sensory impressions, as you might call them—subconscious odors, images, and sounds summoned from how long past?—from the time, four-and-a-half years ago, when you first cradled her in your arms?—from her puppy days, when squeaky toys were almost constant business?—from your first serious hunt together, she barely seven months old, chasing as many flying sharptail as she flash-pointed over your ancestral, Dakota grasslands?—from her first limit-day on Wisconsin grouse, early in her second season, after the morning rainstorm and into the humid midday of leafy late-September, when she so etched upon your mind what has become her signature, the point that seems to last forever, the stance she will not break, no matter your boot-stomping, and the result of which is often an immediate grouse or woodcock in the face of things, that you sometimes wonder if her disposition to hold fast isn't one of her ways of responding to your age?— from which, if any, of the intervening hundreds of hunts, walks, and runs does she take the terms of her sleep and the restoration of her energy?

Or is it that she dwells only on what you call the recent past?—the anticipation of any moment when the two of you may be out together again, leashless, exposed, and "free" in the only meaningful sense there can be, not a release from connections or restrictions, not by any means, but the condition in which you comprehend that from which you are not free—as at the height of October last, when you worked like a precision duet in big country, hardly missing a note or glance or gesture with each other? Or those four waning, cold days of last month, on only one of which did you give her a bird to bring to hand, your grouse of the winter solstice? Or even, perhaps, despite their accompanying irritations, the dawning moments of early fall among cattails and phragmites, when she was engaged, half against her will, in teaching yet another puppy (your younger son's then six-month-old, highly athletic golden Lab) the vital premonitions of duck call and gunshot, and the basics of reading pothole-country breezes?

If all your ratiocination seems terribly anthropomorphic, it's probably worth remembering that you're pretty much stuck with your anthropomorphism. And it's certainly worth appreciating the fact that bird dogs are especially adept at exposing your anthropo-logical limitations— "Woof." Whether you're equal to them or not, there are obligations implicit in these relationships, commitments you must somehow weigh against your arthritic condition and your climatological forecasts.

In the evening's meantime, as it were, your *Wheel of Fortune* seems to have become *Jeopardy*—or better, perhaps, *Antiques Roadshow.* If the ambient outdoor temperature and your osteod age continue to hold you back, you need to consider the rather simple thought that Jessie hasn't given a squeaky toy a second glance since mid-September, and that the now-eight-month-old female retriever puppy ("Farmer" by name, "Farm" for short, built like a Derby-winning filly) hasn't been out hunting for more than a month. You owe the dogs a good run, at least, which wouldn't take anywhere near the time it would take to make the four-hour, round-trip drive to some accessible cover where the season's still open.

But consider that there's virtually no snow on the ground, neither here nor on those distant islands of Sand County aspen. Perhaps in the difficult marshes that separate and surround the islands, but very little, if any, beneath the occasional clusters of pines, or on the south-facing oak edges with their berry shoots and occasional chokecherry, where for years you have undertaken one last January hunt, which usually means no more than two hours of walking, as often trudging, in heavy or crusted snow—in one, at most two, coverts—and when you're lucky, a bird or two flushed—or if you're extremely fortunate, a good point or two, and perhaps even a shot.

Maybe in the aspen-cut to the south of the road that leads to the cranberry marsh, where there were no birds two years ago—but where last year, after two hours of heavy work, Jessie swung upon a foot of snow in fading sunlight into one final point for the year, one fabulous point, held and held in thick cover, for one last shot and a glimpse of a departing bird—where (how many years ago?) there were four or five grouse, two of them together at the end, with two of Jessie's predecessors pointing, whichever one backing the other, and one of the birds proved to be a red-phased January possession—and where, some years later, now that you recall them, two birds found by utter chance, after yet another two hours and a wide mile of seeking, under the thicket of a downed oak, one of them treasured a quarter mile to the car and home for a midwinter meal—matters of sustenance.

With but twenty days remaining in the lawful season, and your hope fixed upon a day when the temperature must rise to a sunny thirty degrees—or now even to a cloudless twenty-five degrees—your visions seem to be becoming increasingly hazy so that the day after tomorrow (to be thirty degrees and cloudy) looks briefly hospitable, until you hear about the anticipated rain and accumulating snow—and tomorrow, January 10, just a few days beyond Epiphany (twenty-two to twenty-four degrees and cloudy, preceded by a night of ten degrees), begins to look like about all the Red Gods are going to grant you.

So you go to bed thinking less of grouse than of two cabin-fevered dogs, trying not to think of giving Jessie one last hunt in this year of the down-cycle, or of receiving from her one final bird to bring the season to a fitting end. You set the alarm for 7:30 AM, and try not to think of how pointless the hours of driving for a two-hour hunt through midday will doubtless be. You drift off thinking that she will enjoy herself in any case, and that puppy Farmer will find every boisterous moment informative.

You get up more or less sleeplessly at 5:00 AM to take two ibuprofen and turn off the alarm. You rise, in a manner of speaking, less pained but more doubtful, an hour later than you've intended, and with far-fetched dedication, get your act together, pick up the energized Farmer ("Good morning, Farmer. How's the Farmer?"), and hit the road—two hours west to those islands of aspen.

As with Aldo Leopold in *A Sand County Almanac*, you think, perhaps, that "There are two kinds of hunting: ordinary hunting, and ruffed-grouse hunting"—and "two places to hunt grouse: ordinary places, and Adams County"—and maybe even "two times to hunt in Adams: ordinary times, and when the tamaracks are smoky gold." But you try to convince yourself that there's a third time to hunt Adams—another extraordinary time, beyond the gold dust of autumnal tamaracks.

You try not to think of the mile-long hunt into the corner where the drainage ditches meet and late-season grouse occasionally find some refuge. You no longer have the time. You try to repress that downed oak surrounded by the aspen-cut, concentrating instead on some cover more immediately approachable, some place in which you may have just a chance to make the most of your foreshortening time.

You think, perhaps, if no one is there, of the nigh impassable stuff along the haphazard south edge of the slight ridge that runs east from the dead-end where you sometimes park the truck, where the wildlife management plan left everything but the trunks of the big oaks that were cut ten years ago or more, the shin-bruising stuff that, with new growth, means even the dog can't work in a regular pattern, no matter the wind. You think of the January grouse found more than those ten years ago, beyond the eastern end of that stuff, not much more than two hundred yards from the dead-end, in nearly two feet of snow, grouse—four, five, six—out in the marshy patches of willows, when two of you with two dogs couldn't trudge much farther, and you got one on the very last day, in the last few hours of the season.

Or you recall the single grouse found out that way in what may have been the following year (if it wasn't one of the years when you had to hike in because the road was drifted shut), the single grouse, the only one of the day, that rose (and had to rise) into an afternoon sky, and fell to be found among blowdowns on the opposite side of the thickest cover around. And the islands across the marsh to the south by a couple of hundred yards, and the little pine plantation, and the heavy growth along the ditches that flank the road you drive in on, not much more than a half hour's hike to cover them all, where turkey tracks once so fascinated the then ten-month-old Jessie on her first January hunt, so entangled themselves with the tracks and scent of grouse, that you were fortunate to get one fluky shot and one serendipitous bird.

If no one else is there, a slow mile west off the highway with the dogs now getting antsy—if someone else is there, you'll have to reorient yourself, reconsider, retrace your mind tracks—and another, slower half-mile north on the rugged road of frozen sand, along the flanking heavy cover until the dead-end comes into view. No one is there.

So the dogs may tumble from the truck, race around and around on a light dusting of last night's snow, checking out this and that, marking with a selective squat you know not what, the Brittany's head high upon a southeasterly breeze, speeding back down the road for a hundred and more yards, and pulling the inexperienced Farmer so far beyond her retriever's instincts that she comes zooming back on the direct line of a long, imaginary, retractable leash.

While the walls of canine cabin-fever are warping outward, you place your own rather random mark upon the edge of the forest and make your way to the back of the truck, first for a good stocking cap, then for Jessie's bell-collar (you no longer need to mince more than a word or two to find her gently presenting her muzzle; she knows what the bell bespeaks), and finally for your vest, gloves, and gun.

As you take your first steps on the trail to the east, the dogs running too far in front of you, you think, perhaps, that there's an almost oxymoronic quality to this January grouse hunting, a blend of nearly impossible opposites—an almost hopeless smiling, perhaps, with the dogs and the fresh air and the cluttered view ahead. You don't much treasure the thought of the heavy cover to come, but there's no turning back now without crushing a certain Brittany's soul. It's a kind of commitment to a process with no clear end in view, a sort of half-intentional exploration without much by way of anticipated discovery—except, of course, through the dog, vicariously.

Time to get off the trail, whistle Jessie around—the puppy, unable to command our attentions, alternately gallumping along behind her or running back to you, trying to make some sense of what you all are doing. Locate, if you can, a passable deer trail heading in what you think of as your preferred direction—east for a ways, then finding yourself impeded, south, away from the dog, before climbing over the back side of a blowndown oak, and then east again, drawn by her intermittent pauses, tail wagging, nose thrust under a log, or up against a clump of grass, glancing at you, and again and again for the next few minutes, as you wait upon her experienced revelations—nothing doing, apparently, except the residual scent of rabbit, vole, squirrel, and deer.

Time to head south—in part, at least, because she now wants to work south, if not southwest—turning slightly back upon yourself then, and soon whistling her to the edge of the marsh you must cross to get to those southern islands.

In the awkward, frozen hummocks of marsh grass, you move slowly, trying to take your cues, where you can, from the narrow runnels of deer or, once upon a time, muskrats, listening for the bell that invariably heads for the nearest woody growth—which, in this case, is a long stretch of impenetrable, head-high willows—and thinking with affection, of how much she has learned, how well she knows, quietly whistling her over when her bell stops out of sight, and then leaving her to her own devices when she has satisfied herself that you are crossing east by southeast rather than south, somehow understanding that you want her to work the west edge of the east-most island first. With no steady trail to guide her usual figure eights, she knows that in cover like this you work irregularly.

So that on this particular day, you come to the south island circuitously, in a ragged, indecisive, semi-elliptical pattern across the iced-over marsh, through breaks in the willows and alders, and wrong upon the southeast wind—from the east and even a bit of the southeast rather than the north or northwest—in large part, because you've somehow found yourself wanting to cover more ground, or you've wanted Jess to cover more ground.

Shaped like an elongated boomerang that curves from east to southwest—a hundred yards deep at its deepest, and no more than three feet higher than the surrounding marsh—the island of light grass, berry shoots, and scattered aspen will eventually lead you on a course across the wind, and gradually out to the sandy road a quarter-mile south of the truck—but not yet. For the immediate future, you need to head west, and even a bit northwest, toward and along the outside curve of the boomerang.

Hence, you must slow down, pausing here and again as Jess loops out and back along the near-southern edge of alder, angling on the wind, adjusting her patterns to the changes in your direction while you, in turn, coordinate your flanking movements westward upon this heavily glaciated upland.

You wait then, until, trailed by a tiring puppy, Jess crosses your apparent path to reach on out to the island's northern margins, and then to turn west, southwest, and back on south toward you.

If there is much fortuitous in these latter days of grouse hunting—if the essence of the hunt is a matter of somehow expecting the unexpected, even against the day's and time's imposing odds—you must, on occasion, have thrust into your human mind's eye some image, some appearance, nearly miraculous, as when, with but the slightest of foreshadowing signs, Jessie's head rises in surprise to her west, wrong way on the wind, and she freezes, a knowing glow upon her face, and you know by now that she knows that you know.

Caught in her tracks, she shifts her uneasy stance but slightly, a short foot at most, and against the odds and ends of aspen trunks and branches, a grouse rises, almost straight up, as if to sit in a tree—without a snowball's chance on the same trajectory at the same speed—and a second grouse comes slanting, tailfan spread, too tightly above and across your left shoulder to the southeast.

The day's and the season's and even the years' hunting thus comes to its end in the almost overwhelming moment—for you a kind of tearful joy, for the dogs now running behind you to the east, you know not what, but you cannot help thinking for the older one, at least, something comparable—"Bring, Jess . . . bring."

Turning back toward the first bird, which must have taken some time to fall straight down, you watch as Jessie races to find it—stone dead, as we say—and the young Lab piles into scattering leaves and plumes of snow to seize it, to bounce her way back to you, to present the prize she thinks she has won, and then to leap and peck at it, until it disappears somehow in your vest.

At such a juncture, on a snow-dusted island of aspen in a northern January, the dogs nibbling bits of snow beside you, there is little point in going on. Against your reasoning, late-season doubts, all considerations seem to have converged in the moment's end.

But moments do not so end. Duration demands otherwise. You have some 800 yards yet to walk to the truck—and the dogs, the dogs are not about to stop hunting, not now. The older one is almost insisting on the direction of that second bird, southeast, into the wind, and you have no interest in disappointing her.

Quite the contrary. So off to the southeast you will go to cross another strip of marsh, to rise slightly to another island, this one more open and expansive than the last, and to let her work all its edges, out and back, up and down, scanning it and contiguous covers thoroughly, paying close attention to each of your suggestions—knowing, as she does, that there's a bird out here somewhere—until it's time to turn around.

With a good half-hour behind you now, you head northwest, then west, crossing your own tracks, revisiting the point of the original flushes, reaching out in deeper loops downwind, and coming out upon the road that will take you home.

About all that's left is the heavy cover flanking the east side of the road to the north; but Jessie hardly gives it a moment's notice. She heads on directly across the road, down and up the banks of its western ditch, and straight on through some seventy-odd yards of ragged knee-high slash—downed branches, stumps, whips of aspen, grassy new growth—the half-acre swath of a recent cutting.

Only when she gets to the inward edge of the clearing, does she turn to read your direction, to find you and the puppy waiting and watching from the welcome level of frozen road. Only then do you signal her north, only then do you take a step toward the truck and home, only then do you hear the thrum of a bird flushing from the edge of the road well ahead of you, wide open, and too far out—but with the Farmer now racing north in pursuit, you cannot (and should not) resist a pointless shot.

Within thirty seconds or so, Jess has returned from the far reaches of the clearing and, within another thirty seconds, has made it apparent that this now long-gone bird took flight from the tip-top of a three-foot tangle of upturned roots—and more, that the bird had company, which must still be around—facts now confirmed to your limited, human senses by the imprints of two distinct grouse tracks in the fresh snow on the iced-over ditch. Up and down the edge of the road she goes—ten yards up, ten back—into the ditch and out again—while you and the puppy wait upon her quick readings of the evidence, which soon take you across the ditch and into the downed branches and stumps, for ten irregular yards, and then twenty, not far—until she turns almost back against you, left, into the wind, head high, hopping over and around two or three blowdowns, and into a point.

No longer inquisitive, she stares slightly downward, looking as if she can see into and through the clump of grass and branches no more than a yard in front of her nose, and hardly more than thirty feet front-left of you. She is pinpointing everything that matters for the nonce, giving you in the process the nearest thing you can get to a guarantee in the sunless clearing of a late-season afternoon.

Both of you know for certain what is about to be discovered. She is telling you precisely where it will appear—while you, head high, are stepping slowly toward the mark, hoping against hope to return the favor of her certainty. But the Farmer, off your right flank—the young Lab, not yet so much given to deliberation, now closing rapidly upon the mark, now dead downwind at twenty feet—now also knows what revelation is at hand, and that she, and only she, will be its final cause—plunging her imprudent snout, head, shoulders, immediately beneath her mentor's nose and into that clump of grass and twigs, to capture that revelation or possess the discovery or, if nothing else, to force it out into the open where you can deal with it, flying not where you might expect it to fly, not any angle of upward or outward into the wind, nor any degree of left, but low and close and clear to the right, no more than shoulder-high, fast across in front of you, an entirely open shot, a bit awkward, but successful—*bring*—the dogs so fast in their pursuit downwind that they both overrun the bird by thirty yards or more.

Gun empty, you cannot help but stand upon the instructive scene, watching Jessie turn abruptly, running back those thirty yards (the puppy closing on her tail), shifting briefly in the conic breeze of scented gunpowder, and pouncing to secure her bird—*hers* this time, as she will have it. Standing, bird in mouth, in a little break beneath a berry bush—and confronted with a determined youngster—she pleads with her eyes for you to play your role. She parries the puppy's insistent thrusts by dodging this way and that behind the berry bush, until finally she can extend the bird to your outstretched hand, with a serious growl for the Farmer—"*Okay, Jess,* I've got it—*Okay.* Good girl. Jessie's bird." And as the puppy leaps at your grousy hand, "Good Farmer."

The quarter mile north along the road to home continues with the Farmer behind you, trying to get a sniff of your vest, while Jessie swings well off the road on the flight-pattern of the bird that flew wild some ten minutes ago—and the distant sound of its departure from the top of a tall pine. How much she knows.

As you walk up the road, you think not simply that the dog's anticipations have proven more dependable and sustaining than your own, but that she has proven once again her capacity to bring you out of your late-season doldrums—that without her expectations and interpretations, or what you can make of them, you can have little perspective on your own.

As you think, the dogs now both trotting slowly ahead of you, some rather dreamy reflections run through your mind—what a brief, lasting time. The season of the year has come to an end you could not imagine even an hour ago, and you can now wait upon next year's season with some considerable contentment, the moment almost serene when the dogs are curled together on the back seat of the truck, and you know again for certain that there are moments, however brief, when the fortuitous and the fortunate are synonymous, however loose the usage.

The Dewbird of Sappiness

Bruce Guernsey

No matter what you actually name them, bird dogs always end up being called something else. "Doodle," "Dolittle," "Duodenum," "Dufus," "Dewbird"—these were just a few of my dog Dewey's nicknames—and if it's true that the number of nicknames is an accurate measure of love, then Dewey was worshiped. I even called him "Dwight" on those occasions when we had to have a serious talk about something, like his not retrieving woodcock, for example. "Dwight," I'd say, looking down his overly-long-for-a-Brittany beak and into his sweet brown eyes—"Dwight, your namesake, Dewey Evans, could catch anything out there in right field. Remember that catch in the '75 series against the Reds? Just pretend you're him next time, okay, and bring the bird back."

But Dufus never would, though he loved to point them. He'd hold and hold and so would the bird then, *whee*, up it would whistle, towering above the alders, and, *whack*, if I was on, down it would come on the other side of the bog. Dewbird would be after it in a jiffy, in love with mud and water as he was, but out of his mouth would come the bird just as fast as he'd tried to fetch it. "Damn it, Dolittle," I'd yell, and end up

(Illustration by Victoria Wollen-Danner)

Bruce Guernsey's Dewey.

sloshing my way to where he sat there trying to get the taste out of his mouth. With all that mouthing he was doing, I swear I could hear him talk, maybe trying to explain himself, "Hey, I'm sorry, but timberdoodles taste like worms."

That's because Dewey was a wit. I mean, this hound was smart, and not the easy kind of smart like learning "sit" or "stay," and I have proof, such as when my father and I got our first deer together, a real nice eight-point. Obviously, to me at least, so special a deer had to be mounted, and I was in the living room admiring this new addition to our decor when Duodenum trotted in. I wondered what he'd do, maybe growl a little or maybe even point, but he cocked his mathematician's head instead and made a beeline for the next room. This went on five or six times, back and forth between the two rooms, so I went in to see what Doodle was up to, and there he was staring up at the wall. And why not, it suddenly occurred to me. Where's the rest of the deer? He was trying to figure it out. And why would any animal stick its head through a wall to begin with?—something he must have mentioned to my wife, who insisted I take that awful thing down.

And then there was that incredibly cold January day with the wind ripping right out of the Rockies into east central Illinois. There's no place colder in the world than these open fields out here when the wind blows like that, but it was the last day of the pheasant season, and my friend Johnnie Mack Simpson and I were going out no matter what. But that was something the silly dog already knew, and he was panting by the door before I'd even made coffee. "Such clairvoyance, Sir Dufus," I said to him, "and so early," and off we went to pick up John.

There was a deep creek about thirty yards wide that cut through a cornfield we liked to hunt. Even this late in the season, a rooster or two always hung out in the thick grass between the stubble and the water. "Let's start from the bridge and work the west side first," I said to John, not meaning to give orders but because our guide, Mr. Dewey, had already bounded that way. There was no use trying to whistle him back: none of us could hear a thing in the fierce wind and with our hats pulled down over our ears besides.

We'd gone a couple of hundred yards doing various Marcel Marceau imitations to try to keep the dog close when a cock bird flushed wild and hooked towards the creek. John made a good quick shot and knocked him down at the edge of the field, and the chase was on: the bird into the grass with Doodleness on his trail, then, splash, into the creek they both went. But it was no contest. Midway across, the bird was in my gallant doggie's beak, then out they came on the other side, one shaking and shivering Brit, and one very startled cock pheasant.

"Here, Dewey," John started to yell. "Here." But Dewbird didn't move, other than to tremble in the wind, soaking wet. "That's my bird, damn it! Tell your dog to bring it back!"

I tried to reassure John that his pheasant would not get away and called to Dewey myself, but I knew he wouldn't budge. Instead, he was pondering, something to do with Newtonian physics no doubt, cause and effect. He looked at John, then me, and then at the water he'd just come out of and at the bridge a quarter of a mile away. Hmmm . . . "I'm not going back in that icy stream for anything. Sorry, guys," and off he went with Johnnie Mack's baffled bird blinking away, and J. Mack himself hopping about like Yosemite Sam, "Bring my bird here, you no-good varmint!"

And Dewey did, of course, going all the way back to cross the bridge as any sage fellow would have done, then ambling proudly up to us as if he had a peacock in his beak and not the recently expired pheasant he dropped at my feet. "Good dog," John said, as I helped him stuff the bird in his coat. "Good dog." Dewey wagged his stub happily and shook ice crystals all over John, then winked my way and off he went.

But now to the dark truth about this clever pooch and how he came to be that way: he hung around with cats. We'd always had a one or two, so when Duplicity came along, he grew up with them and learned their ways. He even baby-sat for the occasional litter that inevitably showed up. The kittens would clamber up his fur when he was lying on the floor, scoot along his back to his Frenchman's nose and leap, then circle back to do it again. The mother cat didn't seem to care and seemed to have the hots for Dewbird herself the way she'd rub against him, fluff her tail in his face, and purr-r-r-r.

The oddest thing, however, was his friendship with a chubby kitten we named Pudge. Perhaps because they were both named for Red Sox players, Dewey would sneak into the garage and pluck the little cat from his nesting box and carry him off, the way he once carried around a butterfly that later flew away as if untouched. The same kitten each day, the same one out of the seven in the litter—it was amazing. Then out in the yard he'd lap and lap wee Pudge all over, then tote him back to the box, wet as a newborn. They were inseparable for years after that.

"Your dog's a sap," Johnnie Mack said, when I told him this story. And there's no doubt that Dewbird was, and no doubt, too, that his being a cross-dresser had something to do with it. "We are lumberjacks and we're okay," and Dewey, too, it must be told, dressed in women's clothes—or more accurately, in the doll's clothes my three-year-old daughter chose for his outfits.

★ ★ ★

We got Dewey the first fall after we moved to Illinois in 1978. I'd always wanted a bird dog, having for years hiked cornfields and kicked brush piles without one, and now was the chance because we'd bought a house with a few acres in the country and there would be plenty of space for a pup. But I also wanted to have the dog around inside, to have him with us. "You'll ruin him doing that," some guy at the local gun club warned me as I watched him throw his dog into the trunk of his car. "Thanks for the advice," I said, and knew for sure I wanted my wife and kids along when we went to look for a pup.

An ad in the paper led us to a local kennel that had a litter of Brittany spaniels for $55 each. That seemed high to me then, which suggests how little I knew about buying a dog, and I may well have looked elsewhere except for the long-nosed, gangly little guy that followed my kids everywhere. They insisted, and their mother and I agreed, and home we went with our first dog. A few days later, the Red Sox lost to the Yankees in that notorious Bucky Dent playoff game, and in memory of my beloved but defeated team, Dewey got his name, which somehow leads me back to the aforementioned cross-dressing issue.

If I could think of this puppy as a baseball player, why couldn't my three-year-old daughter think of him as a doll she could play with and dress up? Thus, my would-be hard-hunting hound soon found himself arrayed in bonnets and blouses, tee shirts and tights. "You'll ruin him doing that!" I heard the guy at the gun club say again as Doodle would appear festooned with ribbons and bows. Ruin him? The heck we did. He was the best-dressed bird dog in Coles County, Illinois.

He even had a favorite hat, a Beetle Bailey kind of cap I'd put on him when we'd head for the fields. He'd hop in the front of the old beat-up Saab we had and wait for me to strap the seat belt around him. There he'd patiently sit with his long legs splayed out in front of him and his crumpled cap on, its visor down the length of his beak. Stopping at traffic lights caused some consternation for those waiting next to us who'd look over and see what they did.

But Dewey was all business when we'd get to a field, and he could run from dawn till dusk. Sadly, however, there were fewer and fewer birds each year as Earl Butt-head's farming policies had their effect. Fence-line to fence-line plowing meant the end of hedgerows and other cover across much of the Midwest, and Doodle and I would often go out for a whole day and find no more than a pheasant or two. He never gave up, though, and was tireless despite the lack of game.

It was around then that someone suggested I try squirrel hunting, and when I began to read various recipes for Brunswick stew, I decided to give tree rats a try. And why not? We lived in what was one of those pockets on the pool table that is Illinois. Our little section was unglaciated and full of steep ravines and hogbacks where white oaks and shagbark hickory abound: a perfect spot for the fattest fox and grey squirrels I had ever seen.

This was no hunt for a bird dog, however, and I left Dolittle in the garage and sneaked out the back door to climb the wooded hill behind our house. I found a spot with lots of cuttings on the ground, loaded my .22, and made myself invisible.

My wife had no idea of my afternoon plans and, of course, let the dog out as soon as she came home, a half hour or so after I'd locked him up. I was four or five hundred yards from the house and well above it when I saw this white and brown-spotted, long-legged bloodhound cut across our back yard, race through a field, circle back twice, sniffing his way along as he madly followed exactly the same serpentine trail I had made, then around my tree three full orbits before he ever looked up and in front of himself sat me. Thus was born the best bird 'n squirrel dog ever made.

He learned what we were doing almost immediately and sat perfectly still just next to me, if quivering counts for "still." Oh how that little dog would tremble, but he never moved an inch. Instead, he watched the branches for any kind of motion, his eyes rolling about like Marty

Feldman's. But as soon as Dufus spotted a squirrel, he'd stop shaking altogether, on point but from a sitting position. I didn't have to do a thing, except shoot straight, and when I did, he'd retrieve russet foxy or shadowy grey like a quail, then snug up beside me to scan for another.

All that mast on the ground also meant a huge growth in the deer population in our area during those years, and I decided to give Bambi a try as well. My father came out from back East to hunt, too, and we got that wall-hanger eight-point the first season out. Poor Dewey was much dismayed when I'd gear up in the early morning but would leave him behind. My wife wasn't too happy, either, because he'd whine and cry, waking the kids and her, so after the first deer season, I put Dewey in a kennel to save his sanity and my marriage.

I hadn't yet taken up hunting with a bow, but Johnnie Mack had and used to come out from town in the late afternoon to hunt behind our house. One night he came back ranting and cussing about a buck he'd hit and couldn't find. It was pitch black by that time, but we hiked around with lanterns, anyway, like the townsfolk after the werewolf and with the same result. "My buck," The Mack moaned, sounding like someone I'd heard before bewailing his carted-off pheasant. "Where's my buck?!"

"Come back real early tomorrow. I know how we can find it," I said, looking down at the thirty-five-pound wooly wonder leaning against my leg.

John was back before the sun, and off we stumbled with the dog along, though Doodle gave me that quizzical look of his, wondering what kind of hunt this was without any weapons. It had rained some over night, and the blood trail was mostly washed away, so we didn't have much choice but to spread out and head up a steep hill where the deer had gone. Four legs good, two legs slow, and Duplicity was out of sight in a second, and nowhere to be seen when we reached the top. I called and whistled, but there was no sign of him anywhere. It was as if he were on point, holding as he would forever and waiting for me to show up.

"That's it! On point! Dewey's on point somewhere," I yelled toward John who cupped his ear to hear what I was hollering about.

"I tell you, the dog has found your deer and is pointing it," to which John replied from fifty yards away or so something about "full" and "shit."

So on we searched, but as the mist began to clear and the sun to make us blink, what's that I see, off there through a lumber yard of tall grey trunks and down a slippery hillside? A little patch of snow, methinks, but an oddly furry patch, it seems. Sure enough, that was my bird dog with his first buck, and a whole one at that, with both a head *and* a tail. The deer had died overnight, and John was ecstatic, promising Doodleness a hunk of back strap. He even gave the boy a kiss and hugged him plenty. But Dewey didn't quite believe him, I could tell, and was soon off romping the woods towards home. Pointing his first buck can make a bird 'n squirrel 'n deer dog hungry.

But the most famous of this dog's many feats was the eternal point he held in front of an audience of hunters, plus the game warden, my father, and me. Pop was nearing the end of his hunting days, but he wanted to come out to try for some birds one more time and to watch Dewey hunt again. The Illinois Department of Resources had set up a program for pheasant stocking on land leased from local farmers, and I had been lucky to get two permits for one of these hunts, so off we went, Dewey strapped in the back seat this time, but still wearing his cap. He drew the usual much-amused crowd when we pulled into the parking lot of the Conservation Office, but this was old-hat to him, as it were, and he never once blushed, waiting in the car as we went in for a lecture from the warden about how not to kill one another. Each group was then assigned an area to hunt and cautioned that there was absolutely no shooting until 9:00 AM *sharp.*

My father and I got to our field a good half hour before that, however, and I was about to open the Thermos when, *whew* in the confines of the car, let's just say it was easy to tell that Doodle needed out. He made it on time, did his business, but then started acting birdy, sniffing around a small brush pile no more than twenty yards from the car. Then suddenly, he went on point. And a hard point, too: flat, low and locked in.

"That your dog?" I heard from the window of a pickup that had pulled in behind us. Each hunting area could hold up to a dozen hunters, and they were now just arriving and checking their watches.

"How long will he hold?"

"I guess we'll find out," I answered, and the countdown began.

Poor Dewbird. He couldn't figure out what the hell I was up to: "Here I am with a rooster at the end of my nose, and you're shooting the shit with a bunch of guys about the time of day. And who's that guy dressed in green anyway?"

Yes, that's my dog, I told the warden, and, yes, I know I still can't shoot for another fifteen minutes, and, oh, was I nervous because my old man had just told me there was no way in the world that he'd take that shot when the time comes if the dog was still holding. That meant I was on stage for a crowd that had gotten bigger and bigger, maybe twenty or more by now and included my father, *my father,* but so what because I'll bet Duplicity's up to one of his cat-learned tricks, and there's no bird at all and no way to miss when there's no bird but, wow, are my palms sweaty as "ten, nine, eight," the warden is announcing the five-four-three seconds left, and I am heading for my execution but pump a shell in anyway moving up behind the statue that was once my dog, but what dog can hold like that for some thirty minutes with people all around when *gobble, gobble, gobble* was the last thing I remember until *Dewey, Dewey, Dewey,* and everyone is out of their seats and cheering like he'd just hit a grand slam and is rounding the bases with a big fat pheasant in his mouth, the goofy Dufus forever in slow motion like it was tomorrow and not twenty years ago.

Long may he run.

The Dogs in My Life

Jim Harrison

Our greatest politician, Thomas Jefferson, said that "good wine is a necessity of life for me." I agree but he should have said, "Good wine and good dogs are a necessity of life for me."

Maybe it's as wrong to call a great man like Thomas Jefferson a "politician" as it is to call a grand sporting dog a "dog." It's too categorical. For instance the best dog of my life was an English setter named Tess over whom I shot at least 1,200 birds, including grouse, woodcock, four kinds of quail—Bobwhite, Mearns, Gambel's, scaled quail, and also sharptails and Hungarian partridge. Bird hunters are invariably sentimental about their dogs unless the animals are outright incompetent. With Tess the actual proof was simply in the numbers, though with a dog, that's never more than part of the story.

I imagine that within the vast number of dogs in America the categories of "use dogs" and sporting dogs are small indeed. Half the year I have my studio on the Hard Luck Ranch near the Mexican border. This is improbably rough cattle country, and rounding up or moving cattle from one area to another would be impossible to do efficiently

Jim Harrison with Tess, his English setter.

without cowdogs, which are usually purebreds or mixes of blue-heeler, Australian shepherd, border collie, and sometimes Catahoula leopard dog to give them a bully edge, the latter occasionally excessive as Lisa, a female Catahoula here, who had to be given away after she tore a horn off a recalcitrant bull. She was fairly large and liked to sit on my lap, though this affectionate nature didn't embrace misbehaving cows. Just the other day a covey of Gambel's quail wandered through the barnyard in among the dozing cowdogs, who only reacted with boredom to an occasion that would have electrified a bird dog.

Once on the ridge summit of Hog Canyon near the Mexican border we were sprawled on the grass resting from the steep climb when Tess, also prone on her side, went into a full point in that position. My hunting partner noticed it first and nodded, and at this same moment a Mearns quail cock marched past her nose and then between us.

It was an extraordinary afternoon as a little earlier Tess had pointed a few feet below the crown of a hill too steep for us to scramble up, then held the point as she slowly slid backward some hundred feet or so to the bottom where we stood. We call this being "staunch to point." Another desirable word and characteristic is "intensity."

★ ★ ★

To start at the beginning I've always trained my own dogs but I wouldn't offer this as a necessarily wise move. My first bird dog in 1964 was an extremely full-chested and muscular bitch named Missy. From the moment we picked her up in northern Michigan she in fact became our trainer. As a pup she could scale tall bookcases to play with the cat. We were quite poor at the time, living in a drafty rental for forty bucks a month in Kingsley, Michigan, with a furnace that couldn't raise the heat past fifty-five on the coldest winter days. At the time of getting Missy I was trying to grouse hunt with Verl McManus' old beagle, who had a singular talent of pattering around the woods treeing grouse at which point he'd yip. I'd pretend the grouse had just barely landed or was on the verge of taking off when I popped them out of trees, and then one day I shot one on the fly flushing down between aisles of pines. The beagle naturally looked at me with admiration.

By the time Missy was six months old, I knew I was outfaced and took her to a trainer; he said euphemistically "that's a lotta dog," as she climbed with some success a fir tree in his yard to get at a squirrel. Sad to say for both of us, we moved that fall to New York's densely crowded Long Island just after Missy had learned a new trick. After I ran her she'd re-enter the yard at top speed and leap over the entire hood of our car, brake with her front feet while her momentum would pivot her ass around so fast it would drag her backwards a few feet. Quite a dog.

A university community is no place for a sporting dog or sporting gentleman. We had two years of solvency but at the price of boredom for someone who had grown up around woods and water. I was in my mid-twenties and never took a real job again. The rest of our life has taken place in the immediate area of trout fishing and bird hunting, and where I could train a dog on wild birds right out the back door. Missy had taken to excavating our suburban yard, and upon my coming home from a wretched day at the university, she'd hear my car and explode upward from under the ground like a creature in a horror movie.

Sad to say, but soon after coming back to northern Michigan, Missy came down with fibroid cancer and died. When I dedicated a novel to her many people were upset, assuming that one of our children had died, and were further confused when they discovered "it was only a dog." How can I forget the way she entered a pasture woodlot as if it were full of grouse and then the ground shook as she drove a big herd of Holsteins toward me as if they were her gift and she was wondering why I didn't lift my shotgun.

There was an interim then when I only hunted with friends and their bird dogs as if I couldn't quite bear the memory of Missy. Starting around 1970 Guy de la Valdène came up every fall for grouse and woodcock shooting, and he had a lazy, incredibly neurotic Lab bitch named Rain who despite her "put upon" attitude was a superb upland game dog with an uncanny nose. She was equally good at ducks down on Lake Okeechobee in Florida, though she had to be lifted gently into the boat.

To fill our dogless space at the time, we bought two farm dogs, Airedale terriers, with the male whom I called Hud coming from a bear dog strain in Arkansas. "Hud" was well named because his favorite activity was screwing the garbage cans at mid-morning everyday. It didn't look all that much fun to the owner but he obviously enjoyed it. He was a big boy and soon got in trouble for ripping off a barn door to get at a female in heat, and tunneling under a kennel to mate with a neighbor's pretty boxer. He also knocked men off snowmobiles when they crossed our yard. The other Airedale, Jessie, who was female, hoarded the bowels of entire cows the neighbors butchered. She would hunt but getting a bird back from her was a wrestling match.

My hunting life changed for the better when Guy de la Valdène sent us a young yellow Lab from England's Sandringham breeding. I properly called her Sand and she was hunting well by the age of seven months, learning more from Guy's dog Rain than I could teach her. This is a rarely mentioned item in a trainer's vocabulary, but a young dog learns very well from watching and hunting with an experienced dog. You are "guiding" rather than training the animal and your most important function is to discourage bad habits. Once the dog comprehends that you are partners, and hunting depends equally on both of you, the process is three quarters of the way home. An occasional light spanking can be in order on young dogs, but it too severely wounds the dignity of an older animal. The best tactic I've developed is a stern word and a light ear pinch. If you love to punish, pick on someone your own size. Many hunters carry over illusions of control from their day jobs. They want what some call "lawyer dogs," kenneled dogs that only get to hunt a couple days of fall and are still expected to cover the ground in a tick-tock, metronomic fashion. They are expected to be as efficient and obedient as a legal secretary. The half-dozen top bird dogs I've known in my forty-year hunting life have all been dear companions of their owner's daily lives.

I got so used to following Sand's superb nose that I'd occasionally get lost, which is no fun at all in Michigan's Upper Peninsula, where my favorite area is a dozen miles from anything. You're more likely to get lost when the hunting is good.

I soon could tell from the way Sand's butt wiggled if it was a grouse or woodcock. She often retrieved birds that I was unsure I had hit. She went through a short period where I caught her trying to bury grouse, and then she would sit on the dirt pretending she couldn't find the bird. I thought this peculiarity might have come from her convalescence after being hit by a snowplow, with her medical bills coming to $10,000 in contemporary money. We called a trainer in Pennsylvania, a friend of Guy's who said, "Kick her in the ass. She's trying to hide the bird to eat later."

She did have "eating problems," as many Labs do. Once on the way north I stopped at a tavern for a much needed drink and on returning to the car, Sand had eaten a pound of butter, a dozen eggs, and some bananas. The next trip I put all of the sacks of groceries on the car roof when I went into the tavern, then had a few extra drinks and forgot them, so that when I drove off, I recall clearly the sound of three magnums of good wine crashing to the street.

A singular charm in Sand was never losing a downed bird even in the thickest Michigan cover, a common event with big running pointing dogs that only wish to find more birds. The biggest problem with Sand—other than she was part pig—was her fear of bears. Dozens of times I would drive to an area I wanted to hunt, and she would jump back in the car if she scented bear. If I forced the issue she would walk behind me tight to my legs. Once in Sand's late years when I was hunting both her and Tess, we came upon a bear in an alder thicket that growled before running away. Tess growled back and Sand disappeared. I asked Tess "Where's Sand?" then followed her more than a mile away to find Sand hiding behind a stump and still shaking with fear. I was always mindful that an English setter had been killed on my Upper Peninsula property before I bought it. Small bears tend to be underrated. A bear hunter I met had a hound that needed 280 stitches after a run-in with a bear that was not that far beyond cub stage. When you skin an adult bear, you see a musculature that makes Arnold Schwarzenegger look like Mary Poppins.

The arrival of Tess brought on the true glory days of my hunting life. At the outset I was lucky to have Nick Reens as a friend, neighbor, and hunting partner. Nick has managed, along with a few others, to breed a select number of litters out of an Old Hemlock strain. These are big-lunged dogs ranging from seventy pounds for a bitch to a current male, Joe, who goes at 110 pounds. Though utterly docile and sweet in the cabin or house, these are big running setters suitable for the southwest and Montana, though they shorten up in the denser cover of northern

Michigan. When cynics say that our dogs are "too far out," we've learned to give a pat answer, "That must be where the birds are." Nick hunts as many as five at once, and they act as a massive vacuum cleaner for the game birds in the area. One day on Drum Hadley's 500,000-acre Gray Ranch in New Mexico, three of us bagged thirty quail on a cold, windy day while another group hunting short running eastern setters shot only four. The possible downside to this strain of setters is that the owner must be in fairly good walking shape. Though of serene dispositions, these dogs don't care if you have a sore foot or a hangover.

Curiously, it took a while before I did as well with Tess as I did with Sand. A fine pointing dog can promote a certain laziness in your attention span while with Sand I had to watch her every moment. I knew Tess would hold the point, but I was a little slow in learning how to approach her while hunting solo. With a hunting partner the avenues of escape are more limited. I gradually figured out it was better to come up on her from the side rather than directly from the back. This afforded me a clue, as her eyes often followed the scent line. Sometimes in sparse cover she would lay out flat on her point, which setters did earlier in their tradition, and when she had to reposition she would often crawl very quickly on her belly. Like any good grouse and woodcock dog Tess kept a sharp eye on the direction missed birds were flying in order to re-point them. I've long given up this practice under the idea that if a bird escapes once, it's sporting to let it be home free. There are specific exceptions to this rule. One day in Montana it was blustery, and the Huns wouldn't hold to the point but would wild flush well out of range. Because Tess had such a sharp eye, we were able to pick up fifteen singles.

Her main drawback was a weakness for rabbits and ground squirrels, though this penchant was usually under control. Chasing a jackrabbit can blow out a dog on a warm day. I have never understood the attraction of ground squirrels for dogs unless it's the peculiar sharp squeak these rodents make. My cabin can have a half dozen red squirrels in the yard and the dogs yawn but they can't resist ground squirrels. And dogs can have additional oddities. Tess never once acknowledged the presence of a horse or cow even within a herd of either. I could also tell when she was a bit bored, and then I would take her to new cover where she had never hunted, which delighted her. Many dogs don't figure out how to control running

Gambel's quail but Tess did, circling way out like a good pheasant dog and turning them back in my direction. This is pure hunting instinct rather than simple intelligence. Despite my affection for English setters, there are a dozen breeds with more apparent intelligence than setters. My wife's English cocker, Mary, would have made Tess look like Big Dumb. (Mary has even figured out the proper time for me to get up in the morning and when it's time for my afternoon snooze.) In defense of Tess, her sole interest in life was finding game birds, with ground squirrels and eating dinner a distant second and third. The only food she ever begged for was the skin of fried whitefish. If I give her my leftover breakfast oatmeal with raisins, she finishes the oatmeal but leaves the raisins in a neat pyramid pile. She turned away in disgust and embarrassment when I offered her yogurt as a joke. Our last hunt together was a tear-jerker. We were over a mile from the car in a rough canyon near the Mexican border. She had given me two points and then quite suddenly collapsed. I carried her out over my shoulder with some difficulty and a week later had to have her put down. I thought I was mentally prepared for this moment but then I broke down in what mediocre writers call "uncontrollable sobs." This has been true of the death of all our dogs, I suppose because I have never had any impulse to rate animals in levels of importance. We are fellow creatures.

In Tess's mid-career, when Sand was still alive, we got Kate, a female Airedale that was a delightful girl. She lacked the feistiness of our earlier Airedales, Hud and Jessie. My wife Linda gradually figured that this was true because Kate imitated the behavior of Sand and Tess. Occasionally her true nature would rise, and Linda took her to obedience training where she won best in class. Kate, however, saw no relationship between the class and her life on the farm and continued her behavior, which could politely be called "independent," backing off into bushes with black, glittering eyes when she decided a demand was unreasonable. I noted that she responded best to the extremely non-ironical requests of our younger daughter, Anna. Dogs are first to sense self-doubt in your voice. Once while hunting with Richard Ford and his wonderful Brittany, Dixie, I heard him say, "Dixie, please behave, I've been working hard." The writer Tom McGuane used to deliver elegant speeches to his English pointer Molly, who evidently preferred the music of the spheres. In contrast, my neighbor Nick Reens who is absolute master of his five setters rarely speaks to them until after the hunt, and they are intensely orderly dogs, assuming you can handle the idea of big runners.

In the late years of Tess's career I got another puppy from Nick and we named her Rose. The mother was Sam, who had a problematical early career after the trauma of being confined in a dog trailer while some kids were setting off firecrackers. She mostly tagged along with us for two years until we were hunting one morning in South Georgia on Jimmy Buffett's property, and Sam quite suddenly decided she was over her trauma and began hunting beautifully. Back home she would regularly run the half-mile from Nick's house, scratch at our door, say hello, turn around, and run home. Rose's sire was Nick's prepotent Mack, who was also the sire of Tess. Mack was as good a grouse dog as I had ever hunted behind.

Frankly, I had had some doubts about getting another setter because I was by then in my mid-fifties, and the early training period can be a real workout which translates into "you are going to bust your ass." I thought that Rose had no more than eighty percent of the intensity of Tess, but this is partly because my own intensity had begun to wane. Tess regularly hunted perhaps seventy days a year or more in Michigan, Florida, Montana, and Arizona. With Rose I had started hunting half days and had reduced my kill to much lower levels. One August morning in the Upper Peninsula, Rose had twenty-nine woodcock points in less than two hours. I was slow to admit that I enjoyed this training run as much as hunting. As I became a little more squeamish and had further reduced my kill, I'd simply yell "bang" at the flush, and that was fine by Rose, whereas Sand would look at me with disappointment whenever I missed. She liked the flavor of everything.

Rose's biggest drawback is that she's what's called a "competitive bitch" and doesn't like to hunt with other dogs, and if she does, she tries to beat them to the cover. We lost her for three days in a vast area south of Safford, Arizona, when she too successfully outran all of Nick's males. I'd like to say she learned something from this harrowing experience but I don't think she did. After that I only hunted her alone or with dogs that didn't mind her being out in front.

I gratefully accept that Rose learned a lot more hunting with Tess than she ever did from me. She learned to honor the points of Tess because when she broke a covey, Tess growled and snapped at her and after that with my help she honored. This one-day lesson wouldn't have worked without her stern aunt. Rose has also been spectacular at singles. One day in New Mexico after a friend's dog had bumped a quail covey, I shot six singles while my friend took a hangover nap.

Rose's main drawback has been her love of water. She grew up beside a creek in Arizona, beside a big pond on the farm, and next to a river in the Upper Peninsula. One day we got two grouse within minutes of leaving the car, and the second wounded grouse whapped Rose in the face several times. I generally try to avoid hunting near a river, but this time we were close, and after she had subdued the grouse, I knew she would head for a long soothing swim. I don't mind this or her other daffy antics because I am older and more than willing to doze against a stump until she returns. Rose's downfall came last summer in Montana in her ninth year when she was struck twice by a rattlesnake in our yard, and one fang broke off in her right eyeball, blinding her. She was already half-deaf, but her recovery from the snake took several months. The venom affected her brain or sense of smell, or both. In the Upper Peninsula she bumped woodcock though she held steady to a number of grouse. On a few occasions she seemed not to recognize me. I didn't push but let her try to recover at her own speed. She'll point doves in high grass though she flags a bit and turns around to look at me explaining "dove." She's had some nice quail points this winter, but not many, mostly because of the precipitous decline of birds in our prolonged drought. Many times when her beeper collar signals a point, I've found her lying down looking at the mountains.

Rose is now ten and I'm vaguely shopping for another pup. I'm seriously thinking of slowly ending my hunting life with an English cocker like my wife's dog Mary, whom I could easily teach to be president (or at least a senator), run a corporation, or write my novels. One day on a walk Mary scented quail and crawled like a marine toward a covey. This breed of dog could definitely become a multi-species expert.

One day near the end of the season, Rose flounced around and trotted back to the car like a gaited horse after pointing a large covey of Mearns quail. I suddenly remembered reading that, in the seventh century, the Church decided dogs can't go to heaven because they don't contribute to the church. If true, then I don't want to go either. I'm very poor at dates and numbers, what happened at what time in our life, but if my wife mentions a name of a dog we've owned and loved, I can recreate the dog's life with us, and consequently my own.

When Rose passed on I made a rather dramatic misassumption. I was in my late sixties with some health difficulties and decided I was too old to train a big running setter pup. I thought about a French Brittany because my friend Dan Lahren had an excellent one named Jacques, over whom he had shot a hundred Hungarian partridge when the dog was only about nine months old. Jacques was also a fine companion in the drift boat when he fished with us up to seventy days a season. He'd look at us questioningly when we didn't cast to a rise he noted.

Instead of thinking through the whole issue of a new bird dog for my senior years, I was swept away by rather literary sentimentality over memories of the aforementioned Lab, Sand, who was also a good companion. I completely forgot the downside of training Sand in my assumption that another Lab would be far easier on my old body than another setter.

Zilpha (the name of my wife's favorite relative) came from the great breeder Dennis Anderson in Minnesota. Her parents are from a hunting estate in northern Scotland. From the first day she was a bully little bitch, improbably active and frolicsome but a good learner. She is smaller and much more muscular than the outsized, rather snouty American Labs. Ever the athlete, at six months she jumped over the high stucco fence surrounding our winter casita near the Mexican border. I said "no" and she never did it again.

I haven't given up on the idea, but she is simply no good at quail or Hungarians except for the singles after the first covey flush. It's a bit of a mystery because she did well on ruffed grouse and woodcock on our two trips back to my true homeland in Michigan's Upper Peninsula. On quail and huns she is too much a *charger* after picking up the first scent, unmindful of my physical slowness and occasional inattentiveness. With a good setter you can drift around in a semi-dream state waiting for a point but with a Lab you have to relentlessly pay attention.

She's wonderful on doves. When she was only year-and-a-half, she retrieved 157 doves eating the 158th on the last day of the season. She pretended she couldn't find the bird, but there were a couple of feathers protruding from her mouth which, when I opened it, was plumb full of feathers. She was embarrassed.

This has to be enough. As an older hunter I'm not very acquisitive anymore, and for peculiar emotional reasons I can no longer hunt woodcock so that there will be no more hunting trips to Michigan.

When suffering occasional bouts of insomnia, I think of strategies to slow her down on quail and huns; I come up with attaching a fifty-foot log chain weighing five hundred pounds to her collar. Any crossness I have is outweighed by her comic qualities. A couple of times when we've seen big javelinas, she runs frantically in place at my side counting on me to restrain her. She did commit the unlikely act of chasing away a bull that was threatening me and once snuck up on a covey of Mearns quail, allowing me to get an equally unlikely double. Good or bad, it's hunting. I'm apparently better at imagination than life itself, and I've often imagined all the dogs in my life working a particular big covert near the Kingston Plains in the Upper Peninsula. It is pleasant to allow them life again. We bag a few birds on a cold, clear October afternoon then return to the cabin and start a fire. They all love short-rib broth and *reggio parmagiano* on their kibble, after which they sleep in a pile before the fireplace.

The Other Man's Dog

Randy Lawrence

The Murph was crazy. At least that was the opinion of Roger Reho, the harried UPS driver who forded my pack of setters, pointers, and golden retrievers whenever he made a delivery to our farm. He'd bought Murphy as a pup and said he couldn't do a thing with him.

One afternoon, over a signature for a package, he asked, "Who trains your bird dogs?"

I looked over the jostling, crotch-sniffing mob and confessed I was the guilty party.

"What would you charge to work Murphy for me?" I was between teaching jobs. The last magazine piece I'd sold brought $150. How crazy could Murphy be?

On a handshake and a $50 deposit, I agreed to train another man's bird dog.

That weekend, Roger Reho dropped Murphy off in our barnyard. The little orange-and-white setter exploded out of his travel crate, a wild-eyed, slobbering mess. When he wasn't lurching at the end of his

(*Courtesy of Randy Lawrence*)

Randy Lawrence with English setter Banjo.

lead, he was using it as a sort of canine Maypole ribbon, winding it around and around his owner's legs.

Reho was too busy reciting names of luminaries in Murphy's pedigree to notice. I recognized most of the names from captions in the *American Field*, dogs that fairly crackled and sparked, posed with a gallery of wind-burned riders, lathered horses in the background.

The "crazy" in Murphy was pure drive. When Roger took the dog to the grouse woods, "the Murph," as Reho called him, did what his genes knew. He ran.

The last three times out the previous season, Murphy had been picked up miles from where Reho had parked his truck. Only once was he actually recovered on the same calendar day the hunt began.

"He's birdy as hell," Roger insisted. "Bird crazy! And he's got a ton of point. But I don't have the patience to work him myself. What time I have, I want to spend grouse hunting. I don't know what you can do for him, but if he'd just stay with me and come when he's called, I think he'd make a dog."

He handed me the end of the leash and a check for the one month's tuition. As I stuffed the check in my shirt pocket, Roger turned back to his truck and reached something off the dashboard.

Grinning, he tossed over a Mighty Mouse squeaky toy. "The wife thought it'd help take some of the edge off him if we played before we hunted."

Reho shook my hand. "I'll call in a couple of weeks," he said, sliding into the cab of his SUV.

Murphy didn't even notice his owner was leaving. He was too busy yipping, growling, and straining to get at two fat mourning doves puttering under a bird feeder.

Braced against both the leash and Murphy's fever, I stared down at Mighty Mouse and squeezed. With that squeal came the first wave of panic: a guy was *paying* me to fix his dog. For the next three days, I kept Murphy in the end kennel where I could watch him from my writing desk. At no time was he still. He bolted from one end of the gravel run to the other, ricocheting off the wire panels, anxiously scanning the sky. Songbirds. Crows. Buzzards. The BATF 'copter, low and slow, snooping out dope patches. The mere shadow of a flyover turned Murphy inside out.

When no birds flew, he panted. He bounced in place. He whined, fretted, and muttered. My own dogs eyed him the way a psychiatric ward full of patients looks at the new guy who needs his meds adjusted. I told myself I was letting Murphy get acclimated to new digs. When my wife complained about his occasional fits of barking, I told her Murphy was homesick, and that I was studying him. In truth, I had no idea of where to start with a wack-job dog I'd not raised from a puppy.

The fourth day, guilt kicked in. I took down the stiff, forty-foot check cord, put on a pair of light deerskin gloves, and walked to Murphy's run. He paid me no mind. Instead, he pressed against the kennel fence, drooling at robins hopping across the lawn.

The snick of the gate latch triggered a white-and-orange slapshot toward the opening. I butterflied like a hockey goalie, scooped the dog in both arms, and groped for his collar with the clip end of the cord.

Just as the snap closed, forty-seven feet of cord burned through the palms of my gloves before I could squeeze a grip. Murphy hit the rope's end and lost his feet, slamming down hard on his side.

Instantly he was up, shook himself, then bolted toward where he'd last seen the robins. Leaning back, I let the rope play out, then up-ended him again . . . and a third time, then a fourth . . . before I could finally reel him back, hand over hand. Never once did he stop leaping and struggling. Not once did he acknowledge that I was on the other end of the rope.

When I had him beside me, I knelt, sweet-talked him, petted him. No dice. What he wanted was to be away. For Murphy, "away" was where the birds always were, where the birds always went.

I looped a half hitch around his flank and tried walking him at "heel." Murphy twirled. He twisted. He tangled himself in frustration and the first real rage I'd ever seen in an English setter. I'd lift him, get him organized, then step away. In seconds, he was aimed in the opposite direction, oblivious to the snarled check cord choking at his hips, his head constantly on a swivel, looking for birds.

I suppose we wrestled like that for twenty-five minutes, a dervish of a dog and an increasingly panicked, phony-baloney trainer. When I finally surrendered, it was all I could do to lift the struggling dog and stagger back to the kennel. He stopped for a few gulps at the water bucket before kicking back into his manic sky patrol.

Later in the day I tried again. All I got was a fight. I tried a third time. Same thing. Certainly, it was time for Plan B. The only problem was, I didn't have a Plan B. What I did have was a place with no birds.

We'd bought our farm from a former teaching colleague of mine, an erstwhile poet who raced mountain bikes on the weekend and planned to retire on an ultralight airplane dealership. In a county with the highest unemployment rate in the region, I'm not sure to whom Casey planned to sell those perilous one-man crafts, but he grew into something of a local celebrity, flying his plane over a neighborhood known more for Amish buggies than retro homages to the Wright brothers.

There was oil on the property, too, and with the proceeds raised during boom times, Casey had built a beautiful metal-sided pole barn, a sort of hangar/showroom fronted by a long runway in the bottom field. In five years, he managed to sell precisely one aircraft. That was the one he bought for himself.

On our watch, we fenced the runway for horse pasture and converted the hangar into box stalls and an office. After chores the morning after the first lesson fiascos, I set up my typewriter on my grandfather's big steel desk, kept down at the pole barn, then went back up the hill to fetch Murphy.

I had learned a long time ago that, as awkward as it was, it was better to carry a dog than to continue teaching him he could misbehave on the end of a line. I hauled Murphy, clawing and struggling, in my arms all the way down from the kennel. Turning sideways into the hangar's small side door, I pulled it closed behind me, then snapped a short, twenty-foot check cord to Murphy's collar before letting him down. Murphy dug into the dirt floor, trailing the rope behind him. He scurried around the barn, sniffing and marking and trying desperately to make any sort of bird fly. I rolled my battered office chair up to the word processor and pulled up a rejected magazine piece, a spellbinding treatise on gun fit I'd coaxed another long-suffering editor into considering.

It was a long time before Murphy wound down in the cool, low light. Every few minutes, he'd flop down, panting. If I turned to look, he'd be up and off again.

I have always thought we should take our training to wherever the dog was. But before Murphy, I'd never tried to hook up with one who operated in another galaxy. For that entire morning, again that evening, and all of the following day, Murphy stayed trapped in his manic preoccupation. Only the smells of that barn registered with him. I was simply transportation to and from his kennel cell.

But that second night, just before quitting time, Murphy rushed up to snuffle around the desk. I ignored him. He went away, then came back, this time to give my chair the once-over before trying to hike his leg on it. I drove him off with a sharp, "Achh!" then turned back to my work. From the corner of my eye I could see him standing ten yards away, studying me as if noticing me for the first time.

The next morning, whenever he slipped near, I'd let one hand drop to stroke him whenever he was in easy reach. The come-bys came more frequently. They seemed calculated to cruise just close enough to earn a pet each time. He squirmed more than he fought as I carried him up the hill at the end of the session.

Midway through our evening session, the desk became Murphy's home base. He'd linger to be petted. I could take a light hold on the check cord, say "Murphy, come" and coax him back in to me for a pat, before quickly letting him go.

I remembered an old horse trainer friend who insisted, "They all sell out for somethin' sooner or later. You just gotta figure out the price point." I took to keeping treats in one desk drawer. When I would see him sidling over, I'd give the command—"Murphy, come"—as if it were my idea instead of his. If he came in, stood easy, I'd slip him one of those little liver bites.

Later, it did begin with me: "Murphy, come." At first, there was always a treat; later, the treats alternated with a quick pet or head scratch before I'd say, "Alright" and turn back to my keyboard. Murphy needed to learn that it was up to me when it was our time, and when our time was over. Every day he became quieter. Every day he became a little more self-assured.

Every night, I'd type Murphy's progress into my journal. It occurred to me then that schooling a dog for another person was a little bit like the technical writing I was doing for the shooting magazines. It required attention to detail, a sense of logical order, a never-ending search for better ways to communicate, a fair bit of skill . . . and, bottom line, was mostly about the bottom line—the pay check. Worse yet, it skirted the part of me that had craved connection with bird dogs in the first place.

From the time I first worked at a shooting preserve, apprenticing to a pro trainer, to the day I drove to Michigan to choose my first English setter puppy, what I had wanted most was the kind of collaboration that bridged the chasm between dog and person. I wanted to cast the natural world the way they did, through their speed and tenacity and uncanny sense of smell.

With my own animals, it was no holds barred. I couldn't possibly get close enough. A client dog, I had to hold at a distance, creating enough intimacy for that dog to want to work with me, but not too much so that the transition back to the owner was more difficult than necessary.

When he first came, Murphy felt no connection to any person or any thing other than the visual cocaine of *bird*. His nose only heightened the sensation. What I had to do with Murphy was craft a partnership, then rebuild his bird interest from the nose on back.

Roger Reho, like most of the men and women for whom I trained later on, took all of that as a matter of course, something for the pro to work out before handing back the dog. In their way of thinking, a "trained" setter, pointer, wirehair, or shorthair should be like a fitted gun—something that a professional shaped to fit the shooter. It could be stowed away, then taken down on the occasion of a hunt and always perform as expected. There was no need for intimate knowledge of the thing; it was merely a tool another person adapted for them.

Later, I'd learn that most clients want to be outfitted with some semblance of the clicker that manages their television, TIVO, DVR, satellite radio, and other entertainments. There's no reading the dog. No checking the wind. No thinking about what the weather is like now, or has been for days, or what front is coming in to the area. No sense of the cover, no real understanding of a particular game bird's proclivities under certain situations.

Such people make it all about the dog understanding them on their terms. There's not the slightest interest in learning how and why the dog makes whatever voodoo he do to make a fidgety game bird set for the "Gun" to flush.

The corollary to this is that somehow, a pointing dog makes the bagging of game if not easier, at least more efficient. Since birds in the bag are the only measure of the day, the dog's performance is taken for granted if it's to Hoyle. However, when the whole pastoral tableau explodes into mayhem—the birds flush wild, the dog runs amok, the "Gun" empties his gun just about the time he probably should have taken his first considered shot—it's all going to come back on the dog. By extension, nearly all who have paid good Yankee dollars for dog training will blame it on that lazy ass crook who didn't deliver Robodog on the right frequency in the first place.

Meanwhile, Murphy was opening up his bandwidth. The indoor time away from bird distractions had allowed me to tune in to a dog whose high intensity nature had insured he spent a whole lot more of his life locked up than in the company of his owner. Before we could ease into "formal" lessons, the kind every client believes he's paying for, Murphy needed to believe in me enough, trust me enough, to want to join up. So Roger Reho spent about half of his month's tuition toward my sitting at my desk, courting Murphy.

By the start of the third week, without the distractions of any and all winged things, Murphy bought into the half hitch around his flank and walked grudgingly at heel. Two sessions later, we graduated to a heavy slip chain collar, more forgiving than the narrow garrote style sold at most department stores, but still an effective reminder of where he belonged in reference to my side.

From the chain, we transitioned into the lead snapped to his nylon collar's ring. "Whoa" was introduced as part of "heel," switching off between commands, using his name each time. None of the sessions lasted more than fifteen minutes; most were shorter.

We were making the connection that a hand-raised puppy, brought thoughtfully along, establishes soon after weaning. At the end of the third week, I stashed a shoulder bag with two homing pigeons on a high shelf down in the barn. When Murphy had settled in for his morning session, I ducked into that bag, letting it hang on my right side, then scooped up Murphy's check cord and brought him in at heel on my left. We "heel/whoa-ed" our way to one of the big front hangar doors, and I dragged it open about ten feet.

We made two laps, heeling and whoa-ing around the inside of the barn before I gave Murph the word—"Whooooaaaaa." I slipped a pigeon out of the bag and tossed it toward the open door. The big white bird battered into the sunlight, Murphy jumped once, twice . . . then stood, quivering.

I was quivering, too.

I bent, gathered him up and set him gently back at my side, repeating the command: "Whooooooaaa." When I released him with "Alright, 'Heel!'" he tossed a couple of glances over his shoulder toward that open door, then got back with me for two more circles of the barn.

The third time around, I whoa-ed him, and sent the second pigeon careening away out of the bag. This time, Murphy leaped after, came up short on the lead, and struggled a little bit while I brought him in to heel. I made him stand there in that block of sunshine, holding him steady when the pigeon made two passes within sight of the open door. I turned him away, walked him to the desk, tethered him to a ring I'd screwed into one of the barn's support posts, then went back to close the sliding door.

Hot damn. Maybe I was a dog trainer after all.

That all vanished when I called Roger Reho with a gushing progress report. It was easy to tell that he was decidedly underwhelmed. Three weeks in and we hadn't even been to the woods yet? I tried to explain what we'd had to do just to get Murphy with the program, how far he'd come, how we were going to make the transition away from the barn. All Roger wanted to know was what I'd charge for an additional weekend. He and "the wife" were going to be out of town, and he'd pick "the Murph" up on the following Tuesday. I had nine days left.

We stayed two more days in the hangar, up to four pigeons a session. About half the time, Murphy held steady. Somewhere in the dark recesses of his fevered mind, he'd made a connection: "There weren't birds away. There are only birds where *we* are. So that's where I want to be."

We took that connection, and bags of pigeons from the big loft near the house, and moved out of the barn to the runway pasture. When Murphy stood staunch through a flush, I'd flip another bird out of the bag and spin it out in front of him. Before long, he believed that as soon as one pigeon left, another one was going to appear, and that if he stayed put, he'd get to see it.

Finally, I let him go, dragging the longer check cord. Instead of running straight lines away and back, he was beginning to quarter, only because that kept him in closer proximity to me. When Murphy swung by in position that I could step on the check cord, I'd fly a pigeon, step on the cord to prevent a relapse chase, and whoa him to a stop. Tight-roping up the check cord, I'd get out on front of his nose, a hand upraised to warn him to stay put, then fly another pigeon.

The last weekend, we swung into the big alder swatch that lay in a low spot on the property line. There were tweety birds there, and Murphy noticed them . . . but that was it. He was still running, and running hard. But after every cast, he'd swing by across my front, hoping maybe, just maybe, he'd get to see another big white pigeon go spiraling off through those black, twisted branches.

Roger Reho came on Tuesday and followed Murphy and me through the whole program—the barn, the runway pasture, the alder swale, then on up into the edge of the neighbors' big woods. Murphy hunted fast and wide, but not deep, flying by on his own, checking in when I called him, stopping at the flush of the pigeon. When I could stand on the check cord, I'd fire the little .22 blank pistol, muzzle close to the ground to dampen the report. When Murphy jumped, I'd set him back, "whoa" him, and fire the gun again. What I wanted Roger to see that we were well on our way to steady to flush and steady to shot.

Mostly what Roger saw was the face of his watch. He had something else going on that evening and needed to get back to town. He said he was sorry we hadn't worked any quail or pheasants, and that maybe I ought to think about getting some. I handed him a training journal I'd printed out, ran down the command sequences, told him what he needed to do to build on what Murphy had accomplished so far, and gave him a whistle just like mine, still in the plastic wrapper. Meanwhile, Reho's dog was lying on the gravel at my feet, snubbing his kennelmates shouting at him from their runs. When I handed over the lead, Murphy hesitated, then fell in at heel to the tailgate of Roger Reho's truck. I pretended to have something urgent to do in the house and didn't watch them load up and roll down the driveway.

Over the next twenty-five years there would be other dogs. In his cups, Stevie bought a puppy two years in a row at the Ruffed Grouse Society banquet. Both came to the farm to be trained: Greta, the shorthair with mad skills and the athleticism of an Olympic pole vaulter, and Zac the bimbo Gordon setter with all the brains of the plastic cups his owner had emptied during the bidding.

There was an American water spaniel called Byrne who chewed through two pieces of rebar to escape an above ground kennel and who suffered a virulent case of Little Man's Disease, staring down the biggest retrievers he could find before dancing back with dead roosters nearly as big as he during our pick-up work at a driven pheasant shoot.

Ghillie stayed when his owner confessed he couldn't pay his training and board bill, offering a dog I didn't need instead. Later that summer,

I carried Ghillie out of the low prairie sandhills when a landscape full of sharptails flushed in staggered waves, tolling him off on a toot that nearly killed him in the September heat. He went on to hunt for a portly gentleman who belonged to a local club and doted on released Huns and chukar. Ghillie was a star on those birds and was fed into a facsimile of his owner. Together, they trundled around the hunt club grounds. When Ghillie died, the man stowed his guns and moved on to other things.

Maybe the best of them all was the one I couldn't untrack. Babe was a back-yard-bred setter—pretty, neurotic, and almost impossible to correct. When owner Bob DeMott came to fetch her home, she did what she'd done throughout her schooling, pointing a planted pigeon, then darting back around to huddle behind my legs, establishing another timid, trembling stand.

I had done all that I knew to do. Bob shrugged off the sorry display, took her home to hang out under his writing desk, and let her ride loose in the truck when it came time to go into the coverts. Woodcock were his passion, and they were the making of his tiny, tri-colored partner. In time, there were grouse, too, and they became her crowning glory.

For Babe had the knack of setting birds in times and places other dogs could not. If I told you how many seasons in a row she went without a misstep, you would not believe me, so I will only say that the dog that was perhaps my biggest failure in training went on to forge a partnership that was most dazzling in the field. How could anyone have predicted that?

This winter, there is Banjo, daughter of a good dog who stayed with us several summers ago. I have no idea what she will become, other than the last of other men's dogs to come here for training. She is agile and talented, a delight some days, as dark and inscrutable as a Zen koan on others. But already, I can feel the deep pull between us, the tie I have to resist if she is to go on to become another man's dog, the one I covet most between my own pointers and myself. It is a connection I crave like air, one that, no matter the payday, I can no longer afford to deny.

It is September on the prairie, October in the alders, November among the grapevines and tulip poplar slash, December on the shaggy edges of Amish-picked cornfields. It throbs with an urgency and beats with a rhythm that is nothing less than my own pulse.

Blessed

Sydney Lea

A *dog you love should live as long as you do.*

How often now have I said this to myself since I began hunting over pointing dogs? That was fifty-seven years ago, when, at nine, I toted my single-shot .410 on some of my father's shorter forays into the field. I didn't shoot much game over Dicey (named for his Lucky Seven marking), but when at long last he died, I recall—more vividly than I do most things from that time—how I protested the plain *injustice* of it all. Like my father himself, Dicey was surely meant to endure forever.

I have grieved for a number of dogs since, in ways quintessentially similar to that first: for Hector, who had that uncanny knack of pointing up at a limb-perched grouse, who still busts the brush of memory; for the first Wes, whose doggy smile so endeared him to me; for Gus, who in his prime wandered off on my wife as she took a short hike in our woods, not to return, and who shines with sleet in my mind's eye—a certain fabulous late October hunt, no matter the chill weather, near my Maine cabin.

Bessie. Sam. Belle. Wes II.

Sydney Lea & English pointer Pete.   *(Courtesy of Sydney Lea)*

And those are only the pointing dogs. There are the retrievers, too, somewhat fewer but no less dear.

I recall reading an article in the dreary *Psychology Today*, as a person may do in dentists' or optometrists' waiting rooms, whose thesis was that two weeks at most comprised the span of heartache after one's dog dies. (That was more than the single week the cat-lovers got.) The author of that piece, I suspect, never owned a dog, or at least not a working dog, just as so many child-rearing "experts"—Locke, Spock, and Piaget—have never known parenthood. Maybe I'm the exception that proves the rule, but I doubt it. In any case, I think sorrowfully of all my gun dogs, and I've done so a lot over the decades.

And joyfully, too: it's not only that I can summon grand old days with each, but I also recognize that if one of those adored dogs had in fact lived as long as I have, there'd be only the one to adore. *Death is the mother of beauty,* as poet Wallace Stevens famously put it, and true enough, the athleticism, the grace, the quirky personality of every one of my dogs burned themselves into my consciousness, and at length into my remembrance, not least because in my soul I understood how briefly I'd get to treasure him or her.

In my most heartbreaking dreams, however, I never imagined that Wes II's life would prove so fleeting. A foursquare muscle merchant with the heart of a bull, he seemed as solid as earth itself. When, having just turned seven years old, he came up lame one morning, I took him to our veterinarian, foreseeing perhaps a few doses of Metacam and then back to business as usual. We had just returned from eastern Montana, after all, where for six seven-hour days we'd stalked the Huns and sharptails and ring-necks of the prairie, and where Wes had seemed nothing but Wes.

"He's been hiding this from you for a long time," said Diane, "and I can't see how." The X-ray showed shadow where bone should have been in his left shoulder, the cancer that ravenous. It seemed nothing could be done. A surgeon's second opinion matched Diane's. Being a surgeon, he proposed that we might right then and there do a radical amputation, but he was honest enough to predict no more than an extra six months on earth for Wes as a result. I couldn't imagine this stout creature as a tripod. I drove home in tears. As it turned out, Wes lived that six months, and several more, without any surgery. I got word of a Cornell-trained vet over in Burlington who incorporated traditional Chinese medicine into his practice. The doctor's acupuncture, a dietary change, and some herbs—together with Western narcotics—erased Wes's limp overnight and gave him, if anything, a little too much energy. But like the other two consultants, the Burlington doctor cautioned that his own treatment would work no miracles: it would be palliative, not curative.

Virtually all the pointers I've trained and hunted have had one thing in common: they've been almost as unenthusiastic about swimming as your average tabby cat. But Wes plain *craved* the water. Every August, when my family arrived at our Maine camp, which sits on a sixteen-mile lake, he rushed out to the end of the wharf and—like a champion Lab, all four feet in the air—made his entry.

He would then paddle around literally for hours. No need for September roadwork to harden Wes up for bird season; by the time we got back to Vermont he was nothing but gristle.

Not so long ago, his ashes floated away from that wharf. I am barely a twentieth-century man, let alone a twenty-first. So my eventual recourse was entirely uncharacteristic: I searched the Internet for a pup whose genetic makeup was as close to Wes's as I could find. I didn't necessarily desire another Aquadog, but I did want one equally biddable if possible, an ace in the field and also a good guy to hang out with in New England's much too long off-season.

I was looking above all for a scion of Snakefoot, one of the many champions in the Elhew line developed by the late Bob Wehle. I have heard some call Elhews the most over-rated dogs in America and others call them anything but. One thing they are is famously biddable, which is not a thing always said about pointers. Indeed there are wags who claim that the breed got its name because, having been asked a question like "Where's your dog?" an English owner's frequent response was to point in the direction of, say, Hungary. I have had four Elhew pointers, two brilliant and, to jump ahead, a third prospectively so. Each of these was a Snakefoot descendant. Max, the odd one out in this list, was lovable, eccentric . . . and not a good gun dog. And not a Snakefooter. Yet I have a feeling that I had a hand in Max's hopelessness; I failed to recognize him early enough for the soft dog he was. I therefore very probably and stupidly raised my voice one too many times; the result was that he'd start off like a champion, and then, fearful of making a mistake, he'd more or less quit hunting.

My example should be a warning, chiefly to myself, to anyone who thinks of pointers as somehow bomb-proof. Most of mine have been, but I may well have squandered the considerable talent of the one who was not—all of which simply means that my own inclinations for the genetic strain that resulted in Wes (and his predecessor Belle) has in all likelihood—like many if not most dog-related inclinations—its share of personal superstition. Be all that as it may, my search took me to a kennel in Arizona, of all places, and I picked my pup on the basis of a photograph alone, a thing I'd never done before. That was in December, but by airline restriction he couldn't be shipped until the weather warmed up, which in our north country meant May. This gave me some interlude, likewise, to brace my wife—as in my cravenness I hadn't yet done, Wes still deceptively hale—for the addition of a fourth dog to our pack. In short, I never met Pete (as my youngest daughter, who names all our dogs, had dubbed him) until he was already nine months old. Scarcely ideal, but it would have to do.

I liked what I saw the minute I uncrated him at Bradley Airport down in Connecticut: he was not so blocky as his predecessor, but he had an even deeper chest, so deep that to one unfamiliar with the breed, it might even look freakish. Oh, but he was a handsome specimen . . . except that he had pretty bad dentition, an under bite so pronounced that at times his whole lower arch would jut out over his top lip. With a muzzle that tended toward the short side, Pete's countenance looked in such moments as much like a boxer's as a pointer's. Like the rest of my family, I have come to delight in Pete's sudden changes of aspect: just now he looks as though he belongs on the cover of *Pointing Dog Journal;* and now he looks like a cartoon goofball. His ill-placed teeth, I thought, might have an unanticipated advantage: he'd not be *able* to chew up any birds in his maiden hunts, even should he want to (as it turned out he did not, but I get ahead of myself).

There have been times in late years when I almost believed the disease that brought the second Wes low to be somehow contagious. I had too many friends, hunters and non-hunters alike, who were losing their own dogs to cancer. But there were even more important human creatures in my life who confronted its horrors: my noble and generous pal of forty-four years, Strachan Donnelley, would die of a stomach tumor around the time of Pete's first birthday; the hilarious and moving poet Jack Myers had survived other cancers but was having now to wait for a liver transplant down in Texas; a lovely local woman, Ellen Ryan, had already passed on the winter before; and my beloved brother-in-law, a Massachusetts police officer, was recuperating from a brutal round of chemotherapy while I was training my pup.

What brother-in-law Chip has taught me—and what, at the risk of sounding preachy, I think all of us should bear in mind, though we rarely do—is that, in his own words, the best things in the world happen every day. After his first bout with cancer and its hideous treatment six years back, he described raking his front lawn, for example. He mused on how lousy a chore it once had seemed. Now he asked himself, "How could I *ever* have thought that?" I mention all this because, as I worked young Pete on quail from a bird launcher and on a few released pheasants last summer, and as I deeply felt the loss of Wes, often calling the new dog by the old one's name, the illness and suffering of my wife's brother, especially, was much on my mind. It chiefly reminded me that I was and am a blessed soul, and that I therefore must cling to what, and above all, whom I love.

All that seems so perdurable can vanish in a heartbeat. Even with a pointer as tractable as Pete, there were frustrations, as anyone who has started a dog from scratch knows there must be. But a young dog breaking a point on a bird and cutting rope-burns into the palm that holds the check cord—well, it wasn't drinking a liquid that was either hotter or colder than a certain prescribed temperature and thus feeling as though your mouth were full of razor blades. It wasn't watching the skin of your arms and legs flake up and peel from the flesh, your veins turning to grim black tattoos. It wasn't going cold turkey from the OxyContin without which you couldn't have endured. Once, when my wife praised Chip for battling cancer, he wrote that there was no fight involved; you just *took* the mauling: "It's like having two thugs show up at your house, tie you to a chair, then beat the shit out of you all afternoon. A week later, when you're starting to heal, they show up and do it all over again." I've always been intrigued and gratified by training dogs, but now to steady Pete to flush and shot seemed an utter luxury, a sort of grace that I didn't somehow have to deserve, any more than good Chip deserved his illness and the wretched treatment it required.

My wife reminds me that every new dog I make is my favorite ever. She's likely right. There may well be some sort of psyche-preserving mechanism at work in me to make that so. I must therefore be self-skeptical, must stop short of saying, after this rather brief time with the new man, that Pete's my best of all time. He may go south in his sophomore season. I've seen it happen. What I *can* say is that for now he is the quickest study I have ever handled. I try to keep my commands to any working dog as few and simple as possible. I have four for my pointers: "heel" (mostly so that I can confidently walk the dog back to the truck along a tarred road); "all right," which sends the dog on; "whoa" and "dead," which need no explanation; and after a spell, if I've been scrupulous and consistent, "whoa" drops out of the repertory.

Pete learned "heel," as God will witness me, after about ten minutes on the check cord. "Whoa" was a bit longer in the learning, not in the yard but when I launched quail; it came with astonishing speed, nonetheless, and has not needed a refresher since. "All right" was, of course, a snap. Because pointers are not famous for their retrieving skills, I didn't insist on a fetch back to hand. "Dead" only meant I needed him to locate whatever just got knocked down in the puckerbrush.

For my money, training a pointing dog is really a matter of respecting and refining the dog's instincts, and then getting the hell out of the way. As a friend of mine, a first-rate professional handler in our Northeast Kingdom, once put it to me: "Some guys pay me $2,500 for training their bird dogs, but most of it should go into training *them.*" Or, as the late Bill White of Washington County, Maine, once advised me when I was green at this business: "Soon as you learn that your dog knows more than you do, you'll be ready to use him right." Pete got so steady on planted quail that, even when he could actually see the dumb little things on the ground, he held; and it was gratifying that in actual woods, away from the tall grass meadow where I worked him on the quail, he made excellent finds and points on the pheasants, never mind the heat and dryness of August and September. But half tame quail and domestically raised pheasant are one thing. Soon enough I'd be off on my annual hunting trip to Montana with Pete in tow—and wild birds are quite another proposition.

We began in the Bear Paw Mountains. Usually I put off the western trip till November, because the New England season for ruffed grouse, which will always be my favorite bird, is so short that I don't want to miss any of October. I'd gone west early in the season this year only because I hoped that the sharptail—not yet having been much hassled—would be a bit more cooperative than the ruffs, and more so than they'd be themselves later along, holding well enough that Pete could get his nose into them. And the shots would be over open country, not the split-second affairs that our dense local woods afford, if they afford any at all.

The sharpies' wing bursts and squawks, and their tendency to move before flushing, confused my pointer some, but only for a forenoon. After lunch on that first day, we were lucky enough to find quite a few birds, near enough to one another that there weren't many breaks in the action, but not coveyed up either, multiple eyes and ears conspiring against us.

There was a stiff mountain wind that first afternoon. We hunted into it, and Pete soon had scent. He went on, high-headed as I wanted him to be, not sniffing along like a vacuum cleaner, a trait I despise, and in the ten or twenty seconds between his making game on the first afternoon grouse and the point, I swore I saw the metaphorical light bulb flash on. From that moment forward, whether he was into a single grouse or a covey of Hungarians, he looked for the most part astonishingly like a seasoned dog.

I have hunted and fished for so many years now that what I do can bring out a jadedness in me. To fool a big brown trout, for instance, is in later life more satisfying than thrilling. I gave up deer hunting more than a decade ago: it didn't mean enough to me anymore to compensate for the endless hours of scouting, stalking, sitting, gutting, dragging, butchering. I still hunt turkeys, but rather casually, unwilling to cruise for hours in pursuit of a gobble; a tom responds to me from where I set up, or he doesn't and I go home. To this day, however, I have an electric response to a dog holding a wild bird. The flush and shot are secondary.

And there Pete was, locked up on that sharptail, the prairie grass rippling around him, the air sweet as flowers. I did not say "Behold a miracle" to myself, but I sure to God felt something to that effect.

Maybe my hunting—or rather my dog-handling—life, for which I have sustained such enthusiasm, has qualities echoed by my writing life, for which I have sustained the same. Neither life has anything to do, Lord knows, with money or reputation, at least not in my case. Rather its seduction is that enlivening process of setting out in pursuit of what Yeats called the "click": a moment when all your ranging and false starts and backtracks and frustrations and experience and intuition all somehow flow together, and you suddenly come right onto what it was you've been looking for all this time. That's a miracle, too, a payoff for having invested what you have invested in your life.

But all this may be subject for another inquiry. What's more, there's frankly something in me that resists the allegorization of my days afield: it's a boon that what my dog and I and the game do together is *not* encoded, that it is direct and unmediated. That's what keeps those days so fresh and dear.

So back, precisely, to the field.

Our next stop was a hardscrabble ranch way up near the Saskatchewan border, whose population of smaller birds had diminished significantly over the ten years we had visited there, but whose pheasants were still numerous. Now anyone who, like Dick Cheney (to whom an unfond good riddance), knows pheasants by way of some godforsaken hunting preserve—well, he doesn't know pheasants at all. The wild variety, especially if they've heard a few rounds of gunfire, are nearly as smart as our own ruffed grouse: like them, wild roosters know how to keep something—a creek bank's shoulder, a hedge of willows, a single cottonwood—between themselves and the gun. Flushed, shot at and missed, they will fly a half-mile if need be. And of course they will run.

Oh, how they'll run.

I was uneasy about leaving the grouse and the Huns just as Pete had pretty much gotten the hang of them and traveling onto a terrain full of ring-necks. Those running tendencies, I believed, would baffle my pup all over again. I'll simply say that he took another forenoon to wise up, and then he got the knack of moving with the bird until he could pin it—if it was pinnable: some pheasants, of course, just run plumb out of the countryside.

Anyone reading this may, like me, hate the article in the outdoor magazines that claims a dog can do everything but brush the author's teeth and fold his laundry, especially if that author takes credit for these alleged virtues. Lest I sound like one of that type, let me say that my youngster, indisposed to any mistakes I now can see, will *not* be flawless. I have never owned nor beheld a dog to fit that description. What he is is a precocious pup, and I suspect he'll only get better as I provide him with more and more exposure—if, that is, I remember Bill White's counsel:

my pointer already knows a lot more than I do. I just need to get him into the cover, give him exposure, and let him go.

What will Pete's foible or foibles be? The first Wes would bring a woodcock halfway to me, then drop it and roll on it. Sam was a model citizen till his second season, when, rather than retrieving as he had the first, he got . . . roughmouthed. Well, I understate: the first bird of season two was again a woodcock; I got to Sam just as the bird's feet were about to disappear into his gorge, as if Sam were a snake and the bird a frog. I subsequently had to force train him to point dead, not retrieve at all. In *her* second season, Belle wouldn't pick up a woodcock in the first place. For all of that, these were good animals, and were so first because of genes and second, again, because of exposure.

Yet I underexposed Pete at the ranch, having no choice.

On our second evening there, I got sick. Very sick. Back at home, my wife and two of our children had recently contracted Giardia, a dreadfully debilitating parasite, and I began to wonder if I had now gotten a delayed dose of the same. I didn't know how else to explain the loose bowels and the retching that kept me up almost till dawn.

As it turned out, Giardia was not the villain, and I still don't know what was. It certainly wasn't the ranch owner's cooking or her water, which I had been eating and drinking for a decade, and of which my longtime hunting partner Peter Woerner had consumed no less than I had this trip. I wouldn't take much food for a while, but the most painful effects of this stomach bug diminished considerably after that one nasty night. The illness left me, however, with next to no energy. I could horsewhip myself through a morning, intent as I was on filling Pete's mouth with feathers and keeping the human Pete company; but after each midday break I was done.

As I sit here today, I feel about as fine and fit as a man my age has any right to feel. Since Montana, I have spent a peaceful and productive week at my Maine cabin, each day getting Pete into the ruffed grouse and the occasional woodcock (the latter of which I have let fly for the past decade, so radically have their numbers diminished in my lifetime; the retrieving problems I catalogued a moment ago are thus more or less irrelevant now). All but retired from college teaching, I'm dreaming up a Midwestern trip for later in the year. It's as though that enervated few days at the ranch had never happened.

I'm lucky enough never to have had any serious or chronic medical problems, but like anyone else, I've had episodes of compromised health, from occasional flu to a self-inflicted chain saw gash that required a hundred stitches and a hundred staples. In those times, unable to do the physical things that are my very life's sustenance, my spirits have sagged, if I may euphemize. And whenever I recuperate, I give myself the same familiar lecture: count your blessings; don't forget what it's like when they're suspended.

Like most people, I surmise, I soon forget my own admonition, sound as it doubtless is. It's a bit like the caution one gives oneself after losing some beloved friend or relative: remember what's important in life; be an even better companion to the ones who survive. And then the busyness of life flies in to blind us.

All of this makes me think that the events and reflections I've recorded up to this point are, for the most part, a bit *beside* the point. And yet in several ways I do owe whatever may be worth saving from them to the point of the pointer I praise—and to that awareness of what my brother-in-law and others have been through in the past few years.

On our last day in Montana, I went afield after breakfast, which for me had consisted of an unbuttered slice of toast. (I was still sick enough not even to mourn the more-than-hearty meals, each of them featuring some form of beef, that we always share with the wranglers.) The weather was dispiriting: a stiff east wind full of drizzle and a warm enough temperature that the prior day's dusting of snow started melting, the mud underfoot transformed to what the locals call gumbo—clay so adhesive and heavy that homesteaders used it to construct their very houses some generations back. With every step, the clot on my boots fattened, and it wasn't long before I had a sort of gumbo snowshoe.

I had been tired even before I left the cookhouse. Under these conditions, a single hour had me pretty well played out. Some vestige of macho pride, but more importantly that urge to keep Pete's nose into game, kept me going just the same. But the pheasants had gotten wise and scarce since our first few shots.

Still, something wondrous ensued.

I needn't even close my eyes to see what I saw about an hour later. There's a certain low mesa about three miles north of the ranch, the creek running tight to it but a swath of gamma grasses, perhaps fifty yards wide, flanking the creek on the east side. I stop and lean against a lone cottonwood in the middle of that meadow, as beat as beat knows how to be. My legs are anchored by fatigue and the gumbo. The raindrops are seeping down the back of my neck. We haven't moved a bird, or at least none close enough to shoot at, let alone for Pete to point, in some time.

A warm and palpable wave of gratitude washes over my body and soul. There's my young dog, bold white against the grey of that mesa and the tawn of that grass, quartering with so much energy and enthusiasm you'd think we'd been finding rooster after rooster.

I love the way a pointer moves, enough so that even when I'm shooting over a friend's superb setter or Brittany, I feel something has been left out of the movie. That's no indictment of or condescension to other breeds; I've seen some real world-beaters without an ounce of pointer blood in their arteries. I'm talking only of a sort of spiritual energy that both charges and soothes my own psyche. Head high, chest mighty, sinew rippling throughout his frame, Pete seems, for me, an embodiment of physical perfection. What drive. What agility. What bodily *intelligence* in his every gesture.

Like Wes II and all his much-mourned predecessors, Pete will probably be gone before I go (though a sexagenarian should govern his assumptions). Death may be the mother of beauty, but the dolor of sickness seems to mother certain benisons, too.

The Only Honest Way to Eat Poultry

Thomas McGuane

On a bright and cold October morning in Montana, my dogs Abby and Daisy, the Pointer Sisters, are in my closet helping me select my clothes. On the left end of the rack are everyday clothes; on the far right are coats and ties for the occasional urban jaunt; and in the middle, clothes for sport, especially hunting. Here sit the two girls, tails whisking the floor between the shoes. They moan, grumble and pant wishfully while my hand hovers over the coat hangers. I shouldn't do this as dogs don't enjoy being trifled with. They know where the thorn-proof pants hang, since the red suspenders dangle to eye level for them, but they watch my hand. I don't move; Abby turns to stare at my boots with such longing she must think they can scoop me up and take me into the hills. Finally, Daisy can't stand it and barks at me: I pull the hunting pants from their hanger and with a cry of triumph they scramble out of the closet to watch me dress. Let others withstand the elliptical trainer, the rowing

(Photo by Laurie McGuane)

Thomas McGuane with Abby & Daisy, the Pointer Sisters.

machine, and the NordicTrack. Mama wants two partridges for tonight's table and I will walk long miles hoping to get them.

I can tell myself that I take my dogs afield because they want to go, and yet when the hunt is on, its urgency spreads from them to me as they course through rivers of scent; I am tugged along in a state of rising alertness and renewed addiction. The Pointer Sisters are running and gasping for my truck while I lug their water jug in one hand, the shotgun in the other, while trying not to step on my untied bootlaces. They run round and round the truck to keep it from getting away before I can take them to the hills. Now they peer from the aluminum boxes, happy to be on the wagon and to hear its hearty engine start with a roar, as if glorying in our carbon footprint. It's an unusual east wind and I ponder the places that will let us hunt into it, to gain the scents and ambrosial trails that lead us to the quarry. Dogs, gun, shells, and supper—all in a row. It seems about right.

There have been several hard frosts and the morning is young. Those rattlesnakes not yet denned will be too sluggish to matter. The cattle have been gathered from the hills and now it all belongs to us. The hawks are up to the same thing we are; and it is possible to feel the competition of the Northern Harriers as they course low to the ground in the very fields we hunt. The light from the East and the bright serration of new snow on the mountain ranges surrounding us seem to bind a vast country together.

The dogs wait behind the truck as I rattle some 20-gauge shells into my pocket, slide the plastic water jug into the game bag behind my back. I walk a few yards in front of them, turn and tell them that they may begin. They leave at a blistering rate and in a very short time are rifling through the buck brush and chokecherry stands, across the broad juniper savannah, crisscrossing each other's trajectory with a reciprocity it took them a couple of years to work out. I potter along on two legs, gun action open and dropped across my shoulder. I seem to be drawn by the wind behind the dogs as if I were sailing. Abby succeeds first, stopping to point as though she'd hit a wall. From a nearby rise, Daisy sees her and backs. If anything on either dog moves, it is because of wind. They are inanimate objects in the landscape. My heart races as I step into a chaotic covey rise of more than twelve birds, partridges everywhere. I manage to scratch down one and Daisy retrieves it. At the end of the day, this is all we have, one partridge. It will go into a salad. The carcass is cooked to make a liqueur to go over the kibble.

There is so much in the air suggesting that hunting is an anachronism that it's easy for a hunter to feel he is an anachronism, too. An old fishing friend of mine said, as we headed home from an agreeable outing, "I thank God I'm not a day under eighty." I'm a meat eater and have the teeth to prove it, but greatly pity the creatures in the domestic meat businesses. An industrial chicken factory gives me heartburn and Thanksgiving is a tragedy for turkeys. I don't wear camo, don't belong to the N.R.A., and haven't been to a gun show since the jovial grandmother sitting behind a pile of machine guns said to me, "Goblins get in your house you'll love having one of these." I have no great enthusiasm for family tradition but my father and grandfather were hunters, and I cannot remember a time when I didn't wish to hunt. Like most who have hunted all their lives, I have grown quite austere about what I harvest for our table—some for sustenance, some for ceremony.

The dogs are everything, and they want to hunt, too. Bird dogs plead with you to imagine the great things you could be doing together. Their delight is a lesson in the bliss of living. As Bob Dylan says, "You've got to serve somebody." I serve my dogs and in return, they glom the sofa. Too many hunting dogs live depressing lives in kennels with automatic feeders and waterers, exercised only enough to keep them ready for work.

All vigorous pursuits bring real change. As I keep track of my dogs in broken country I notice that my memory improves, particularly short-term memory—no small thing at my age. The hills that at the beginning of the season seemed so laborious roll beneath me. One does not set about doing these things as a salute to the Protestant ethic but rather by noticing the land, the weather, and the dogs and by allowing a sympathetic chord to rise to the hunt.

When our northern season ends, the backslide begins, a fearful dullness and the prospect of thickening. The dogs hardly wake up during the day. Something must be done and the longer quail season in the south beckons. West Texas is beckoning too, one of the few places left where mean and deceitful are not considered virtues.

I don't face the facts of late fall in Montana until the whistle freezes to my lip. "Girls," I announce, "we're going to Texas." In two days, Abby, Daisy, and I are asleep in an Oklahoma motel, a dump with truckers snoring through the walls. We've just done an 800-mile nonstop and are stunned, in bed with the TV running, and I'm trying to get motivated to drive the last stretch. I step out of the artifice of my truck and I'm some place that, in all its weirdness, is not home. I have a tummy ache from the simple fact of eating along the highway. Is this worth it? But a day later a covey of Bobwhites flashes up through mesquite branches, Daisy locked on point and trembling from head to toe, Abby backing and listening to the report of the gun while I drop to one knee and await Daisy's retrieve.

My season ends in the south with old friends Guy and Jimbo, five dogs on the ground at once: the Pointer Sisters; Jimbo's radar retriever Dixie; Guy's recently retired Brittany Obie; and Obie's successor in the field, the valiant Briget. We are like parents at a school play and privately root for our own dogs. The hills sweep under old moss-hung oaks and tall longleaf pines. The morning frost is gone by nine. The pretty black ponds are alive with wood ducks and cranes. We had to get this out of our systems: the Super Bowl is about to start. Guy prepares the mood with stone crab claws and a platter of roasted quail. We watch a somewhat fragmented game between never-ending commercials. At halftime, a lunatic with a microphone runs around in tight pants bellowing to the crowd. My host sighs, aims the remote, and shuts it off. The day had started quite early: it would be a good time to feed the dogs, clean the guns, and turn in.

Now the long wait begins before we can do this again. Off season, the reports fly: Kansas has a few birds, Oklahoma looks spotty, West Texas coming back, wheat in Saskatchewan still not combined, bad spring freeze in Montana, Arizona desert birds droughted out, prairie chickens on the rise, ruffed grouse cycle on its way and if they've got woodcock in Louisiana they aren't telling. No sense taking anybody's word for it; we'll see for ourselves.

Auggie Doggie

Craig Mathews

If you're a fan of 1960s television, you might recall the cartoon, "Quick Draw McGraw," with its co-stars Auggie Doggie and Doggie Daddy. In late May of 1990, I got my first real bird dog. I named my tiny female German Shorthair pointer Auggie Doggie and, of course, I became known as Doggie Daddy. This is our story.

The first time I saw our new puppy was when my wife Jackie brought her to our fly-fishing store after picking her up at the airport. The dog had been flown in from an Iowa breeder in a tiny portable kennel. I saw Jackie drive in and met her at the door. I will never forget Jackie, toting in the kennel with our puppy, saying, "This little girl already has a lot to say. She has been barking and grinning at me since I picked her up." Peering into the kennel, I could see a very small dog with oversized ears and a curious smile on her lips. The tiny puppy, mouth open with her big smile, had her tongue curled side-to-side, an inherited trait that nearly seventy-five percent of humans exhibit, but not one I'd seen before in dogs.

(Photo by Jackie Mathews)

Craig Mathews with German shorthair Auggie Doggie.

Auggie took one look at me, her Doggie Daddy, dropped her head back, and let out a bark followed by a coyote-sounding howl. Our fourteen-year-long show was just beginning.

I had already done my homework, reading and rereading several books on training pointing dogs, so that first summer I started with Auggie. Since this was my first pointing dog, I was determined to flawlessly train my pup. I was almost paranoid after hearing and reading of improper training methods and how one could destroy a potentially great pointing bird dog puppy simply with one improper command.

Auggie, though, was one of those dream dogs to train. She basically trained me. She had the patience to wait for me to come around to proper methods. She could take my temperature, so to speak, and let me make mistakes, which then sent me back to the books to figure things out. She led the way, stuck with me, and by mid-summer, she was making good progress in showing me the light.

We were making great strides, with the opening of Montana's bird season only two months away. Then our first tragedy struck in late July, when Auggie was only five months old. As she waited patiently at the fly shop door to be taken for a short walk, the phone rang. Jackie answered it while I continued talking with a couple of customer-fishermen at the door. We didn't notice Auggie, who crept out of the building to the front walk, pointing robins on the lawn. A stray dog on the other side of the road attracted her attention, and she began to cross the roadway. We heard the screeching of brakes, followed by a thump, then the sickening wail of a dog in severe pain.

For the next month she would lug around a full cast on her front leg, but we continued our training. By opening day of the 1990 grouse season, her leg had healed and I announced that my Auggie Doggie was ready for wild birds.

On her first day in the woods she locked up on a solid point, and I shot my first grouse over her. All the while she stayed on point, steady to wing and shot—even as I retrieved the grouse. Anyone who has trained a pointing dog knows I was in heaven! A short while later she pointed again, and once more I pulled off a lucky shot that sent the ruffed grouse falling to the ground. Auggie again remained steady to wing and shot. This time I decided to allow her to retrieve the "dead bird." She returned with a lovely male grey-phase ruffed grouse. I knelt down and took the bird from Auggie, thinking how great life was, how time was on our side, with many more years and grouse to come in the seasons ahead—the way the air is cooler in early September, the way the leaves on some quaking aspens are turning red and gold, the way the distant Madison Range carries an early snow for an astonishing horizon, and the way the sky is so big and blue that this could only be Montana.

That first season I began keeping a detailed journal of our daily bird jaunts, along with photos, dates, times, and places we hunted, noting weather conditions, number of birds flushed and taken, crop contents, the sex of birds, and a tail feather from each. My journal tells of us ending that first year with exactly 100 grouse, and I was more than pleased. My friends who came along on daily hunts in September and October were amazed at young Auggie and our success. And when the season closed in November, I began counting the days to the next grouse season.

In her first year of bird hunting, Auggie and I developed that special synergistic relationship known to bird hunters who have had the distinct pleasure of owning a dog that understands and appreciates its friend afield with the gun. Too, the hunter who can do what the dog tells them to do, much like fly fishers who do what the river tells them to do, will always be far more successful. Auggie taught me patience, to trust her instincts and her nose, and to shoot accurately in order to avoid her icy glare when I missed a wing shot I should have made. Those times when I tried to sit her down and explain how I missed the bird were about as effective as talking to a winter wind. After I apologized and walked a short distance away, she'd seemingly forget my shortcomings and begin her energetic search for another grouse for me to miss.

★ ★ ★

The following two seasons went much like the first and we added Gambel's, scaled, Bobwhite, and Mearns quail along with pheasants, sharptail and sage grouse, and Hungarian partridge to the list of birds we pursued afield. This added even more days to the fifty-plus we already spent chasing ruffed and dusky grouse in Montana and Idaho in September and October. Now we would pack up and head to Arizona,

South Dakota, New Mexico, and Texas. We'd spend nearly 100 days in the woods, prairies, mountains, and fields.

★ ★ ★

In her second summer Auggie began showing interest in larger critters. One morning I'd let her out of our house at daybreak to use the ladies' room. She'd usually return quickly to the back door and bark to come in for breakfast. On that late August morning I heard her bark, and when I went to let her in, I found her nose-to-nose with a grizzly bear in our front yard. She was bobbing and weaving like a prize fighter, barking and false charging the huge boar grizzly, which gave me a look that conveyed, "You had better get this little doggy away from me before I rip it apart." I was a nervous wreck for the safety of Auggie, my pride and joy, and after considerable coaxing, I got my little warrior safely inside. The bear promptly ripped down six of my wife's bird feeders in our yard. This happened more than once each of the following summers, even though we took the bird feeders down so as not to encourage bears into our yard. Each time Auggie would run at the bear(s), bobbing, weaving, and barking, with me, bear spray in one hand and a .357 Magnum pistol in the other, yelling at her to "come in this minute."

Then there were the times she decided bull moose were not to be tolerated in her yard. Several times I had to come to her rescue, or so I thought, as she pranced and danced between the moose's hooves as they tried to punch her lights out. She'd look at me, Zen sentiment in her eyes, and run in and out and through, as the moose juddered and bumped and stomped in an attempt to trample her to death.

In her third season on a September morning hunt, Augs and I took a break after the long hike up to the Trapper Creek divide. We sat listening to horned lark songs and the keening of the morning winds. Updrafts became strong from the valley below when suddenly she lifted her nose to scent, and moved snakelike through the white bark pines, nearly the length of a football field, to the edge of a small draw. There I saw her lock up on solid point. I approached, kicking the Idaho fescue and stunted huckleberry bushes, attempting to flush the bird, all the while searching for it hidden and hunkered down in the thick cover. My 28-gauge AyA side-by-side at the ready, I slowly and nervously tiptoed toward her, prepared for the big grouse to flush in an explosion of wings.

I came up to the steep drop into the draw, passed Auggie, still rock-solid on point, and peered over the edge. Not twenty feet in front of us, a huge sow grizzly with her two cubs stood up and looked at me. I glanced at my dog, who returned my look as if to say, "It's gonna flush, and you'd better not miss this time!" I quickly retreated, grabbed my companion by her pink collar, and made tracks out of the area. I did what grizzly bear specialist Doug Peacock told me to do: "Look big, talk loud." As we moved off I glanced back at the bear, her cubs rolling and playing at her feet, still standing her ground, glaring at my tiny dog. The big sow weaved from side-to-side and squinted through its tiny, gleaming eyes, trying to make out what that little white dog and guy with a scatter gun were doing disturbing it as it peacefully rooted for pine nuts at 9,000 feet.

As I retreated with Auggie in tow, but still within sight of the bear, a covey of dusky grouse flushed wild. Auggie looked at me in her enigmatic way, and I had to tell her, "I'll explain later; for now, just keep moving as fast as you can."

★ ★ ★

Near the end of our third bird season, Jackie, Augs, and I decided we'd chase pheasants on the Crow Indian Reservation and along the Big Horn River south of Billings, Montana. The weather forecast called for snow, but our little Auggie was in tremendous physical condition having hunted, nearly nonstop, for the past sixty days.

Arriving at our first spot on the high benches above the river, we took a short lunch break and marveled as the endless fields of prairie grasses bent and moved in the distance like waves on the sea. On our first hunt, late in the afternoon, she pointed a rooster. We moved in and flushed it out of thick cover along a small stream, and it fell to the ground with our shots. I sent Augs to retrieve the bird. As she crossed the frozen stream, the ice gave way and she disappeared. Frantic, Jackie and I ran down the bank of the small creek searching for our dog. We began breaking ice along the stream and yelling her name. It seemed like eons before, fifty yards downstream, Auggie's tiny head poked up above the ice. As we all headed, cold and wet, the mile back to the truck, about halfway there Auggie began to stagger. I picked her up and ran the rest of the way. Once we warmed her up, she seemed fine, but we took no chances. We drove the 350 miles home that evening.

The next month we drove to Amarillo, Texas, to shoot Bobwhite and scaled quail on a friend's ranch along the Canadian River. I began to notice a change in Auggie; her stamina wasn't as strong, and where before she would devour her meals, she now refused to finish her food. And, while we only hunted a couple days in Texas she seemed tired. We cut our stay short and headed to Nogales, Arizona, where we were scheduled to hunt Mearns quail and visit a veterinarian friend.

Auggie rested for a few days while en route, and when we arrived, she was eating well and seemed ready to climb the nearby mountains in search of Mearns. I made an appointment for the following day with our friend just to be sure of her health, and we hit the mountains. Two hours later Jackie, the dog, and I found ourselves miles from the truck. We had taken several birds, thanks to some nice dog work. Stopping for a water break, Jackie, Augs and I enjoyed the warm sun and sank into a reverie. We fell asleep and awoke an hour later as the sun began to dip below the mountaintops and the temperature cooled. We decided it was time to call it a day.

But Auggie would not get up. I would stand her up, but she'd sink back to the ground. My heart raced. It was at least three miles back to the truck through rugged country. I gave my shotgun to Jackie, picked up Auggie, and began the long walk back. I hadn't gone more than a few yards when she seemed to come out of it and began to lick my face. I lowered her to the ground, and it was as if she'd stored strength in her body over the past few years and now could call upon it when she needed to act. She picked up her pace and followed us to the truck, not hunting, just following. The long walk back was glacially slow, and it was well after dark when we arrived at the truck. We knew something was terribly wrong with Auggie.

★ ★ ★

That night Jackie and I agonized over our taking Augs into the tough mountain country on the Arizona-Mexican border to chase quail that day. Jackie reassured me the dog "would be fine after seeing Dr. Tad tomorrow."

The next day the doctor took skin scrapings off several lesions on Aug's legs and ears and sent them to labs around the country for analysis. He advised us to head back to Montana to be near our local vet. He indicated he suspected a terminal disorder in our dog and said he'd heard of a couple similar cases: "To be real honest, things don't look good." He promised to call our local vet, research the diagnosis, and work out treatment if there was any.

Jackie and I packed up immediately and headed north. I can still see Auggie sitting like a vigilant grandmother in the back seat of our pickup truck as we set off for home. We drove the 1,200 miles non-stop, arriving at midnight in a late January blizzard. We put ourselves to bed, planning to drive the seventy miles to Mike or Eileen White's veterinarian office the following morning. At 6:00 AM, when I tried to wake Augs, she was unresponsive. I sped to the vets' offices.

The following few days were touch-and-go. Mike and Eileen conferred with Tad, our friend and vet from Arizona, and worked with university and independent labs to conduct analyses and devise a treatment. The bottom line seemed to be that Auggie would live a month or two . . . at best. She lacked adrenal function, her thyroid was not working, and there were other complications. She was started on experimental injections along with a couple of oral medications.

Jackie and I moped around the house for weeks, then months . . . Augs moseyed along behind us, appearing to pick up stamina and steam with each week. We decided to get another German shorthair pointer since we knew Augs, not even three years old, could never, would never hunt again.

Soon Emma, our new dog, was with me daily for training and long romps in the grouse woods. We didn't take Auggie out of our yard for fear of what could happen; we put her in a glass house. I'd brag like a proud father about how great she was for the three short seasons she was afield with friends and me. We'd taken more than 300 ruffed grouse, as well as hundreds of quail and pheasants, partridge, sage and sharptail grouse too, all over her sure, steady staunch points. Now, though, Auggie was out of shape, having gained several pounds from prescribed meds of steroid shots and pills. Her characteristic little smile and curled tongue, along with the twinkle in her eyes, were gone.

The following spring, with Auggie and Emma in tow, I started out down our long driveway for a walk. Emma got birdy near some aspens, not fifty yards from our house. Auggie, following up behind Emma, locked up solid on point . . . her first point in nearly two years. Emma backed the point, and I walked in to find a hen ruffed grouse nested at the base of an aspen not five feet off the drive. I took both dogs by the collar leading them away from the nested grouse. I could not help but notice Auggie's huge smile and her eyes twinkling brightly in the afternoon sunshine.

Later that summer, the grouse hatched her chicks, and I became the proud stepfather of eleven baby ruffed grouse. Auggie took great pleasure in hunting, locating, and pointing the active brood as they moved about daily, feeding on clover, beetles, and grasshoppers. She became stronger and lost weight; her attitude seemed to improve daily. She wore her determination to hunt again like an invisible suit of armor. In August, after conferring with our vets, we made the decision to hunt Auggie again, nearly two years after she was given a month or two to live.

Auggie's glass house days were finished; she was back hunting in the grouse woods with our friends and me.

★ ★ ★

For the next eight glorious seasons, Auggie would hunt birds with us. Ruffed and dusky grouse, Hungarian partridge, sharptail and sage grouse, Gambel's, Mearns, scaled, and Bobwhite quail would freeze under her steady points, and some would fall with our shots. Life was never better and time was on our side, with many more birds and seasons ahead.

One morning, it was just Augs and I hunting up ruffed grouse along the Gallatin River in southwestern Montana. Morning mist hung low and stayed in the valley like a relative. We had moved a small covey of birds, and I'd taken a mature grey-phased male with the second shot from my 28-gauge AyA. We stopped to clean the bird by a small spring entering the main river, and I sat on a moss-covered rock and marveled at the intricately mottled back feathers of the bird as it lay in my hand. I looked at Auggie, wiggling on her back in the grasses and slurping water from the spring. For all my missed shots and mistakes, I would often look at her and she'd look back at me with those big-brown eyes and forgive all my shortfalls. I wished I could do the same.

★ ★ ★

I swear, as most bird dog owners will, that their dogs can reason. We believe that great bird dogs think through a bird hunting issue or problem. For instance, after dealing with the bird above, Auggie and I walked a short distance from the spring, where she made game on another bird. With her white stub of a tail wagging a mile a minute, I knew the bird she was scenting was a wise old bird. She'd follow the scent a short distance, then she'd backtrack and redirect me in a wide arc to come on the running bird from another direction. Often we'd work with the wind in an attempt to head off older, wiser birds before they made it to impenetrable downfall or a dead-end canyon cliff. As before, I confidently followed, knowing Auggie's thoughts had taken wing and she was now ruminating on finding the bird as we went. This happened frequently, especially on wise old dusky ruffed grouse. The typical deal would play out when, after moving a hundred yards or more in the opposite with-the-wind direction, she'd suddenly stop and circle back into the wind and towards the escaping bird. Most times she'd lock on a solid point and I would have to remind myself time and again to trust her. On this day it was no exception and we scored another mature grouse over her sure point. This time as we stopped to clean the grouse and Augs rolled in the grasses and absorbed my praises, I noticed how old she looked.

Her muzzle was grey, her eyes clouded with cataracts, her breaths shorter and harder. It was her twelfth year in the grouse woods, ten more than anyone had predicted for her. We sat along the river and had a talk.

★ ★ ★

Most humans have experienced the unfailing love, loyalty, honor, faithfulness, and more that a dog can give. I have learned when a bird dog makes a promise, nothing is going to change that promise. Dogs do not lie or cheat, and they talk the way their parents, grandparents, and distant ancestors have passed down to them. We as dog owners/hunters cannot make or hold promises, we can only make deals with our dogs. We say things like "just one more bird and we'll call it a day," or "one more shot and I promise I will make it." We know, even as we promise, even as we give our word, that we can't stop with just "one more" of anything.

But sitting along the river on that September day in 2001, I made a promise to Auggie. I promised that, when she became so old that she could no longer wag her tail, no longer see, no longer get up to go outside on her own, I would let her go to the big grouse woods in the sky.

We had three more good years of chasing birds together. In all, Auggie lived nearly fifteen years of a good life, one that initially seemed doomed to be cut short when she was just two. But she beat all odds. She pointed and retrieved thousands of birds. She lived through Addison's and Smitt's, sugar diabetes and valley fever, pneumonia and more, and never quit.

Several times in those weeks before she passed on, she could barely crawl from beneath the desk where she slept. She'd limp and whine the short distance to the back door to go out. But when I would ask her, "do you want to go out?" she'd wag her tail furiously, and I'd pick her up and bring her down the steps.

That last time, early in October as a heavy fog clung to the Madison Range near our house, I brought her out for her final visit to our back yard. When I asked her if she wanted to go outside, she didn't wag her tail, and she could not get up. She could no longer see me. I felt she was asking me to fulfill my promise, and I did. As I write this, nearly five years later, the tears still well up.

Auggie and I shared a final promise, as well. We had visited several spots where I thought she might like to be buried, but we never seemed comfortable with any of those locations after talking about them. She'd always go back to her all-time favorite spot, in our special room with guns and ammo and photographs and bird journals. She is there today, in a tiny heart-shaped urn, along with a paper ink-stamped with one of her paw prints and dozens of photos of our junkets together.

Many will say, "It's just a dog." They'll caution one not to anthropomorphize, not to think of a dog as having feelings or being able to think. I like to imagine Auggie is steady staunch and pointing scent, with the grouse under her point hidden in the huckleberry brush, holding deep in the tangle of pine grasses. Auggie has scored again. I move in, and the grouse flushes, and I shoot straight, and the bird crumples and falls. Auggie remains steady to wing and shot, and only moves to fetch the bird on my command. She returns with the beautiful grey-phase ruffed grouse, full of herself, strutting back, bird in mouth, feeling proud. She's never failing, always loving, steadfast, and faithful. I can see it in her eyes that she's thinking, "Let's not be here too long; time to get going as there are more birds ahead."

The Flying Saucer

Craig Nova

The pleasures of bird hunting are best summed up in an essay that almost all bird hunters have read: José Ortega y Gasset's *Meditations on Hunting*. Among other things, Ortega y Gasset says that one of the pleasures of walking into a cover where a dog is pointing a bird is that the hunter lives in a state of only being alert, which is what it was like before we became self conscious, before the invention, if you can put it that way, of a sense of self. This experience really is the ideal.

I've had this experience, and there is another quality that I'd like to add, which is that at some moments I have had the sense of a special kind of communication between my dog and me. A cover I used to hunt in Vermont is not far from the Connecticut River, and in the fall when the flights of woodcock are in, this is a wonderful place to spend an afternoon with a dog. I like to consider particular moments: my dog, an English setter, quartering the ground ahead of us as we approach a stand of whip-stage maple. The breeze flows downhill from this place and the dog gets birdy. The odd thing is that I have had the sensation, as strange as this sounds, that I can smell something, too. Maybe it is just the litter

Craig Nova's daughter Abby & Brittany spaniel Jack.

of leaves in the stand, those wet places where the earthworms wait and where the woodcock like to drill for them.

The dog points. I walk up, stock under arm, and when the bird gets up, it is as though I am not thinking at all. The barrel swings up and toward the bird. *Bang.* The bird slides down as though there were a large piece of glass between me and that autumn sky, at once so pale and so hauntingly blue.

So, this is the ideal. It takes work to have it, and this work is worthwhile. It seems to me that this experience is particularly worth having in the modern age, which, if nothing else, makes us think that the natural world only exists on the Nature Channel. But, this being the modern age, we have some new tools in bird hunting. Mostly, of course, these are expressions of new technology, and while they have been around for a while, the experience with them can be less than perfect. And so I'd like to add, as a sort of asterisk to *Meditations on Hunting*, my experience with the new technology of bird hunting.

I began using this stuff in a way that is as innocent as a teenager fumbling with his girlfriend in a car. I had no idea what I was getting into with new technology, but I could feel the attraction of it, which is to say that I could feel the attraction of the ideal. And maybe this is behind the seduction of all new technology: it helps us, or seduces us, or leaves us with the illusion that it will help in that pursuit of the way things should be, whether a novel or an afternoon spent with bird dogs. And how are you going to resist this notion of the ideal being more available? You might as well ask a young couple in the front seat of a car to give it up, and as everyone knows, that just isn't going to happen.

The first thing I started using was a substitute for a bell. This was a thing that looked like a sort of half-length of a flashlight, and it was worn on the dog's neck like a small barrel filled with brandy. It made one tone, a sort of horrible squeaking, when the dog was moving, but when the dog stopped or when it pointed a bird, the device made another. The first time I heard this noise—that is, both of them, the running sound and the pointing sound—I thought, God, that is like an alarm at a toxic waste storage plant.

But here is the attraction of technology and the method that we use to change the way we think about things. It occurred to me very quickly, or maybe it just happened, that when the beeping started, it meant that the dog had found a bird, and soon this noise, which had been so horrible, became sort of beautiful if only because of the message it was sending. And, much to my shame, I abandoned the small, lovely bell.

So I started hunting regularly with this thing, and the small difficulties I had with it should have been a warning. That is, the thing, the device, the Electronic Pointing Device (hereinafter called the EPD, as though it were a variety of financial instrument that also didn't work out), had a switch so that you could turn if off if you were moving from one cover to another. The on-and-off switch worked fine—that is, it would have worked fine if the EPD only sat on a shelf in a sporting goods store, but given the nature of the old apple orchards I hunted in Vermont, and the cane and brush and whip-stage covers I hunted, this switch could easily be turned off just by the clutter and difficulty of the brush. And so I started covering the switch with a piece of electrician's tape, but then this had to be pulled away from the switch to turn it on or off, or from "0" to "1" in computer-speak, and this meant the adhesive began to wear off so that the tape didn't stick after awhile, and so the switch wasn't protected. This meant I needed another thing to put in my car, a roll of electrician's tape, when I took my dog to the covers I hunted every fall.

But this minor difficulty was only prelude. The land directly behind my house in Vermont is pretty good woodcock and grouse cover. My office was at the end of the house, in the attic, and since the house was built against a hillside, I could walk directly out of the attic into the small orchard there. Often, in the fall, when I was at work, I would look up and see ruffed grouse in the apple trees, or hear their drumming, which in Vermont, anyway, always sounded to me like someone trying to start a tractor.

One afternoon, I put on my vest, took the shotgun out of the cabinet (locked, because of my kids), and put the half flashlight on the dog. I want to say, sort of parenthetically, that while I am going to give some technology a little grief here, the shotgun was an exception: an AyA, made to measure on the strength of some movie option, two barrels, 20- and 28-gauge, light as broomstick. Anyway, I took the shotgun, put the half flashlight (the EPD) on the dog, a bone-headed Brittany that I still think of with great fondness, and went up the hill with the device making that *squeak, squeak, squeak.*

This was one of those afternoons in Vermont that comes after a still night when the trees have mulled. The leaves make perfect circles around the maples, just like those in a garden architect's plans, and since the ground is covered with these yellow-and-pink circles, the sky and every object in the late afternoon is covered with that warm pink and yellow light. It isn't only a physical thing, but something else, too, and that color with its dusty quality, like a woman's powder, suggests a connection to other days in the fall through the decades, or centuries, or millennia. Although, I have to add, this light has another quality, too, which is the suggestion of mortality and time that is beyond human beings. Surely, this combination of beauty and mortality is near the heart of bird hunting.

We went up the hill. The dog mostly quartered his ground in a regular and pleasing way, not too far out, not too close, and he was pretty good with birds, that is, he didn't bump them very often. I fell into that familiar mood, at once alert to the place where I was and yet mildly contemplative, as I heard that *squeak*, about the usual things—kids, books, publishers, movie people, etc. We got to the top of the hill, where wild apples grew, and I remember taking one down and having a bite, the small apple covered with a kind of dark rust but still cold from the nights that were cold enough to freeze. The moisture cut the thirst. That blue sky was just beyond the scrub of the orchard. The device made that steady beeping, and I approached, still tasting the bittersweet apple, and a woodcock got up, seeming to go straight up, and then, bang. A little weight in the game pouch.

The *squeak* seemed to diminish a little, but I thought about that smell of gun powder, the taste of the apple, and I guess I was a little lost in that Ortega y Gasset moment, or the aftermath, which is a familiar relaxation that I didn't want to give up. So I went around the edges of the orchard, and the *squeak* diminished, and then, with a sort of thrill of recognition of what was happening, it disappeared. And no beep, either, no pointing, just silence.

Bird dogs have a sort of perfect sense of when they can fuck up. It is as though they are in communication with you, or they know you are watching, but if you moon off, or lose track of them, they instantly do what you think they have been wanting to do all along and now have the chance to do. Or maybe, in this case, as in many others, the dog found a woodchuck or some creature and took off after it. Friend Bob DeMott once told me that he had a dog, Spike, who took off under these circumstances to have sexual congress with a porcupine. Spike, needless to say, was a bold dog, especially since he seemed to enjoy this episode.

So the dog had taken off. He had done it before and he did it again, afterwards. I tried the whistle. Nothing. And at least I had done enough work with bird dogs to know that if the dog doesn't respond to the whistle it's a good idea to shut up, since if the dog hears it and doesn't respond, all you are doing is teaching him to ignore you. It takes a few years not only to know this, but to be able to act on it.

I did the usual thing and started looking for the dog. Jack was his name. And the truth is that on a day like this one, even that wasn't so bad, since I knew he would turn up, although every now and then he had gone cross country, and I had received a call from someone miles away who had found the dog and looked at his collar, where I had my name and telephone number. This is particularly galling if, say, it happens when you have been hunting a cover on the other side of the state.

But I did a little rough hunting, trying to turn up some game by myself, although I kept an eye out for what I was now calling a bone-headed mutt. And, of course, my mood was getting darker in the part that keeps track of dogs and their antics. Still, the air was warm, the landscape filled with that pink and yellow light. More apples to eat. I shot another woodcock.

It began to get dark. That pink and yellow began to turn blue, like a delphinium, to a darker blue, and as I went, I thought of a D. H. Lawrence poem, "Bavarian Gentians" and these lines:

Bavarian gentians, big and dark, only dark
darkening the daytime torch-like with the smoking blueness of Pluto's gloom,
ribbed and torch-like, with their blaze of darkness spread blue . . .

Well, it would have been an ideal afternoon, if it hadn't been for the dog. I turned homeward, back down the hill through the places I knew, where there was less brush in the stands of mountain ash, and as it got darker, I finally saw in the distance the glow of the windows of my house, the light seeming to be like the domestic itself. Of course, when I came in, bringing a whiff of the cold, my wife said, without looking up from the table where she sat, "Where's Jack?"—although I have to say that this wasn't a real question so much as a way of confronting the fact that the dog had gone off. Again. But it was one of those things that we didn't worry about too much.

I put the shotgun away, locked the cabinet, and made a mental note to save the woodcock feathers for a friend who used them to tie flies. Then I went downstairs and had a drink. We ate dinner. I kept listening in the dark for the sound of that device, that *squeak, squeak, squeak.*

Up the road from my house lived a veterinarian, a man I much admired and who often looked after my dogs. At night, recently, my wife and I had heard screeching, a kind of wild call, and I said to her that if I didn't know better I would say that it was the sound of a mountain lion, and she dismissed me, sort of, and then the next day when I was out for a walk, the vet said, "Did you hear the mountain lion last night?"

The vet had a wife, a lovely woman who on this night was alone, I think, because the vet, in those days, had a practice of looking after animals in various zoos. The next morning I heard through the town grapevine that something odd had happened the night before. Had anyone seen a white or blue light in the sky? The sheriff had had a report (was it the vet's wife? No one could say) that a flying saucer had landed just up the road from my house, or, at least, the report was that there was an eerie beeping that could have only been from another world. Well, the dog finally showed up, late at night, and I suppose that the sound of the electronic device could have seemed, to someone who didn't understand about these things, otherworldly, or at least the work of an alien.

So you think I would have been warned. Between the electrician's tape and my neighbor thinking that a flying saucer had landed in her back yard, I should have had second thoughts about technology. But, as I say, the pursuit of the ideal is strong, and the seduction of technology in this pursuit is even stronger. And part of this seduction is the belief that we can avoid unintended consequences, or that technology can be applied in exactly the way we want, without any trouble.

In fact, the same pattern that applies to the difficulties of medicine and zoology can be seen in the use of technology with bird dogs. For instance, when we first used antibiotics, we didn't realize how quickly bacteria work their way around the mechanism of a particular chemical, just as we didn't think or were amazed to find that when we tried to poison rats, they soon worked their way around the effects of D-Con, and that in order to kill them, we have to be constantly changing the poisons we use.

So, I plunged in. The next item on the list was a device to help train the dog—another collar set up to shock the dog if the dog did something it shouldn't and also, and far better for training, set up to make a tone (another tone) to warn the dog that it was going to get shocked if it didn't, say, respond to the whistle. As everyone knows, the training that is done with the dog avoiding a shock is far, far better than just getting shocked.

But, of course, here is where the unintended or unimagined quality comes in, and maybe there is something in this fact that all bird hunters might take into account, if they haven't already (and, you know, the ones who have been at it for awhile, I think, probably have). In my case, and in the case of people who first started using these devices, I quickly discovered that the dog was a lot smarter than I had thought. I learned very fast that that the dog knew the difference between when he was wearing this collar—and would behave perfectly—and when he was just wearing a bell (or an EPD).

So the next step in fighting this unanticipated result was to get a dummy collar that looked and felt just like the real thing. The dog now wore this all the time, and when you wanted to train him, you switched collars, taking off the dummy and putting on the real one. But even this had its troubles, since some dogs were smart enough or sensitive enough to know the difference between the two. And if you hunted him with just the dummy, he would behave in ways that left you considering that dark place where you kept a list of bone-headed bird dogs. The next item, of course, is that many dogs are smart enough to know the precise range of the transmitter, the little wand-like thing that the trainer or hunter has tucked away in his vest, and as soon as the dog gets beyond it, he is going to be free. And he knows it.

Well, I have been through all those stages, from seduction to hope, to that state in which I looked at all the junk I had acquired and, like someone who has strayed from the place where he should be, realized that it was all illusion. Or, at least, for me it was.

I think the failure of technology has a number of lessons. You can see a lot of them in its use with bird dogs. For instance, the person who begins to use some new device to work with a dog suffers from a sort of Bonapartism, a rush of power that gets in the way of common sense and good training. The worst part of this rush is that people forget the dog. And what the dog knows. The dog, as any bird hunter will tell you, likes to hunt, and that the way to make good bird dogs is to hunt with them. The old, hard work with a dog is what makes a good one (within, I hasten to add, certain limits of the Bone Head Quotient), just as it is important to remember that not only do you know the dog, the dog knows you. The best days I've had were ones in which I was relaxed and sure of myself, not futzing with training devices and the rest. Or the best days came when I had worked with a dog all summer with a quail recall cage, and after I had spent a lot of time rewarding good behavior. And more than anything else, I think Ortega y Gasset's comment that the pleasure of hunting comes from living in a state of alertness is enhanced by having spent the time to get to know a dog and having spent a lot of time hunting with him.

Technology has its place, and I wouldn't deny that for a moment, but my experience is that it is a good idea to be careful with it. For instance, Dave Albright, a physician friend, told me of a study he had read about technology and productivity in medicine. The study looked carefully at mortality rates in an intensive care ward for premature babies, and the authors of the article found that physicians spent so much time looking at a laptop computer, they weren't watching the premature child, and that this, of course, had led to a decline in the quality of care.

So I like to think of those afternoons in Vermont when the light was pink and yellow, and I went into a cover with a dog I knew well. These were the occasions when the dog got birdy and when I thought I could smell something, and when, without benefit of anything aside from a bell and a gun and a dog, I had one of those afternoons when I could be just alert. And when, as the bird got up with that rush of wings, I simply disappeared.

The Prime of Their Lives

Howell Raines

My wife Krystyna and I had planned to end the season in February by hunting Bobwhites in the Florida Panhandle. Instead we finished two months early and on another continent. On the day after New Year's, on a golden afternoon in the rolling grain fields of Europe's bread-basket region, we found the perfect moment to quit until next year. It is a supposed benefit of reaching the age of sixty-five that you get wiser about such pursuits as fly fishing, bird shooting, and taking care of dogs. I never put much stock in that rumor, but I think that's what happened that day. With five plump Polish pheasants in the game bag, our little pack of four—Krystyna and me and our German shorthaired pointers, Pokey and Clara—had completed the mission we had pursued throughout our gypsy autumn. Nothing we did after that day could provide a better ending to the coming-of-age of Pokey and Clara.

You'll understand why when I explain a bit more about the places we rambled and the dream that drove us. Although neither of us had ever trained a puppy from scratch, Krystyna and I could see during the

Howell Raines with German shorthairs Pokey & Clara.

first two years we worked Pokey and Clara on put-and-take shooting preserves in Pennsylvania that we had a couple of prodigies on our hands. We also realized, as both passed their third birthdays in the summer, that come fall we had a chance to do something special for our talented odd couple. Clara, fast and high-strung in the field, cuddly as a kitten at home, was our scout. Pokey, aloof and deliberate in movement and manner and, on point, as dead certain as income tax, was the closer. We thought they had earned something special that few dogs and their hunters have time to experience. We would devote an entire hunting season to taking them, week after week, while they were in the prime of their lives and at the peak of their powers, to the best bird hunting we could find.

(Courtesy of Howell Raines)

They had mastered Hungarian partridge in Saskatchewan in September, learned the difficult tricks of ruffed grouse in Montana and Maine in October. Then in November and December we were off to Krystyna's native Poland. Hunters there are mainly interested in deer, red stag, and the formidable wild boars that roam the wide open spaces of interior Europe in numbers that stun Americans. Equally surprising, hunting in Poland has not been under state control or monopolized by the upper classes since the eighteenth century, when the nobles and landed gentry put hunting clubs governed by local citizens in charge of game management. In an uncharacteristic burst of good sense, the Communists preserved this system of citizen-controlled hunting, and it remained intact when Poland secured its political freedom with the triumph of Solidarity in 1989.

These clubs, numbering fifty to 100 members, controlled hunting rights on spreads of 12,000 to 50,000 acres. They set the seasons, strictly enforced limits, and repaid landowners for considerable damage to their crops, done mainly by wild boars in the potato and cornfields. The clubs were proud of their democratic tradition that brought plumbers and blacksmiths into the fields with professors, physicians, and, in Krystyna's mother's little village, a retired prison warden.

Thanks to her friends in a hunting club in the historic Silesian agricultural region three hours south of Warsaw, we were able to buy a hunting permit rarely granted to foreign visitors. We were allowed to pursue only the pheasants, which held little interest for a club devoted to larger game. Our bird hunting began just outside my mother-in-law's back gate, usually in the company of the club's gamekeeper and its president, the aforementioned retired jailer. We tramped to our heart's content along hedgerows between corn and wheat fields that stretched to the horizon in all directions. We reveled in how quickly our dogs adapted to birds that might scamper a half mile before holding and, at other times, erupted from the briars within inches of their noses. These were wild and difficult birds in terrain that worked to their advantage. Even with our shooting sharpened by months in the field, a brace of cock pheasants in a half-day hunt counted as an excellent day. On our first hunts, our game bags might have been plumper if I, a lifelong Bobwhite hunter, had realized more quickly how little I knew about pheasants, and how rapidly Pokey and Clara were figuring out their game of high-speed hide-and-seek.

Pokey showed off his trademark caution on close birds that held in the thickets along irrigation ditches. On the runners, Clara displayed her specialty: smelling birds at eye-popping distances and snaking along behind them through tangled hedgerows. On our last day, Clara was working a bird that took us on a long point-and-creep chase. Worried that a big rooster would flush out of range, I was whistling and "whoa-ing" so much that Krystyna had some advice for me.

"Shut up," she said.

"I'm just trying to help her," I replied.

"Well, you're not. She knows what she's doing, and you're making her nervous."

My reward for shutting up was that Clara found the bird in fine form and I, freed from pestering her, made my toughest offside shot ever. That turned out to be the next-to-the-last bird of the last day of our season. Krystyna got the fifth and last one, which Pokey and Clara pointed flawlessly along an irrigation ditch. It came up in a clattering burst of color from the tall green grass that had survived the early frosts. It kept flying despite solid hits from her 20-gauge, defining a straight, flat line across the corn-stubble. Then at a distance of a good quarter mile, the bird suddenly flared upward. It climbed perpendicularly, a couple of hundred feet at least, becoming a speck in the sky, before falling like a rock into the thick forest at the far side of the plowed field.

"It's dead," said our companion from the hunting club. Speaking in Polish to Krystyna, he expressed doubt about whether we would ever find the bird in those woods. Pokey and I, just the two of us, were up for the long hike across the corn stubble. As we beat our way through a willow thicket, Pokey pointed. Several yards in front of him, resting on its belly in a loose mound of brown leaves, its resplendent peacock colors shining in the sun and unruffled, was our rooster. I couldn't tell if the bird was dead or alive. Pokey, who was born staunch, wasn't going to gamble on whether this unblemished bird was down or just stupid. I walked past the dog, ready for a flush that didn't come. I had to pick up the big rooster and shake its limp body in front of Pokey before he would come off point and take it in his mouth.

An unexpected benefit of our gypsy autumn was that our dogs had become self-taught. The constant exposure to wild birds in all kinds of cover had put an edge on their skills far beyond any coaching that Krystyna and I, as novice trainers, could have provided. I thought back to the afternoon in Montana when we had emptied our guns on a covey of ten grouse that Pokey had found in a spectacular manner, winding them across 100 yards of pine-studded grasslands. "You realize they are now better at this than we are," I told my wife as the birds flew away untouched.

Her smile carried the same message when Pokey and I drew close, and I held up her pheasant. We had shot well and the dogs had worked flawlessly, pointing and retrieving to hand. It didn't take a genius to see that the same rule applies to hunting seasons as to training sessions with young dogs. You always want to quit at a moment of maximum success. By the time we got back to the car that day, my internal calendar had flipped over. I was already thinking about the Quill Gordon hatches in April on Paradise Creek back home in Pennsylvania. As for Pokey and Clara, they would have to wait until next year for the adventure of hunting a new kind of bird in a new part of the world. I felt pretty sure that day on the Silesian plains that there would still be Bobwhites in Tallahassee and that when we finally got there in fourteen months or so, our dogs would not be over the hill at the age of four.

Hunting Close: On Bird Dogs
and Lost Time

Bobby C. Rogers

The first one I remember was a pointer bitch named Lady. We'd just moved back to Tennessee after a few years living abroad—in Crittenden County, Kentucky. My parents were relieved to be on familiar ground again. Both were born in West Tennessee, and though they'd enjoyed warm relations with the Kentuckians, they always knew where home was. Acquiring the dog may have been a way to celebrate our homecoming. My father took a posthole digger and a roll of six-foot fencing and built the pen himself behind the little rental house on Elm St. where we'd settled. He was always having to improve the kennel because Lady was an escape artist. "That was the climbingest dog I ever was associated with," my father still says. Every dog is the *somethingest* dog in a bird hunter's memory. My mother and I would walk the neighborhood calling her name and then wrestle her home to the pen, which my father would have to improve some more when he got home that evening. If it was an after-hours escape, the police might become involved. There'd be a

L-R Bobby C. Rogers, Kirk Elvy, Marc Elvy, Bill Rogers, Jr. with Sam.

knock at the door, and the town's only police car would be parked at the curb with Lady peering placidly out of the rear window.

When I enrolled in Mrs. Margaret Scarborough's kindergarten and my mother was able resume her job as a schoolteacher, it wasn't too long before we were affluent enough to get a second car. It was a used car, of course—our main car, the one we thought of as dependable, had been bought used—but this car was *really* used. It had spent time up on blocks in the shadow of the barn behind Billy Curtis's house out on the Greenfield highway, a tan Ford Fairlane, bald tires and manual transmission—"three on the tree," the shifter on the steering column. The old Ford was to be the bird-hunting car, made for the muddy back roads of West Tennessee. Since it was always only a mile or two between home and the hunt, we carried the dogs—usually one, sometimes two—in the trunk.

"You put the dogs in the trunk of the car," my wife Rebecca repeats when I, perhaps ill-advisedly, regale her with this detail from my childhood. She clearly believes I should be prosecuted for war crimes. It was a large trunk, I tell her. A commodious trunk. The dogs loved the trunk. Lady would come galloping out of the pen straight to the back of the Ford, put her muddy front paws on the chrome bumper, and shoot us a look that said: "Let me in this damn trunk." In later years, we had a custom-made kennel built to ride in the bed of my father's new F-150, but, so far as I could tell, the dogs didn't like it any better than the trunk of Billy Curtis's cast-off Ford. Like the rest of us, they just wanted to get to the field.

"You shut your dogs up in the cold, dark trunk of the car," she repeats again. Rebecca has a look of her own for me.

Bird hunters are well rehearsed at telling their stories, but how to communicate to her something of the unfathomable depths of our love for these creatures?

★ ★ ★

The first time I ever saw my father cry, I was six years old and he'd had to put Lady down. I don't remember the cause. Heart worms, most likely. When he returned without his dog from that visit to the trailer where Dr.

Smith practiced veterinary medicine on every animal in town, he took an old rusty dinette chair from the garage out to where a neighbor's oak tree hung over the fence and threw a piece of shade on our back yard, and he sat there by himself and cried. It may have been twenty years before I saw anything like that from him again. I probably shouldn't be surprised at how tenaciously the memory has hung on in my recollection.

His hunting partner back then, before my brother or I were old enough to take up the sport, was Mr. Gene Hicks, our neighbor across the street. They were always playing jokes on each other. Mr. Gene's pranks were characterized by a certain surreal quality. My father was not above the sin of pride, especially where his tomatoes were concerned, and was given to bragging about the size and dependable sweetness of the Better Boys he raised. One Sunday evening he went out to pull a few tomatoes for supper and found a large and particularly succulent strawberry tied to the vine. Gene Hicks had gotten into our garden while we were at church and left something truly sweet and remarkable to brag about.

Gene kept a Llewellyn named Bob in a shaded pen out behind his shed. A city lot in a town like McKenzie, Tennessee was big enough for sour apple trees and a good-sized dog run with plenty of space left over for your vegetable garden. I remember mowing the grass for Miss Charlotte when I was in high school—the pen was still there, rusted wire stapled to arsenic-treated posts, the shed where the dogs were sheltered leaning a little under the weight of three layers of asphalt shingles, all of it abandoned for years since Gene's death from brain cancer. My father would take him hunting even after his vision and coordination were impaired by the surgery the doctors had put him through to cut out what they could of the tumor, which must have taken some courage and more than a little love on his part when you know you'll both be swinging firearms at close quarters. When Gene Hicks died, my father ordered the flowers for the graveside, an arrangement with a likeness of a quail in flight affixed at its center, not an unheard of request at florists in those parts.

★ ★ ★

Eventually, I would join my father in the field, and my relations with bird dogs would become more, shall we say, businesslike. My father had survived polio as a child—he always called himself lucky, getting through it with just a Walter Brennan-like limp, one leg shorter than the other. Even up through the time I was in high school he could out-walk me on those long, hard, brier-obstructed forced marches we thought of as hunting. It was hard work finding birds in West Tennessee. Hard for the hunters, harder work for the dogs.

My father was a school man by profession, the principal of the town's elementary school, and we often hunted with a local farmer who drove one of the school buses. Wayford Washburn kept a pair of English setters, Bunny and Charlie, who were close and thorough hunters, perfectly suited to their circumstances. My father, maybe because of the polio but also due to the realities of the terrain, preferred dogs that would hunt close—little need for a field-splitting field trial dog on the small farms of West Tennessee. Charlie was the smaller animal, with a less than sunny disposition, even when he was younger. But he and Bunny got along: the teamwork of those dogs quartering a field was a sight to behold. They would patiently hunt out the middle of a grass patch then split at the far end to each work an opposite edge on the way back. Bunny was one of the prettiest bird dogs I've ever seen: black and white, broad-chested and strong, gold around her mouth and gold eyebrow markings above each eye. She had all the tools—nose, stamina, field manners—except she wasn't about to retrieve. No, sir. Charlie did the housework in that marriage. Nowadays, dogs wear enough gear into the field—a brass bell for location, or a beeper collar that sounds at eight-second intervals when they're casting, every second when they come on point, a radio-controlled training collar, maybe rubber booties when the ground's frozen, and a blaze-orange cape for visibility—seemingly everything imaginable save a satellite dish strapped to their ass. We didn't even bring a whistle with us to handle those dogs.

The first bird I ever killed was over Charlie. We were in between fields out on the old Bynum place, hunting down the brambling edge of a gravel road. Charlie pointed a single out of a covey that had come up wild and ragged without anyone getting off a shot. I called out to my father who was still working through the briers behind me that we had a dog on point.

"Go ahead, Son," he said. "Shoot you one."

I took a tentative step or two past the staunched dog and kicked at the brush. I didn't yet wear the size twelve boot I drag around today, but up burst a quail through the dead honeysuckle vines and wild growth that complicated the shot but slowed down the bird just enough to render it makeable for a boy trying to catch up to those lightning fast targets and bag his first quail. I had no idea where the bird would emerge but I mounted my shotgun anyway and by the time the butt plate found my shoulder and my jawbone was almost on the walnut stock the quail cleared the hedgerow. I touched the trigger and the pattern of pellets crossed the flight of the bird, dropping it into the hopeless morass of undergrowth. Charlie didn't pause to ask me for advice. He dug his way into the briers and emerged directly with the folded up bird in his mouth. He spat it out at my feet—not even Wayford warranted delivery to hand. My father had walked up in the meantime, but Charlie had fetched the bird to me. Strange how thrilling it is to have achieved some measure of acceptance from a bird dog. Even the greenest and most callow of hunters can figure out that the dog is the true professional in the field, and it's up to the rest of us to rise to his standard of dedication.

By the time I left for college, Charlie was at the end of his career. The institution I was attending offered a January mini-term. I loved J-term—mostly because I was never present for it. I had lost my part-time holiday job after the Christmas rush, so January was wide open. I was reading Faulkner, and Orwell's essays, and spending a lot of time with bird dogs. Wayford wanted his setters to get as much exercise as possible and I was happy to help him out. Bunny was still strong and could cover ground, but it was clear Charlie didn't have much time left. He was almost blind and totally deaf. When he stopped coming to the report of the gun to do the retrieving, I knew he couldn't hear a thing.

During that long January the house was empty, with my parents at the school and my brother moved to Dallas. I would work the dogs most mornings, getting out to Wayford's house shortly after breakfast. He was of course long gone, attending to some matter on the farm. I'd like to think it was me causing the dogs such joy, that they'd come to recognize my little Toyota with the university decal crunching on the gravel drive back to the pen, that they could pick out the calling of my voice, the sound of me chambering a field load shell into my Browning double-automatic, an uncommon gun my father had traded two old single-barrels and some antique nail kegs for in one of his deals. With deaf and half-blind Charlie it had to be scent: the dry rot of my cockleburr-badged vest, or maybe it was the smell of gun oil off the bluing of anyone's gun that let him know what we were about to do.

"Are you sure you want me to take Charlie out?" I'd asked Wayford.

"Dogs need to hunt," he said. "Where would you want to be?"

"What if I lose him? He'll never hear me call him in." I was just getting used to the idea of responsibility.

"He'll smell his way home, boy. Round about feeding time. I'd be out here hunting him myself if I could."

I would unlatch the kennel gate, leaving it wide open in case the deaf dog beat us back, and off we'd go, hunting the coveys on the neighboring farms, always within a mile or two of the pen, Charlie stiff legged but happy over the frozen ground, hunting close as he always had. We took our time. I didn't mind the slow pace. The birds we missed would be there the next morning. We'd find them or we wouldn't. At some point on most of those hunts Charlie would wander over a hill and find himself upwind of us and that would be the last time I'd see him that day no matter how hard I looked for him, always fearing he was somewhere locked down on point, waiting for a hunter he couldn't hear to come flush the birds, feeling angry and betrayed. But he would always be back at the pen by feeding time. Wayford and I both knew he would be dead when he was no longer able to roam the fields.

* * *

If you spend much time around hunters, you'll find out that the good days are always in the past: habitat's gone all to hell, birds won't hold in any kind of a gentlemanly manner, shells cost too much, nothing's the way it used to be. Same's true for dogs. No dog in the kennel ever compares to the heroics of dogs long gone, and there's always one back in the soft-focused, legend-strewn past that rises above the rest. For me it was Sam, a hardheaded meat dog who wasn't always amenable to reason. He had a good enough nose, a soft mouth, eight miles of field sense, and would even work woodcock when they migrated through, which many of the old-time bird hunters disapproved of. Sam was the one. I only halfway knew it at the time, which is, I guess, about as much as we ever appreciate any of our good fortune as it's being visited upon us.

Maybe I'm prejudiced, because it was during the Sam years that Rebecca came to understand a thing or two about bird dogs. When I took her home to meet the family, she had no way of knowing she was undergoing the quail test. If she didn't appreciate a day in the field or wouldn't sit down to a quail supper with us, just how smart would it be to bring her into the family? Fortunately for my future happiness, we had a good hunt. The afternoon was bright and crisp, the countryside, presentable in its fall colors. My brother had moved back from Texas by then, and he and I went about our usual mostly friendly competition at wing shooting, and on a couple of occasions that afternoon the whole process worked the way it's supposed to: Sam found the covey, the covey held, one of us, probably my brother—don't know why I wasn't shooting particularly well that day—made a shot on the rise, and Sam fetched it up and delivered it to hand. "Pretty amazing," Rebecca said, meaning the dog and not me. After this day I never had to explain anything about quail hunting; Sam had laid it all out for her. That evening at supper, when she was bravely picking at the one fried quail breast on her plate—every quail ever served in that house was fried up in a #8 skillet—my brother, a man of few words, remarked, "Well, it's good you found somebody who won't eat more quail than you can shoot."

When Sam was coming into his prime, some friends of mine flew down from Boston for a weekend of hunting. Kirk and his brother Marc had been down to hunt with us before, but this time Kirk was bringing his dog to find out how he would do on wild quail. Kirk had never set foot in the field when we knew each other in school, but when he decided to take up hunting, he bought himself a dog (field name: Injun) out of Tekoa Mountain Sunrise, which is a pretty good way to get started. "I see you got yourself one of them high-blooded dogs," my father allowed as we admired the classy looks of his setter bred for field-trialing. My father always claimed he could have produced papers on Sam to legitimize his pedigree, but none of us ever quite believed him. "Pedigree's in the field," we all would have said, anyway.

The first thing Injun did when Kirk let him out of the crate was to pick a fight with Sam to let him know who was boss. Sam didn't exactly back down from the tussle, but he sure didn't win it. And we had to admit that Sam looked a little homely next to the noble scion of a legendary bird dog line. He had a perfectly formed head and a beautiful point, his setter's tail flagged straight upward, though I'm inclined to agree with one of our other pieces of family wisdom: "There's no such thing as an ugly point." We made polite small talk while Kirk fastened the beeper collar and training collar on the dog and adjusted his leather holster for the transmitter.

Sam wasn't very sociable on his best day, but he kept his distance from that field trial dog, probably not wanting to get his other ear shredded. I was worried our guests wouldn't see enough action to make their trip south worthwhile, but we shot into seven covey rises over two hunts, which is not bad for wild birds in this part of the world. And Injun did have a classy point. We could tell by the picturesque way he honored Sam's points all weekend. Our meat dog located every covey and all the singles except one. To be fair, Sam did have home field advantage. Kirk was happy to get in the shooting and let his dog understudy with Sam while he found out what a wild quail was like. When Injun had his lone "productive" of the weekend we praised him extravagantly and congratulated his owner.

Injun was young and inexperienced in the rough cover of West Tennessee, and finding the single was proof he had a nose on him, but he never got a chance for a rematch. In the spring, Kirk and Marc were killed in a plane crash flying out of a small airstrip in Dulce, New Mexico, and I came to know something of the melancholy in the field my father must have felt at the passing of some of his hunting partners. The conditions of quail hunting are so consistent—the behaviors you expect of the dog, the shots you're called on to make, the season of the year and the look of the landscape and the angle of the afternoon light, the same brier-gnawed britches you wear year after year—that each hunt resonates with an entire history of being in the field, all you've loved of it, and every way it's broken your heart. In some wise, you can never leave any dog or hunting partner behind, and maybe that's why bird hunters are the most sentimental of men.

On the final day of hunting season of what we knew would be Sam's last good year, I left a meeting early and drove up home to get in one more hunt. My brother came over from the county seat and met us at the little Missionary Baptist church where we would often let out. My father hadn't yet retired from running the elementary school and didn't even take his tie off as he swung his vest on and broke down his old Savage Fox side-by-side. It was the last day of February, a mild day, some winter left on the calendar but not much left in the air. We walked out across the fields behind a bird dog who knew what he was doing, and I can't tell you a thing we talked about, but if we were talking at all it would have been about the way Sam was working the fence row, or how some other dog had worked it on a day just about like this one. A large moon was already up and out of the trees, and when the sun was pulled behind the opposite tree line, no one said anything about going back to the truck. Why not let the season last just a few minutes more? I was thinking of the stories my father had told us of hunting in the twilight shadows over Lady and Bob until he could see the orange flash out the end of the gun barrel when Gene Hicks shot a quail silhouetted against the sky. And just then, down at the lower end of the bean field, Sam staunched into a point, startlingly white in the gloaming.

Bad Habits

F. Daniel Rzicznek

Old Photographs

When I look through the photographs of the many waterfowl hunts I've taken part in, one detail stands out above the number of birds killed, the other hunters involved, the weather, or the location: that is the intensely happy and utterly content faces of the five black Labrador retrievers my family has collectively lived with, hunted with, and loved over the course of three decades: Stormy Weather, Buckshot, Samson, Blackjack, and Bleu. The opalescent eyes, the shifting back and forth from paw to paw, the tongue hanging sideways over the teeth, the ear flipped back by a prevailing west wind across the cattails and marsh grass, and the stare of loving attention that penetrates all the way to what it means to be alive and crazy about the world. When I start to reminisce about the hunts themselves, I remember how the birds were flying, who shot what and when, and, above all, how the dogs performed—how perfectly they brought each bird to hand before returning to heel and waiting for the next flock of plump greenheads (all banded) to cup right into the sweet

F. Daniel Rzicznek, his father & Labs Blackjack & Bleu.

spot, which (naturally) would happen, the three or four inhabitants of the blind rising to each claim a clean double, filling their respective limits.

In reality, there are a lot of missed shots (*easy* shots), dogs whining and (naturally) breaking, along with general cussing, fussing, and arguing over firearm malfunctions, who set the decoys wrong, how the whole muck-up is entirely their fault, and delinquent dog behavior. Secretly, I rejoice in these moments: chaos, anger, regret, dismay—all emotions that are impossible to fake and therefore authentic. Bad dog behavior in particular is something I am passionate about. I admit that when a dog handles well, I feel a stray thread in me suddenly reconnect with what it means to truly be an animal: patience and cunning, instinct and knowledge, passion coupled with restraint. And there is the joy in serving, in being part of a meaningful task, and not giving a damn about anything but making another being happy, a selflessness that humans rarely display.

But that same dog that handles perfectly one day can be completely unreliable and ornery the next. When dogs run amok in the field (even my own dog, when my surface emotions can run from embarrassment to anger), there is a silent part of me chanting the renegade animal on. The intensity and semi-formality of waterfowling (get everything set up in time, place the decoys just right, call well, don't screw up the shot) is enough to make me run splashing across the marsh emitting a high-pitched giggle of insanity. Dogs, from time to time, simply must do this, and when they do, I root for them, even if I'm not quite able to muster such unchecked disregard for the occasion myself. My current dog Bleu got so used to geese falling out of the sky last fall that he would charge out to greet them before they even made it to within a hundred yards of the decoys, only to shoot a puzzled look back at my howls of protest. These dogs know when we're taking our pursuits a bit too seriously, and they know that there is a time for business and a time for pleasure, and hunting is clearly pleasure, albeit a *serious* pleasure. Death, after all, is in the air.

Stormy Weather

My family's first Labrador retriever, Andy's Stormy Weather, was my brother's dog and was devoted to him with an abandon I've been unable to document in any canine since. The rumble of my brother's red CJ-5 Jeep turning the corner would send all eighty-five pounds of Stormy scampering from my brother's second story bedroom (a hallowed shrine where Stormy worshipped while my brother was away), down the steps, across the length of the house, to the side door whose lower half was scratched-through to bare wood from Stormy's pawing and clawing to greet you-know-who. This was a typical occurrence on Friday afternoons in October and November when my brother was attending a nearby college and driving home on the weekends to hunt the marshes and lakes we favored in northeast Ohio.

Around the house, Stormy was never particularly affectionate. He ate his food, slept on his circular bed, and indulged in the occasional walk. But . . . clean a shotgun, pull out a camouflage raincoat, rearrange a pile of decoys in the garage, and he sprang to life—a streak of onyx lightning on four paws, happy to spend the night in the back of the car if it meant a day afield to follow. He lived for the field, and one needed only to watch the tilt of his head to know where the next flock was coming from. My brother recalls him digging into a beaver dam after a wounded mallard until only his tail (slicing the air with abandon) was visible, and then emerging with the very-much-alive duck in his jaws. Another memory involves Stormy sprinting across 200 yards of frozen lake to tackle and drag back a mature, and, again, very-much-alive, Canada goose.

The dog was a consummate retriever, and while I cannot scientifically back him up, my brother claims that Stormy never lost a crippled bird. Yet he once inhaled a dozen doughnuts in roughly three minutes. He also once took a foul, stomach-turning shit in a pit blind at Ottawa National Wildlife Refuge east of Toledo. My unfortunate brother, lifting Stormy out of the blind to chase a winged goose through the fog, encountered some of that foulness on his gloved hand. Stormy, however, found the bird.

Buckshot

Buckshot of Brunswick arrived as a gift from my mother to my father in the summer of 1993. One of Buck's favorite pastimes as a pup was sitting next to me and barking incessantly while I attempted the evening's math homework. Before his second year, in the dead of winter, he succumbed to parvovirus, and the event tore an excruciating hole in the fabric of the house. When Buck died, we had Stormy to soften the blow, but losing a young dog left us all heartsick and grieving. My memories of Buck are colored by both a strange impenetrability and a glowing sense of promise. There is a hedge around him that prevents me from seeing fully what kind of dog he was in the short time that he lived, but I have a strong sense of what he could've been. During training, he would observe Stormy intensely, and the result was an incredibly stable dog for his age. My brother maintains that he showed more natural talent than any of our labs before or after. The wound of his death has been healing for more than fifteen years, but certain words, feelings, and even scents can open that scar new and raw to the few memories I have of him: the light in his eye when I would say his name aloud, the promise of seasons he never saw.

Samson

Samson of Hudson was the first dog I ever called my own. When I visited the litter with my mother and brother, the dog that would become Samson crept over to me and licked my hand. That was the beginning and the end. My brother petitioned me to choose another pup that seemed more dominant, more competitive, but I was a goner. This little black ball of hair that had crawled into my lap was indeed the one. Months later, after we had brought him home, we noticed that one of his back legs was crooked and that he favored it slightly. An X-ray revealed a small but problematic fracture, and the procedure to right it was more than one would ask of a human. He received a steel plate (complete with screws) in his leg, and he took an unnerving pleasure in chewing his stitches out (despite the Elizabethan collar), sending us more than once to the vet with a blood-soaked Samson in tow. He healed completely by the time his first season rolled around and when we returned to the vet to have the plate removed, they opened the scar up and found that his bone had grown around the steel.

Like Buckshot, Samson learned from Stormy how to hunt. One calm October morning found both dogs paddling the same Canada goose to our blind, each with a wing in his mouth. I also remember a mid-November sunrise when my father and I dropped three magnificent, fully plumed bufflehead drakes into the dark blue waves of Mosquito Lake. Stormy and Samson made a relay of the retrieval: Stormy grabbed a bird and brought it to his apprentice, who brought it to the blind, and so on, until the frigid work was done. I can summon a specific, three-dimensional memory from that morning whenever I choose: half light, half darkness, spent gunpowder in the air, the wind stinging my bare hands as Samson drops a small, striking, black-and-white bird on the blind floor—it feels plush and warm in my hand and a bead of blood rolls from the beak, rushes between two of my knuckles and down the back of my hand into the shirtsleeve at my wrist—each bird a delicious bundle from the north, a tiny present from the gods. I think to myself: *I have these dogs to thank.*

Sam was never a very well-trained retriever simply because I was never a well-organized teenager. While my taste for hunting came and went with my moods and interests, his never flagged. The unfortunate truth is that he never learned the basics. Even at nine years old, he would break at the sight of ducks overhead. It got to the point where, in order to concentrate on the hunt itself, we had to secure his lead to a sturdy tree, an act that generated even louder whining when ducks appeared. Sam also had an irreparably hard mouth (irreparable because I waited too long to try and correct this behavior—my own teenage fault). In his later years, when I would see Sam sink his big white teeth a bit too deeply into a wood duck or mallard—not enough to really ruin the bird, but just enough to break the skin and pierce the meat—I could relate, as I intended to take the bird home and do basically the same thing, but within the context of a hot oven, some root vegetables, and a bottle of wine. We had, you could say, an understanding: just bring it back without inflicting *too* much damage and we're square.

A gentle buffoon when it came to blind etiquette, Sam transformed into a champion if you put his nose on the trail of a downed bird. The list of crippled birds he retrieved from under rotten tree stumps, overhanging roots, beaver dams, and just nasty spots in general is too long to recount here, but one particular retrieve stands out. One morning while my father and I were hunting a small beaver meadow fed by the Mahoning River, I winged a drake wood duck. The bird hit the water, took one quick look around, and dove. Experience told me that the bird headed for dry ground, but his lanes of escape were practically unlimited. The backwater was bordered on all sides by thick woods, and wood ducks blend in with freshly fallen maple leaves extremely well. I took Sam along the water's edge and within minutes he was clambering up a steep, wooded hill with his nose in the leaves. He crested the top only to reappear seconds later with the bird in his mouth. He trotted down the hill and dropped the woodie two feet from me. The bird leaped straight into the water and, once again, disappeared. I stood there cursing poor Sam who responded with a look of profound bewilderment. My father, hearing the commotion, came to lend a hand, and we sent Sam across the water to the far bank. His nose hit the ground as he came ashore. And then he vanished into the brush. Minutes passed and my father and I exchanged a silent glance, wondering where Sam had gone and how we would get to the other side of the deep water to find him. About then, Sam popped his head out of the brush with the wood duck once more clamped in his maw. A third retrieve was not required.

When Stormy died, we then had Samson to soften the blow. The mantle of "old boy" passed on to Samson, who nonetheless retained his vigor for breaking at the sight of cupped birds and then chewing on them after they fell. He also learned some new tricks. Samson harbored a disdain for retrieving geese, but became unexpectedly eager to chase them down after a decade of cautiously sniffing them only to trot sheepishly away. Watching an eleven-year-old, grey-muzzled dog charge a half-alive goose on slippery marsh ice should be enough to make even a young heart feel downright childlike. When I go back to it, my blood pumps a little faster.

Sam, despite his flaws, was a joy to hunt with, and when he died, we had no one to soften the blow.

Blackjack & Bleu

In the winter of 2007, after the turn of the year, and after hunting for the first time in my life an entire season without a Labrador retriever at my side, my wife and I made a place for a pup we named Levon Hubert "Bleu" McGuire Rzicznek, and my brother and his family welcomed Emma and Zach's Blackjack. Both pups came from the same litter and both started out as pups do: pooping on the finest rugs in the house, peeing by the back door, yowling in the wee hours, and being generally lovable and eager to learn. We're entering our second season of hunting over them, and while they've each developed their own peculiar habits, they both also show great potential.

Jack, plain and simple, is part rhinoceros—he's just as likely to charge directly (and lovingly) at your face as he is to become a sleepy and immovable doorstop. Jack also has the goodness of heart to indulge the occasionally boisterous antics of my niece and nephew. And, Jack is a back-talker. He sometimes barks back when given a command and the onlooker is left with no recourse but laughter. Yet he is irrepressibly interested in both retrieving things and pleasing my brother who works with him tirelessly. I've taken a slightly lazier approach to Bleu, who on a weekly basis gets more walks around town than he does blind retrieves. As a result, he's somewhat of a local celebrity. The neighbors, the mail carrier, even complete strangers know him by name and often speak directly to him, ignoring my wife and me, who stand bewildered at Bleu's uncanny ability to attract attention. Have we loved him too much, to the point where he loves the world too much? Is such a thing possible? For the better part of a year, Bleu challenged me relentlessly with bringing dummies to hand. What started as dropping the dummy four feet short of my hand quickly became a propensity to run acre-wide laps around me, taunting any step I took towards him with a gruff but playful bark. I think he may be the smartest Labrador to ever live, and that's not necessarily intended as a compliment.

Put Jack and Bleu together, and you get a cross between a wrestling match and a yodeling competition. When we arrive to set up for the morning's hunt, they immediately find a suitably large tree limb to team up on and destroy. Once the limb has been completely humiliated, they just run after each other, occasionally rearing up on their hind legs like spooked horses. When one gets tired, the other will saunter over and give him a playful humping. And then they run some more. If we keep one on a leash and throw a dummy for the other, the results can be terrifying. Jack howls like a banshee set loose on a pack of wayward tourists, and Bleu sounds like a young toddler with a freshly snapped leg. Only when the dummy is safely in the hands of either my brother or me do peace and quiet resume. They are, in short, thoroughly brothers.

Pleasingly, Bleu tends to do better on live birds than he does on dummies. Hunting a half-frozen marsh near Sandusky Bay last year, he retrieved half a dozen birds, mainly teal and ring-necked ducks, directly to hand, only to subtract at least a year from my life three months later by sprinting around the neighborhood for forty-five minutes with a plastic bucket in his mouth. The temptations of car rides, food, and dummies had no effect. Only my wife was able, in the end, to talk him down. This summer, however, he has become much more reliable, and I find myself looking ahead to many seasons at his side, enjoying his company regardless of whether the birds are flying or not. What the dogs I've lived and hunted with have taught me, in the end, is a rich sense of both awe and mischief: the ability to be in tune with the magical possibilities of the world and to also partake in refreshing spats of tomfoolery, sometimes swinging effortlessly between both. Good habits, bad habits, but all of them true to the challenge of living the small but invaluable ration of moments we're granted before it's time to go.

How I Came to Live
with Bird Dogs

Dave Smith

The first dog I loved was a runty little brown terrier from the pound. Then I went to college and never went home. The dog stayed with my grandparents until he died. My father was already dead, my mother had gone somewhere else with her life. In most of the fifty years that followed I had numerous dogs, often Boxers, once briefly a German something, but never a bird dog. I think the death of my father in May of my seventeenth year, one Sunday afternoon after an automobile accident, brutal and apocalyptic, explains why for the fifth and sixth decades of my life I have been owned by first Molly and then Finn, American Brittanies.

Having no father in the hormone-besotted world of boyhood can be dangerous, but I was lucky and a good family embraced me. My closest friend, John Woodfin Speers, who answered to Buddy, as many do in the South, lived on the Elizabeth River in Churchland, Virginia, with a group of kin not unlike the citizens of Flannery O'Connor's pages.

They were country people who worked for the U.S. Navy and after work hours ran a small horse farm for training trotters. Mother Ruth, long deceased, was a painted lady, her mascara everywhere, a pillar of the Baptist Church, and a surrogate mom. Buddy's dad, Big Bruce Speers, now 93, a slender man as hard as a horse's hoof, was a deacon. His brother Grady, ten inches taller and fifty pounds heavier, and his wife, a woman I hardly remember, were part of the family compound. A third brother, Edward, sailed the world as a Navy chief, a duplicate Ernest Borgnine, but when ashore he lived in a small barn where horses came and went. A fourth brother and a grandmother stayed in the biggest house, but I never saw them. These were Georgians, resident in eastern Virginia, and they shared a passion for quail hunting.

In those days quail coveyed as thick as mosquitoes in Virginia. Abundant farmland, water without stint, and not yet the bite of industry and its secondary spread of suburbs like phlegm, this was the country William Styron grew up in and wrote about. You could stand almost anywhere at any hour and hear the iambic Bobwhite calling. There was a similar sound that buoyed me when I lived in Utah in the mid-1970s, my lawn the residence of a large covey of California quail. But I listened for Bobwhites, especially when I went back to hunting in central Virginia in the eighties. Then I moved to Louisiana, then to Maryland, and in neither place was a wild bird to be heard as it was with coveys scattering at the Speers farm when pickups bustled in and out. It had been more habitat than farm, a track, houses, cars, barn, peach trees, unmowed acres, and salt marshes where quail flew to escape. The Speers world was my emotional home.

They were the first and only people I had known who hunted bird dogs, keeping a wire kennel the size of a garage in the front yard of the main house with the usual six dogs, invariably pointers, lean as marines and blooded champions, it was always said with a laugh. They were drops, gifts, some abandoned, mostly experienced. It was Big Bruce's job to keep them ready to hunt, though all males trained the dog that was to hand, as they all hunted with whoever was to hand. During my high school years I walked their fields and those of their neighbors with occasionally as many as eight armed men and boys, most of them Speers, always led by dogs—Peanut, Pickles, Watermelon (called "Red" for short), Lady, Freckles, Alice, among those I recall.

Having abandoned hunting at eighteen when I went to college, I did not resume until I was in my forties. Buddy, whom I scarcely saw for twenty years, died when the Hodgkin's disease he had seemed to beat returned; at his funeral I swam among the remaining Speers, at play in the lovely memories, inventions, exaggerations, and lies that composed any hour spent with them. I met a lawyer who had been our boyhood pal, who invited me to hunt with him in Buddy's honor. Big Bruce, after the ceremony, made me a gift of the scarred 1946 Remington automatic, a Browning look-alike, Buddy had shot for as long as I had known him. Soon other lawyers telephoned to hunt, each with land and dogs. With them I had no significant friendship, but they and their dogs must have offered me something of my youth and my dead friend.

To my wife and children I must have spoken of birds and dogs more than I realized. We were a suburban family. Our dog Red was a fat, farting, companionable boxer. Really, he was my son's dog, not mine. If asked, I would not have said I wanted any other dog, let alone a hunter, having little notion of what that might mean. But I did want one. Even then I wasn't anxious to hunt, though I wanted something. My wife, a woman good at many things and at nothing better than loving people, understood more than I did. She asked people about bird dogs, who had them, what the kinds were, all this before the easy research Google now makes immediate; she determined the choice for us was a Brittany, a dog I had never heard of. One Saturday, on my birthday in December, stealthy as a mistress of espionage, she commanded my sixteen-year-old son to drive 150 miles south into the darkness, to us Virginians anyway, of North Carolina. When he returned to our home in Midlothian, Virginia, he came to my study, where I was laboring over a poem, and placed in my lap the nine-week-old puppy that someone, at the last hour, had declined to take from the breeder. So was my life changed.

Molly, said breeder Mr. Edwards of Greensboro, North Carolina, came of exceptionally affectionate stock, and ought to be treated in kind. She slept upon our bellies, rode in our laps, and took to the closet of my study as if it were a bedroom the Lord created for her. Her white hair was long and silky, blinding in sunlight, the orange mask on both eyes matched by orange freckles that looked as if she had been dappled by

Dave Smith & Brittany spaniel Finn.

curry. The eyes, shiny brown, seemed to know aforehand anything that came into my head. They looked back wherever I looked.

Though I am a teacher by profession and ought to have been competent to train Molly, I sent her to a trainer in the middle of her second year. I wonder why even now. She remained with this Viszla man

(Courtesy of Dave Smith)

for almost three months, living in the small dog shelters all of his wards used—I had seen them and shivered—while she learned the rudiments of finding quail, that point I was as proud to see as I would have been of a Presidential salute, holding it with grace. I am not certain I knew her arrival would change the rhythm of my life, reordering time from my job and writing to take her hunting. Nor did I conceive of how difficult it would be to find birds. When Buddy and I walked up to a farmer's door, asked permission to hunt, we expected to cast the anxious dogs where the man pointed. Now the farmer declined; or he asked a fee. I had no hunting companion, no place to hunt, only Molly, the Remington, and a hunting jacket I wore until I lost it at Richard Ford's house years later, discovering, when it came back to me, I needed a bigger size. But I now had also the start of an adult relationship with my son, who had reached the age when sons see how useless and hopeless and out of it fathers are.

Out of some lingering connection to my grandfather, who had taught me to hunt squirrels, I had taken my son after them enough to foster in him the early desire. He had graduated to occasional pursuit of wild turkey with a neighbor; he had even once stalked deer. One trip quail hunting was all it took, and there was this little character, this Molly, who slept beside my son's bed and who attacked a quail scent as if electric current flowed from it into her. Mostly we took her to game farms and, inept but enthusiastic, we shot the fluttery birds. She judged us somewhere between primitive and poor, and she led our team of three.

At home Molly matched her name, from the first attaching herself to big Red the boxer, who raised her by ignoring her playful chewing and digging. Days inside, nights they were companions in a pen I built with weather access to our yard shed. He was born tolerant; she was born bored. I found her once with a chewed-through tube of Super Glue stuck to her lip. She consumed shoes, tool handles, nails, every material I could name, but never ate one bird. In the field, she was business itself, tolerating no interference from the boys, however big, roaring in to take the fetch when a bird fell. Regrettably, this led her to dust-ups since, being short-legged, she tended to arrive late. Often she snapped at birds she felt rudely pilfered by her peers, sometimes mistaking muzzle for bird. She had not a squinch of fear.

Everyone remarks how individual dogs are, how amazing this is. Molly's stance at a bird is not a thing easily described, but I would know it in a yard of dogs side by side. I would know, as she drops the bird before me, the glance that says "Lucky shot" or the one that says "Are you aware my feet hurt?" She never had a proper lift to her tail on point and she liked to poke up her ears as if to hear what impertinent thing I might say. She made her own decisions. When she had had enough hunting, she would quietly step in beside me, head high, and no amount of chiding or encouraging ever shuffled her back. I think birds could have drawn up in parade-ranked columns by the path and she would have kept rigid eyes front as we headed to the Jeep. Much that endeared her to me I have forgotten seven years after her death, but I see still her last hunt.

Moving to Louisiana to teach, I expected to find an old-time quail population, but found instead scattered plots of state land on which birds were settled before the season, enough to last about a week. Private land was universally leased to deer hunters. State biologists directed quail hunters to Mississippi and Texas, and sometimes to birds. We frequented Covey Rise game farm in Husser, Louisiana, where one day I took my family—wife, two daughters, and son. After a decade of desultory hunting, Molly, now the family queen, had gone a little portly, and her sight wasn't so sharp. We didn't know how not sharp it was. Using a guide because there were so many of us, we followed a Weimaraner named Smoke and a Llewellyn setter named Wheels, apparently on roller skates. At first Molly tried to stick with them; she found a couple of birds placed in short brush. But quickly she seemed lost, darting this way, then that, as if after shadows. She began to stand and bark, then burst forward a few steps as if toward an antagonist, then stand and bark again. She had never made much noise, and this behavior was mysterious. I came to realize that she smelled what was going on and wanted in on it, but she couldn't see bird or dog, could not navigate what must have seemed to her maddening and, finally, terrifying. We did not take her out again. Two years later, blind and stumbling, in Baltimore, she died of cancer, a hard moment I could not face. My wife, loving as always, took her to the vet for me.

Early on I had wished we had not neutered Molly, though it had been reasonable, given that she yowled in heat like a Siamese cat and humped the boxer until he whimpered. Did I want another Molly? No, I thought, wrongly. My son and I had gone through the usual patriarchal combats, but when he had come home from the Navy, having himself been trained by what may have been Viszla men, having transferred to my university, indeed to my house, we became bird hunting companions. A second dog began to look like a capital idea. While Molly still lived, we plotted a choice. Another Molly, of course, only bigger, one whose legs, like those high strutting pointers, didn't bog in short grass, whose hair might be shorter so it didn't snag on inevitable briars, tall enough to be visible above knee-deep cover. We read about the kinds in *Pointing Dog Journal*, tried some out at game preserves, priced litters. A pointer would be like a quarter horse in our spare bedroom. Baton Rouge was hard enough already. Elegant English setters appealed to us, but a long-haired dog in Louisiana suffers more than most with ticks, fleas, and debris our house mother wasn't likely to endure and, for reasons we couldn't fathom, that same dearie had outlawed Weimaraner and German shorthair, to her the equivalent of terrorists.

One summer, after a conference I worked in Vermont, my wife and I, driving home on I-95, stopped to see what Mr. Edwards had in his kennel. Was he still in the business of breeding the little dogs? He was. Having no pups available, only a space on a torn page, he scribbled our name and phone number after he interviewed us about Molly. As we walked past the kennels, we came to a very long-legged fellow who lay without much interest in whatever passed on that warm afternoon. We stood a while as

Mr. Edwards explained he had sent this dog to a doctor whose hunting companion the dog had been for only a year when the doctor abruptly died. The man's wife, with her own life in turmoil, returned the dog to Mr. Edwards. He had thought to sell him, but no buyer had come forth of whom he entirely approved. He put the dog to stud, and it produced fine, tall hunters with the same laconic character that barely raised his head for my fingers. I ordered one just like the doctor's dog.

Mr. Edwards was devoted to his Brittanies. If you bought one, you got a video that showed you how to befriend and then to love them. It said almost nothing about training them. He thought they had hunting in their blood; they trained themselves. If, as I did, you ordered one, it came by air freight, and Mr. Edwards telephoned ahead to say what it might feel in passage, how it might react, and what to do. Mine arrived in a carrying cage for a large cat. I leaned over to see in the turret slits the uncertain but not fearful eyes that were masked almost identically to Molly's. I drove him home and introduced Dave's Finn of Baton Rouge to Dave's Molly of Midlothian. Her response was to pretend he didn't exist. He settled in, delighted to nip her and sleep against her. Red, still alive, sniffed as if it were all simply obnoxious. Molly wasn't much receptive to Finn, but neither was she then hostile.

His size and latent testosterone in due course kicked in. He humped her, asleep or awake, dominant from the start. She whirled and snarled. He learned to match her whirl with his own, a terrific counter puncher, then on her he went. He gained weight and stature rapidly; she grew tormented. The noise she made was endless, and far from agreeable. To Finn, she was the coolest gift a dog could have. He followed her without stint. Along the way he found our pool. Baton Rouge is a great town to have a pool, the only one we had ever had, but our children were now grown, away at college, and we didn't much swim. Finn did. He learned to leap from the diving board, more entranced than any child, throwing himself into the water, shaking off, repeating it.

We sent him away to training, as we had done Molly. We had been referred to a woman in western Louisiana. She was receptive, impressive. I'd call her every week to ask how the student was doing. Always doing perfect. Yet he needed an extra month, or another two weeks, and no good explanation for it ever came. At last she summoned me to pick him up.

Her husband took us a nearby field, put pigeons out, then cast Finn to hunt. He warned me Finn had a bad habit he had never seen, and he hadn't been able to break him of it. "When your dog points," he said, "he sits down. Maybe," he said, "he will grow out of it. Can't tell, but maybe he's just a dud." I had heard by then tales of hunters who bought dogs and, finding flaws or not liking the dog or thinking for some reason they'd made a mistake, they vanished the dog. This loomed in my head like an ache. We'd had Finn for a year now. We'd keep him. But a sitting point?

The very first time my son and I took Finn afield, the first time he saw a quail to point, he sat on his rump, his tongue lagging out. I felt desperate. On the second occasion he pointed as crisply as if he had invented the whole routine. I dismissed fear of his troubles, but something in the report made me suspicious. Finn, like Molly, early on showed a reticence around strangers, but let him examine you and he wallowed in your attention. Still, on three occasions, he had been inadvertently backed into corners by women who then reached to pet him without his permission, and he met each occasion with a snarl and a look that meant business. Had he bitten the first time, I'd have farmed him out, but he had restrained himself. And he never behaved so around a man. He had shown fear of women in his training, a fear he still has though he has never been aggressive. Was this trainer abuse? All I can say is that this dud has a nose, a determination, and a field management that has made every hunting day with him all I could have wanted. He has, I should say, trained himself way better than those who would school him, me included.

Finn is now a portly gent in his tenth year and few humans do not evoke his adoration. He has rarely been able to walk from room to room or floor to floor, preferring to go full tilt before whatever is there escapes, as scattered rugs testify. He is as boyish a creature as God ever made. When he first hunted, his focus was like a cobra's as he vacuumed a field. I have seen him go past a corn row like a greyhound and skid to a point as if a rope snapped his neck. I have never seen him false point. He will back the slightest shadow of a dog on point, but will also creep to get the show on the road. Over the years he has slowed and now heavy foots a field by the end of a second hour, though show him one more bird and look out. He has reserves. Nor does he agree to leave the field, however fatigued, and he will quietly slink from the car where gear is being piled to go home. Few things in life have been as gratifying to me as raising my used Charles Daly 20-gauge over his intense point.

In recent years I have hunted only rarely, always at either Covey Rise or the Gunpowder Game Farm, outside of Baltimore, where I now live. If the boot-hugging quail experience isn't everything, I have an annual hunting weekend in southeastern Ohio, with its rugged hollers and briars, hosted by my old friend, Bob DeMott. Finn has learned the wily ways of woodcock, the main fliers there, and, though his belly comes home bloodied, he seems to take them as long-nosed quail, with relish. Unlike Molly who picked up one and instantly spat it out, and never looked at another, Finn has no prejudice and will hunt and carry pheasant, chukar, grouse, or any worthy bird. As I have my rules, so he has his rules. Steady to wing doesn't cut it for him. If he catches a rising bird, fair enough he thinks. We argue this point. Following that exceptional nose, he has chased birds he's not seen into holes where I had to provide liberation; then he hunts on. I've seen him fetch in crowds of dogs. His rule, however, is that he will only fetch the bird halfway to me, no matter the distance. I don't notice this anymore but it amuses people to see him measure distance with his gaze and drop the bird carefully on his mark. His stubbornness annoys when he presumes it's his hunt I am on, not the other way around, but the electric collar always raises his consciousness. Having for years pored over the gun dog magazines, howling at a prose the equivalent of concrete patch from a tube, I am aware that in this paragraph I am revealing what will seem to those opiners a crude and poorly trained dog. Ditto the dog owner. Each morning when Finn puts his feet on my bed and wakes me, I tell him that's what he is, but, to this, he has no response. Nor do I.

Finn forsakes me only when my son, the lawyer, leaves his wife and son and comes back to hunt, as in the November Ohio foray. Finn then smartly aligns himself with his attorney and pants in flagrant accusations that I must perforce negotiate. My son and I have killed many an hour, and also a few birds, over this living bond between us, leading me to have given him a Brit named Jake, now two years old, with dazzling gold eyes and a mostly liver back, a darling who is as good as Finn himself and even taller. I don't know what my son and I might ever have found to bring us as close as these dogs have done, and all we had to give them was our love.

Still, we didn't go to Ohio this year. I didn't hunt. I may not hunt next year. My son had a fine woodcock season in Louisiana. With his own new baby boy, a weekend hunt here is fiercely hard and costly. He tells me he has heard a quail in his Louisiana suburb, he is sure of it, and I am deeply happy he has the joy that sound induces, whatever one calls it, that two-note on a soft breeze. Yet its absence is bitter to me, its cause maybe changed by farming patterns, pesticide accumulation, foxes, suburb cats, even, as they say in Louisiana, a bunch of goddamn fire ants. It is bitter because I have come to feel we killed them off. Forty years ago, enlisting in that army of Speers, I did not imagine the birds gone from the earth, but few of us can hear them where we live and nothing will return them. Every year Bob says there are no more grouse in Ohio, and the woodcock seem fewer. This is that well-known rock near a hard place.

Who among us wants to retire from what makes him feel alive? Muhammad Ali punched into Parkinson's; at one time, Brett Favre was in danger of becoming a sportswriter's joke. I have long understood the dog, in quail hunting, links me to those men who shaped my life, a life as mysteriously joyful as it is sinister. It isn't so for the dogs, it's all good. They don't wonder about cause and effect, what's not understood, hows and whys. We make the rules; they help us live. Once I saw an old Speers man shoot a dog in the rear-end just to let it know how far out it could hunt. Worked, too. They loved their dogs but treated them as co-participants in a serious endeavor, not as neurotic children.

I brood over the likelihood that we have broken faith in killing so much. Molly and Finn, and those penned Speers dogs long gone, gave the deepest—is it companionship?—a man gets and in return, there is that silence where there was a call you never forget. How is one to go on hunting in the face of such harm? One thing is sure, I can't ask Finn. This year on the day after my sixty-seventh birthday, after I had written the above, he walked out into the snow, had a heart attack, and died. His absence filled my house and my heart. I needed my friend, as I have always needed a field. He would have understood why my wife and I went looking for Whizz, our thirteen-week-old new Brittany, who goes as if he is life itself.

Maybe, for us, he is.

A Good Southern Name

Jeddie Smith

My father and I were hunting quail in the farm hills of Hunt Valley, Maryland. Finn, his experienced Brittany, quartered ahead of us just as he had in his prime. After a while, we worked back and down to the Jeep and broke for rest and coffee. Thermos mugs warmed our hands, with hot coffee steaming the air. In the back of the Jeep, Jake, my Brittany, panted impatiently in his kennel. We switched the dogs and set out again with Jake flying out in front of us.

Finn is orange and mostly white with sheep-thick fur that accentuates his increasingly cobby shape. Jake is liver and white, and he is like a photo-negative of Finn. Dark chocolate covers most of his coltish body, except for white legs that look like a lady's evening gloves and a strip of white across his rump that looks like a racing stripe. It looks like he's been dipped first in dark chocolate, then white. Jake's amber eyes glow with their own light, and at night it seems all I can see are his eyes and that racing stripe.

(Courtesy of Jeddie Smith)

Jeddie Smith & Brittany spaniel Jake.

Where Finn had weaved through the fields, Jake raced about, covering more ground more quickly than Finn could, and he bounced, ears flapping, over brush that Finn four-stepped around. We brought Jake to Finn's leftovers, singles that had escaped our guns to the trees atop a big hill.

We approached a corner of the woods where years ago we had discovered the relic of a 356 Porsche that rusted back into the earth where it had been abandoned before the tall oak and walnut trees around it had taken root. Jake halted, his whole body from raked-out hind legs to pointed nose signaling, "There!" I stepped ahead carefully, glancing at Jake. His eyes were zeroed-in, unblinking, "Right there!" Pop readied the Browning side-by-side that had been a past birthday present from Mom and me. "It's your shot," I insisted. He moved in, anticipating the flush, and Jake held solid. Another step, and the Bobwhite erupted and made for the deep woods, but fell short at the second blast from the Browning. "Dead!" we cheered, "Dead . . . Hunt Dead . . . Dead!" I felt charged as Jake bounded forward into the brush. When he emerged carrying the bird gently, I dropped to a knee, and he rolled it like a gift into my outstretched hand.

Jake was a gangly seven months old. It was his first hunt. His training had barely advanced beyond the yard, and I figured it was risky to hunt him so early, but I had just one opportunity that fall to hunt Jake with my father and his dog, Finn. So, I took a chance. Jake put it all together on his first bird, as if boasting, "What are you worried about? I got it."

Jake continued to point singles and retrieve them when we hit our marks. After stopping again for coffee, we felt confident enough that we brought out Finn to hunt them in tandem. The competition energized Finn, while Jake, bounding about, kept his eyes tentatively on Finn. When Finn pointed, Jake saw him and froze from a dead run. His body was contorted, his nose pointing back over his tail towards Finn. Not a lick of backing training, and there he was honoring Finn in response to some genetic command. Before the day was out, he would back Finn again and again. This was an extraordinary first hunt, but Jake had impressed us from the very beginning.

★ ★ ★

After Hurricane Katrina, apartments in New Orleans were hard to find and the rents exorbitant. My wife, Willa, and I were lucky to find an affordable place in a converted mansion on St. Charles Avenue, where, before the flooding, streetcars used to rumble along the tracks in the middle of the street. Now contractors' trucks were parked all over the streetcar line, rutting it with off-road tires. It was a difficult time. That's when I decided to get a puppy.

I had moved to New Orleans before my parents moved away from Louisiana and had wed Willa, a woman from Baton Rouge. We were married in the first house either of us owned, a 1940s bungalow in Uptown, and we lived like tourists. We were so happy that first year that Willa often said breezily, "This is too good to be true; I don't deserve this."

On the morning of August 28, 2005, she woke me, saying, "We need to leave now! Our lives are never going to be the same." She was right, of course. The radar image on TV blotted out the Gulf of Mexico. Overnight, Hurricane Katrina had grown into a giant that loomed just offshore. With all that we could stuff into our car, we evacuated across the Lake Pontchartrain causeway as Katrina's outer storm bands, like bad omens, rolled low overhead. Katrina blew through the city the next day, and the water it pushed overwhelmed negligently constructed levees, swamped our home, ruined everything we hadn't taken in the car, and upended our lives. Down here, Katrina is simply "the Storm." If you are from New Orleans, you have two lives—the one before the Storm and one after.

There was no choice but to rebuild. I became my own general contractor and hammer-swinger, learning along the way. We had lived in five places in as many months and were anxious to move out of our apartment and back into our home. Somehow, a year later, we were finally finishing the "renovation." Less obviously, we were also trying to recover the rhythm and trajectory of our lives before the Storm. Getting a puppy in the midst of all that was crazy, but at the time the idea didn't seem so nuts. It was just an attempt to recapture something from what the Storm had taken from us. I see now what hopes I heaped on a puppy.

★ ★ ★

I wanted a Brittany out of the same line from which my father's dogs came—Finn and, before him, Molly. They were terrific bird dogs from Mr. Edwards' kennels in Greensboro, North Carolina.

I had lived with my parents in Richmond, Virginia, during high school and my first two years of college at James Madison University in the Shenandoah Valley. When I came home for a holiday break during my first year of college, Mom dispatched me to Goldsboro, a six-hour round trip, to retrieve a surprise present for my father. There, Mr. Edwards handed me a white-and-orange fur ball and instructed me to "hold her up, so she can look about. Keep one hand on the wheel; hold her up with the other. You don't want a carsick puppy." I pulled away holding her so that she could see the passing world. She instantly became so heavy that my shoulder ached and my arm trembled. Faces in other car windows laughed. Fingers pointed. Mr. Edwards had, I'm almost sure, been serious, but I felt a joke had been played on me. I put the pup in my lap and the drone of the road lulled her to sleep.

Minutes from home, she awoke and, without warning, vomited in my lap. "Carsick," I could hear Mr. Edwards judging, perhaps laughing. After I had cleaned up at Lucky's, a gas station near the house, Mom and I surprised Pop in his study, his present partially concealed under my sweatshirt. I can still see him lying on the carpet with his new puppy, Molly, rolling onto his chest. She would become a sensational quail dog.

Occasionally, when I could not interest my father in a quail hunt, I would put Molly in the back seat of my Monte Carlo and drive west towards the Atchafalaya River Basin—by then we had all moved to Louisiana—to hunt woodcock. I had no clue what I was doing. I knew people hunted them, though.

Molly and I wandered the public land of the Basin, and I kicked through any thicket that looked birdy while Molly hunted, I see in hindsight, for quail. Infrequently, we scared up a woodcock, and I managed some shots but never brought down a bird. Molly never pointed one, however, and I realized—finally—that she was indifferent to woodcock. If I had just once shot one, maybe then Molly might have figured out what we were after. I doubt it, though. She didn't give a damn about woodcock. Not too soon after, I quit that pointless folly.

As she got older, Molly grew neurotic, developing trembles and dilated eyes. The last time we hunted her, she seemed to have left her senses in the kennel. She bumped birds, fumbled around, got frustrated and frantic, and fell apart. She retired to chasing squirrels in the back yard and the hunting fell to Finn. I would say that he replaced Molly, but that never happens. Perhaps it would be better if it did, as our best friends are too short-lived.

★ ★ ★

Finn did not share Molly's prejudice against woodcock. We learned this fact years later on a trip to hunt with our dear friend Bob DeMott (nicknamed Big Mott by one of my younger sisters) and his mild-mannered English setters. By that time, my parents had moved, yet again, to Baltimore, Maryland. So Pop and I, with Finn in his kennel, drove west over the Appalachian Mountains, across the Eastern Continental Divide, and down into southeast Ohio where we met up with Big Mott at his home. Our arrival coincided with the autumn woodcock winter migration south, which, for many of the birds, terminates in the Atchafalaya River Basin in Louisiana.

Hunting with Bob demonstrated to me how futile my efforts with Molly had been. I hadn't gone to the right places at all, the dense bottomland that can be so entangling that it is a good idea to carry clippers to cut an open path. Molly's lack of interest in woodcock had been an insurmountable handicap—I might as well have hunted with a cat—and I hadn't given us a chance to start with. Finn pointed three birds, proving Molly's disdain of woodcock was not hereditary. Between falling into a creek and shooting a flushed bird that Bob's setter hadn't pointed, I remember thinking, "So this is how to hunt woodcock."

★ ★ ★

When I tried to contact Mr. Edwards to obtain a puppy from Molly and Finn's line, I learned that he had died and that his kennels were empty. Finn may well be the end of his line, and I thought I might never have the pleasure of owning such a dog. Then I heard that our friends who operate a game preserve along the Gunpowder River had a litter of Brittanies. Two puppies were available, so I sent my parents on a scouting mission.

They reported that Trigger was the sire. We all knew Trigger. He had been the farmhouse puppy, fawned over by everyone. He was dark chocolate, except for white legs, chest, and a thick collar. He had grown long and tall. Trigger, essentially the mascot of the preserve, was never trained to hunt. Once, my father and I watched from a hilltop as Trigger harried a quail from horizon to horizon and back until it gave out. Trigger, when not chained to a post or four-wheeler, moved in blurs.

The dam, Cali, was orange and white. Half of the puppies were liver and white, like Trigger, while the other half were orange and white, like Cali. The largest puppy, one of the two not spoken for, was orange and white and suitably named Tank. The other available puppy, as yet unnamed, looked like Trigger except that, instead of a white collar, he sported a white stripe across his rump. My father said that, when he had approached the litter, the unnamed puppy challenged him with a big-dog bark. He liked that pup right away.

As I had yet to see them, I had it in my mind that Tank was the one for me. I liked that he was the biggest of the litter and that he, like Pop's dogs, was orange and white. Silly reasons, really. When the puppies were about eight weeks old, I went to confirm my selection of Tank. The day was sunny and warm, and Tank and the rest of the puppies sought the coolness beneath a shed. They wanted nothing to do with me, except for the pup that had so boldly yawped at my father. He alone came out, romped around, and wouldn't leave me. I was chosen. Trigger blurred back and forth in the background. With several suspicious sniffs so close our noses touched, Cali seemed to approve of me for her fearless pup. So long, Tank.

★ ★ ★

His name would not come to me, and I anguished over finding a suitable one. Willa, who was anxious about the addition, promised to love the puppy only if I named him "Jake" after a Hollywood heartthrob. A name in exchange for obliged love seemed a good bargain, and thus he became "Jake."

When the time came for Jake to leave the farm where he had lived all twelve weeks of his life, my father collected him and brought him along to a writer's conference in the Tennessee mountains, where he would be in residence for two weeks. I drove up from New Orleans for the hand-off. For several days we enjoyed the mountain scenery and played with jelly-boned Jake. At one of the conference cocktail parties, to which I had brought Jake, I found myself in a conversation with the writer Barry Hannah. He asked my puppy's name and when I told him, he smiled and replied "Jake. That is a good Southern name." I have thought so ever since.

The morning to depart arrived too soon. Pop held Jake while I finished loading the car. The bond that had formed between them was obvious. Jake licked at his chin and Pop smiled through the downheartedness of goodbye. My father had been there from the start; Jake was *our* dog. Taking Jake from his hands and leaving him in the driveway felt somehow mean. As Jake slept in the back seat for most of the drive south, I grinned at his dream-yelps. I did not hold him up to see out, and he did not get carsick. Happiness, indeed, is a warm puppy!

★ ★ ★

As Jake grew, there were many indications that he was birdy. But there was little doubt left when my wife and I came back home from lunch one day to find one of her Mardi Gras masks, constructed of large, colorful feathers and inadvertently left out on the coffee table, strewn throughout our bungalow. Although Jake was not a chewer, temptation had overwhelmed him. The bright feathers were everywhere—a few still drifting in the air—as Jake lay on the cool wood floor, panting hard and worn out. My wife didn't understand my amusement at the carnage until I explained to her that her mask, made of feathers, was to him just a bird, a very pretty bird. He could not resist. It was a good omen.

★ ★ ★

Quail can seldom be found in Louisiana anymore, so Jake and I hunt woodcock. The first time I took him out, we returned to where Molly and I had wandered fruitlessly years before. Now I knew where to go and what to look for, but what would Jake do? We pushed through thickets and briars that snatched my hat, sliced my cheeks, and ripped my hands. Jake looked all business, but found not even the shadow of a bird. As the morning warmed, so did my anxiety. Making our way alongside a bayou, I finally heard the twitter of a flush. Jake heard it, too, and froze, looking for the source. Finding nothing, he turned back to work. Would he, I wondered, be like Molly and not give a damn about woodcock?

Before I took another step, Jake answered my question, his wide eyes lowered on a clump of vines. I moved in, and Jake held even after I missed twice. His eyes flashed back at me, questioning, I have no doubt, what went wrong. "Sorry," I said. As soon he forgave me and resumed hunting, Jake pointed another woodcock, offering me a chance at redemption. I dropped it with my follow-up shot, and Jake jumped forward. Coming back with the bird, he halted about fifteen feet from me, deposited it on the ground, and looked at me as if to say, "I'm a finder, not a retriever." I walked up to him, kneeled, and picked up our first woodcock. "Okay, I'll accept that. You do the finding."

★ ★ ★

My father doesn't live down here anymore, so Jake and I have hunted alone these past two seasons. We rise early, so it's just us and the dark. Jake follows every movement. He knows what the gear bag and gun case mean, but my frayed briar pants stir him most, and he smells them intently as if recalling past hunts and foretelling today's. He becomes too excited to eat. I boil coffee and pack lunch for one, and load the gear and the Remington 1100 my father gave me twenty-three years ago into the Jeep without the bustle that comes with a partner. Jake hops in, evidently knowing where we are going. The rear of my Jeep is his—the seats are down and a canvas tarp tucked down tight so that he has the entire back, window to window.

As we head west over the Mississippi and then out 1-90 over the Morganza Floodway, it's quiet except for the hum of tires. I think of the familiar talks that Pop and I have had going to or coming from a hunt and what I might say if he were here, but there's just Jake's anxious panting for company. I roll the windows down even though it's cold, and Jake flips from rear window to rear window with increasing excitement and frequency. When I turn onto the dirt road paralleling the Atchafalaya River that flows unseen behind the levee, Jake is a constant back-and-forth motion in my rearview mirror. Like his father, Trigger, he moves in blurs.

Over the past two seasons, we have become teammates. Jake knows his range, and when he pushes it and I call "Here!" he turns and reels in without challenge. When I change direction, he races back to get out in front of me without word or whistle. I know better than to try to convince him to investigate a birdy looking spot that he's already passed through—it is barren no matter what I think. If Jake remains on point after a flush, it is no false point—there is another bird in there (and yet, I will always be unready for its rise). When he is out of sight and his brass bell goes silent, I know he will hold the bird until I can get there, at which time their tenuous connection, like a fuse, ignites and the bird breaks free. Jake freezes solid when he has a maybe-bird, except his eyes are loose and follow me worriedly and uncertainly as he waits for me to kick through the brush. Although Jake retrieved to hand the first bird ever shot over him, our compromise is that he does that only when he wants to: he finds birds dead or alive, but he's nobody's delivery boy. That's fine. Jake and I understand each other.

★ ★ ★

So, here we are, on the closing day of our second season, at our hunting spot that we know as well as the house that we can navigate in the dark. But this morning is unlike any I've ever seen. The night's mist froze as it fell, and the dirt road, grass, trees, and leaves, everything, glitters white and silver. We enter the crystallized woods and all is still. Nothing makes a sound; leaves do not rustle underfoot. Even Jake's bell and panting are muffled as he runs, his steaming breath trailing behind him.

I wish my father were here so that he could share this morning and see how terrific our dog is. I imagine what I will tell my year-old son about hunting with his grandfather, Molly, Finn, and Jake when he is old enough to understand, and I realize that I will fail to tell him all that I mean to say, but I will try to remember it all and to get it right. I feed three shells into the Remington and finger the gun's scars. One day it will be my son's, and I hope that it will somehow convey to him all that I can't express. Jake quarters across in front of me in a long flash, reminding me that we are hunting, and his racing-stripe rump disappears into a sparkling thicket. After a bit, his bell goes silent. "Point," I say to no one. I know right where he is, and I plunge forward.

Burt

William G. Tapply

Let's get this out of the way right now: Burt suddenly went blind the summer of 2008 and it was downhill fast. Vicki and I took him to the vet for the last time on December 5 of that year.

However, this story is not about the death of my beloved old bird dog. I hate those tear-jerkers and vowed a long time ago that I'd never write one.

This is about Burt's life.

He was the pick of the males in the litter of Brittanies, a gift from my wife, just eight weeks old when we fetched him from the breeder, a little orange-and-white pup with floppy ears and stubby little legs.

He puked in my lap on his first road trip, on that drive back home from the kennel. This was not an omen. Burt always loved going somewhere in the car—mainly, I suppose, because he guessed it meant a hunting trip, or at least a drive to someplace for an off-season workout, and in any case, a chance to hang out with me. He never puked in the car again, and one of the first commands he learned dependably was "Get in the car."

(Courtesy of William G. Tapply)

William G. Tapply & Brittany spaniel Burt.

When we got home that first day and Burt trundled into the back yard, the first thing he did was squat and pee. The second thing he did was point a moth.

I named him after my old gunning partner Burton L. Spiller, who is known to literate upland shot gunners as "The Poet Laureate of the Ruffed Grouse." "Burton L. Spiller's Firelight" was my dog's official AKC name. I called him Burt.

I was working at home that summer, an ideal situation for training and bonding with a puppy. A hundred acres of woods and fields sloped away from the back of our house, and Burt and I explored every square foot of them. It seemed that he needed only to hear a command once to understand it, and he loved nothing better than to please the man who took him into the woods and fed him and invited him to sleep on the rug beside the bed.

He was housebroken in two weeks. He came when I spoke his name. He followed me from room to room. Everywhere I went, I took him with me. When I said "sit" or "whoa" or "come" or "heel"—or, of course, "get in the car"—he did what he was told. In the woods, he responded to hand signals.

I read some books on dog training. Sorting out the contradictions and conflicting philosophies, I concluded that dogs instinctively want to please their masters, that messages should never be mixed, and that without the right genes, no amount of training will produce anything better than a mediocre bird dog.

I didn't know if the corollary would also prove valid. I hoped that my well-meaning, but decidedly amateur, training program would not negate Burt's stellar genes. Both of his parents were grouse-trial champions.

Marty Connolly gave me a pheasant wing tied by two feet of twine to the tip of an old fly rod, a tool—or maybe a toy—designed to teach Burt to point. The first time I teased him with that pheasant wing, Burt locked on point. I let the wing lie on the ground. He didn't budge. I stroked his back and praised him, picked him up and set him down, and he just kept pointing that pheasant wing. There seemed no purpose to continuing those lessons. Burt loved to point.

He was less than five months old, not even half grown, when October arrived. The books all agreed that he was at least a year shy of being mature enough to actually hunt, but I'd made it my policy to bring him everywhere with me, and even if all he did was run around in the woods while I hunted with my partners and their dogs, I didn't see how it could do any harm.

Besides, Keith Wegener's pointer, Freebie, would make a splendid role model for Burt, and so would Skip Rood's Brittany, Waldo. Both Freebie and Waldo were old dogs—hunting their last season, as it turned out. Both had developed into superior grouse and woodcock dogs. They'd slowed down and gone deaf in their old age, and neither of them could hunt more than a few coverts before they ran out of steam. But they still had sharp noses, and they hunted close, and both of them would rather point than eat.

Burt and I drove to Maine on opening day of grouse season. The woods were tinder-dry, temperatures were in the eighties, and the leaves had not begun to drop. Freebie chugged through a couple of our best woodcock and grouse coverts. They were empty. Burt had himself a nice morning of trotting around on his little legs and snuffling the air. It might have been my imagination, but he seemed to be watching Freebie out of the corner of his eye.

We quit at noon, and as Keith said, "Burt did as good as Freebie."

The following weekend we hunted with Skip and Waldo. Our first covert skirted the edge of a pond. Burt and I followed the hillside, while Skip and Waldo took the string of alders that rimmed the pond.

We'd been hunting barely five minutes when I heard the quick explosion of a flushing grouse between us. I never saw the bird, but Skip, a hundred feet off to my right, fired. A moment later he said, "Oh, hell."

"Miss him?" I called.

"No, dammit. I got him. Dropped him in the middle of the pond, and old Waldo sure as hell won't fetch him. I guess I'm gonna have to . . . wait a minute."

"What's going on?"

"Burt's swimming out there . . . I'll be damned. That bird is bigger than he is . . . He's got it in his mouth . . . He's swimming back with it. I don't believe this."

I hustled down to the edge of the pond, and I got there in time to see half-grown Burt dog-paddling to shore with a full-grown grouse in his mouth. He brought it straight to me. I took it from him and thanked him. He kind of shrugged, shook himself dry, and looked at me, and it was pretty clear what he was saying: "Let's try that again."

Burt pointed his first woodcock that day. Actually he pointed his first six woodcock that day, and when I dropped one in some thick grass, he demonstrated his attitude toward retrieving woodcock. He flash-pointed it, crept up on it, then stood guard over it until I picked it up.

That afternoon, he and Waldo pointed at the same time. Waldo crept forward. So did Burt. From different angles they pointed again.

"They're roading a grouse," said Skip. "Waldo goes slow on grouse."

"Maybe that's what Waldo's doing," I said. "Burt doesn't know what he's doing."

"I think he does," said Skip.

The two dogs—the deaf old Brit and the half-grown pup—moved forward on tippy-toes, creeping, pointing, creeping again, converging from different directions. Finally they both locked onto a clump of juniper at the edge of a dirt road, about 100 yards from where they'd begun.

"Ready?" said Skip.

"I don't believe this," I said.

The grouse burst out and flew straight down the road, the easiest kind of straightaway shot.

I mounted my 20-gauge double and looked down the barrels. The grouse was flying directly at a house.

I lowered my gun. Skip had done the same.

"Would've been memorable to kill that bird," I said.

"Oh, I doubt we'll forget it," said Skip, "the way those two dogs worked."

Later that season I took Burt to a hunting preserve. We spent the day with a guide and one of the preserve's dogs, a lovely shorthair bitch that hunted planted pheasants and chukar every day. Burt had never sniffed a pheasant or a chukar.

The sleek shorthair and little half-grown Burt took turns pointing birds and honoring each other's points. I have no idea where he learned to do that.

★ ★ ★

That winter Burt grew up, and by spring he was long legged and thick chested, a dog, no longer a puppy.

In May, his breeder invited us to go for a run with one of his litter mates to celebrate their birthdays. We met at a state wildlife management area and let the dogs out.

Zoom. They both disappeared. Now and then we caught a flash of white in the distance, one or the other of the two Brittanies crashing through the underbrush, running at full tilt, heading for the horizon.

I yelled. I screamed. I cursed.

They just kept running.

"I don't know what the hell got into him," I said. "He hunted beautifully last fall."

"He's doing great," said the breeder. "He's making wide sweeps, covering a lot of ground. He can really run. You should enter him in a field trial."

"I don't get it," I moaned. "He's acting like a crazy dog. He's forgotten everything he learned."

"In grouse trials," she said, "the dogs are supposed to run big. Burt looks like a winner, assuming he'd point if he found a bird. Would he?"

"Last fall he did. He loved to point. He pointed a damn moth the day I brought him home. Now, I have no idea what he'd do." I was thinking that my little prodigy had turned into a monster.

The breeder explained how Burt's superior grouse-trial genes gave him that terrific nose and those uncanny instincts, but they also gave him strong legs and boundless stamina and the burning desire to range as far as he had to—and as fast as he could get there—to find birds.

Back when he was five months old, she said, he had everything except the legs. Now—and for the rest of his life—he'd have the legs, too, and I better get used to it.

★ ★ ★

We had a lot of adjustments to make. Well, I did. I struggled to convince Burt that he should hunt with me, that if he ran out of sight and beyond the sound of his bell, he wasn't doing us any good. The classic grouse dog, I kept telling him, goes slow and hunts close in thick cover, the way old Freebie and Waldo did, the way he himself did when he was five months old.

He didn't buy it, and I reminded myself that when Freebie and Waldo were in their prime, they liked to range pretty wide, too.

I considered—and rejected—investing in a shock collar. I knew that if I used it properly I might be able to convince him to hunt closer. But I couldn't bring myself to do it. It wasn't so much that I didn't want to hurt him, although there was that. Mostly, I couldn't bring myself to punish him for doing what had been bred into him.

So I yelled and screamed and cussed, which didn't seem to do him any harm and made me feel better.

When flights of woodcock settled into our coverts, Burt worked like my version of a classic upland bird dog. He hunted methodically, moving from point to point, looking over his shoulder now and then to make sure I was with him, and if I wanted him to poke into some part I thought he'd missed, he did it good-naturedly, although he made it clear that if there were birds where I wanted him to look, he would've found them without my help.

He always refused to retrieve a woodcock. He'd find it, sometimes point it, and then he'd stand guard over it until I picked it up. If it was still alive, he'd gently hold it down with a paw.

The trouble was, in our New England grouse and woodcock coverts, more often than not birds were scarce. Burt had no interest in barren cover, so he did what his genes told him to do—he ranged wider and wider, searching for bird scent. He was the dog, he was the one with the nose, and his job was to find birds. I was merely the man with the shotgun. My job was to shoot them.

Burt never minded when I shot and missed. But he hated it when, after all his work, I wasn't in position to shoot. That meant I didn't trust him.

★ ★ ★

It was our annual weekend at Camp Timberdoodle in northernmost New Hampshire. It would turn out to be the last big hunting weekend of Burt's last season, although I had no way of knowing that at the time. . . .

I kept him at heel as the six of us—four men and two dogs—trolled down the long sloping meadow to the alder-rimmed brook. The hillside on the other side of the brook was awash in sepia and burnt umber, the colors of late October. Overhead, the mid-day sun burned thin and yellow through a layer of lacy clouds. There was a pleasant nip to the air. Chilly, but not cold. It smelled of frost and mud and dead milkweed.

We planned to split the brook. Kenny and Ike headed for the far side with Julie, Kenny's young setter. Josh, the kid, and Burt and I, the old timers, would take this side.

While we waited for the others to cross the brook and get into position, Josh told me that he and his bride had recently moved up from Delaware, where he'd hunted stocked pheasants and wild ducks. Loved all kinds of bird hunting, he said. He carved decoys, devoured sporting books and magazines, read everything Burton L. Spiller had ever written. He'd met Kenny at a Ducks Unlimited meeting that summer.

He was, he said, "totally psyched" to hunt grouse and woodcock.

"Burt's pretty psyched himself," I said. "He's going to go charging right down to the corner of the stone wall down there. He knows there are two grouse in there. Problem is, the day's first cover, he's all crazy and will probably bust 'em wild."

"Two grouse, huh?" said Josh. "Cool."

"At least two," I said. "It's way cool."

"I never shot a grouse," he said.

"Hustle down to that corner," I said, "and be ready."

"Or a woodcock, either," he said. "Actually, I never even shot *at* one."

"Today's your day."

I waited for Josh to get into shooting position down by the brook, though I figured it was futile. Burt was sitting beside me coiled like a steel spring, and I knew when I said, "Okay," he'd bolt. He always did in the day's first cover. He'd been doing it for twelve seasons. He'd ram full-speed into the thick stuff, and if there were birds, he'd either be out of sight when he pointed them, or he'd bust 'em wild and bark at them.

Unlike some of us aging hunters, who lived off our memories, Burt, even at twelve, was fueled entirely by anticipation. He loved to hunt—hell, he *lived* to hunt—and I liked the fact that a senior-citizen dog, unlike most of the senior-citizen men I knew, was still full of piss and vinegar. I didn't really mind that he rammed around like a crazy person in our first cover, though if he happened to bump a grouse and give chase, I'd certainly yell at him.

The thick stuff that bordered the brook featured head-high alders, muddy bottom, field edges, blowdown and briars, young birch and poplar, and some old apple trees, with a scattering of hemlock and juniper and thornapple. Mixed cover. Birdy as hell.

Part of me was thinking: "I hope there are no birds here. I don't want Josh to see Burt screw it up." Another part of me retorted: "Don't be a damn fool. It's always better to find birds in good-looking cover than not find them."

Burt sat there, quivering and whining and rolling his eyes.

Josh, on the edge of the brook, appeared to be quivering, too. "So what do we do?" he said. "I never did this before."

"You keep the brook in sight on your right," I said. "I'll be off to your left, and if he does it right, Burt will work the cover between us. Stay even with me. If you see a grouse, shoot it."

"How'll I know where you are?" he said. "It looks awful thick in there."

"You'll hear me. I'll be the one yelling at the dog. Ready?"

Josh grinned. "As ready as I'll ever be, I guess."

I tapped the top of Burt's head. "Okay," I whispered.

Zoom. He tore headlong into the brush, and in about a minute his bell was a distant tinkle that I could barely hear over the gurgle of the brook.

I yelled at him, of course. To no avail, of course.

Then I couldn't hear his bell at all. When that happened, it normally meant he was on point, except in the day's first cover, it could've also meant that he'd just galloped out of hearing range.

I yelled some more, then stopped to listen. No bell.

"Be ready," I called to Josh. "The dog might be pointing."

A minute later I heard Burt yipping way off in the distance. Okay. He had been pointing. Then either he busted the bird, or it flushed. Either way, he was chasing it. Marvelous.

As I stood there, I realized that Burt's yipping was getting louder. "Get ready," I called to Josh.

The grouse came on silent wings, skimming the tops of the alders, heading right for me. He passed over my head so close I could see his beady little eyes.

I turned and took him going away.

"Get him?" called Josh.

"Yep," I said, casual-like, as if I fully expected to hit any grouse I shot at.

About then Burt came crashing through the underbrush. When he saw me, he skidded to a stop and looked at me, and if dogs could talk, he would've been saying, "Oh, hello, there. Fancy meeting you here."

"Dead bird," I told him. "No thanks to you. Go fetch." I pointed at where I'd marked down the grouse.

Burt was back a minute later with the bird in his mouth.

I took it from him. "Thank you," I said. "It works better if you hunt closer to me, you know?"

He nodded, then went over to the brook, lay down in it, and started drinking.

Ten minutes later Burt locked on point near a tangle of blowdown on the edge of an old clearcut. "We got a point," I called to Josh. "Hustle on over here."

I went up behind Burt. "Easy," I said. "Steady, now."

He rolled his eyes back at me.

Josh appeared. "Oh, wow," he said. "Lookit that."

I gestured at an opening in the trees. "The bird'll fly that way. Swing around over there."

When I saw that Josh was in position, I eased around Burt, paused, then took two more steps.

The grouse burst out from under my feet and headed Josh's way. He raised his gun, pivoted, swung, hesitated . . . and then the bird was gone.

At that moment another grouse flushed and cut to the left. I dropped it with a longish crossing shot.

I kicked at the blowdown a couple times, but no more grouse came out.

By now Burt was retrieving my bird. He brought it to me, and I cradled it in my hand. Two shots, two grouse. This was unusual for me.

Josh came over. He was grinning. "Man, was that pretty. Like a painting or something, seeing Burt pointing, and those birds come crashing out, and you shooting it, and the dog fetching it. Awesome!"

I smiled and nodded. It *was* rather awesome.

We'd had at least one solid point, probably two, moved three grouse, taken two shots, and dropped two birds—should've had three, but Josh froze up—all in about twenty minutes. A lot of seasons, that would constitute a decent full day of hunting.

I patted Burt's head. "Sometimes," I told him, "you give me hope."

★ ★ ★

When Burt went crazy, as he often did, I'd dream of the time when he would finally slow down and hunt close, the way Freebie and Waldo did in their final seasons, when they were lame and deaf and on their last legs.

Looking back at it, I'm glad he didn't slow down, didn't grow slowly old and lame and deaf. I'm glad I'll be able to remember Burt as a young dog right to the end, the same floppy-eared pup who puked on my lap and pointed a moth at eight weeks of age, who was full of fire and fun to the end, zooming through the alders and birches in ever-widening circles, hunting for a bird to point for me, ever hopeful that I'd catch up with him and shoot it.

Contributors' Notes

Rick Bass ("Old Dog"), writer, naturalist, and environmental activist, lives in Montana, dividing time between the Yaak Valley and Missoula. Bass is the author of twenty-four books of fiction and nonfiction, including *Colter: The True Story of the Best Dog I Ever Had* (2001); a short story collection, *The Lives of Rocks* (2007), which was a finalist for the Story Award; a memoir, *Why I Came West (2008)*, which was a finalist for the National Book Critics Circle Award; and, most recently, *The Wild Marsh: Four Seasons at Home in Montana* (2009).

Tom Brokaw ("Last Dance for My Ladies"), native South Dakotan, anchored *NBC Nightly News* for more than two decades. He was inducted into the Television Academy Hall of Fame in 1997, elected to the American Academy of Arts and Sciences in 2005, and received the Walter Cronkite Award for Excellence in Journalism in 2006. Author of *The Greatest Generation* (1998) and *A Long Way from Home: Growing Up in the American Heartland* (2002), Brokaw is based in Manhattan but spends as much time as possible at his ranch near Big Timber, Montana.

Christopher Camuto ("Expecting to Be Surprised") is the author of *A Fly Fisherman's Blue Ridge* (1990), *Another Country: Journeying Toward the Cherokee Mountains* (1997), *Hunting from Home: A Year Afield in the Blue Ridge* (2003), and *Time and Tide in Acadia: Seasons on Mount Desert Island* (2009). Camuto has been the book review columnist for *Gray's Sporting Journal* since 1995 and has written the "Watersheds" column in *Trout* since 1998. Chris and Patch—the latter a grizzled, retired veteran of fourteen now—live on an 80-acre woodland farm in central Pennsylvania surrounded by grouse and good woods.

Guy de la Valdène ("Dog Days"), writer, photographer/filmmaker, conservationist, world traveling sportsman, and international gourmand, was born in New York City, but raised in France. He is co-director with Christian Odasso, of the 1974 cult film, *Tarpon*, and author of two highly regarded nonfiction works, *Making Game: An Essay on Woodcock* (1985, 1990), and *For a Handful of Feathers* (1997), as well as a novel, *Red Stag* (2003). De la Valdène, a Contributing Editor for *Field and Stream*, lives in northern Florida and has completed a memoir about his life-long pursuit of gray partridge.

Robert DeMott ("Four Queens"), Edwin and Ruth Kennedy Distinguished Professor at Ohio University, has received five undergraduate and graduate teaching awards. His edition of John Steinbeck's *Working Days: The Journals of The Grapes of Wrath* (1989) was a *New York Times* Notable Book. He is editor of the Library of America's four-volume Steinbeck collection (1994-2007), and he participated in an Emmy-nominated 2001 film for The Learning Channel on *The Grapes of Wrath*. In 2006 he received the National Steinbeck Center's Trustees Award. DeMott has published many other books, including three poetry collections, *News of Loss* (1995), *The Weather in Athens* (2001), winner of the Ohioana Library's 2002 Poetry Award, and *Brief and Glorious Transit: Prose Poems* (2007). Retired in 2007, he lives in Athens, Ohio, teaches occasionally at OU, and spends a chunk of each summer in Montana, close to the Madison River.

Clyde Edgerton ("Bird Dog Ben"), Air Force veteran/pilot and accomplished musician, is the author of *The Bible Salesman: A Novel (2008)* and eight other novels published between 1985 and 2003, five of which have been *New York Times* Notable Books. One of his stories,

"Debra's Flap and Snap," is included in *Best of the South: From the Second Decade of New Stories from the South* (2005). A former Guggenheim Fellow, Edgerton teaches at the University of North Carolina at Wilmington, where he delivered the 2009 Commencement Address. He is a member of the Fellowship of Southern Writers and writes regular reviews for *Garden and Gun*.

Ron Ellis ("The Dog I Belonged To") is the author of the fictionalized memoir, *Cogan's Woods* (2001), and *Brushes with Nature: The Art of Ron Van Gilder* (2008), and editor of the anthology *Of Woods and Waters: A Kentucky Outdoors Reader* (2005). His stories have appeared in *The Gigantic Book of Hunting Stories* and in *Sporting Classics, Kentucky Afield, Kentucky Monthly,* and *Appalachian Life.* With his wife and son, Ellis lives in northern Kentucky, where, besides shepherding into publication *In That Sweet Country* (2010), an anthology of the late Harry Middleton's uncollected writings, he is currently searching for a new bird dog.

Scott Ely ("Hunting Without a Dog"), recipient of an NEA Fellowship and a Rockefeller Fellowship to Bellagio, Italy, has published five novels and three story collections since 1987, several of them with Livingston Press, including *Pulpwood: Stories* (2003) and his latest novel, *Dream of the Red Road* (2007). His stories have appeared in *Boulevard, Shenandoah,* the *Southern Review,* the *Gettysburg Review, New Letters,* the *Antioch Review* and others. "Talk Radio" is included in *Best of the South: From the Second Decade of New Stories from the South.* Ely divides his time between South Carolina, where he teaches at Winthrop University, and southwest France.

Richard Ford ("Foreword: The Beast at My Feet") has published six novels and three story collections since 1976. His Frank Bascombe trilogy, including *The Sportswriter* (1986), *Independence Day (1995),* and *The Lay of the Land* (2006), has been issued by Everyman as *The Bascombe Novels* (2009). *Independence Day* was the first novel to win both the PEN/ Faulkner Award and the Pulitzer Prize. He is co-editor of the Library of America's two-volume Eudora Welty collection (1998) and editor of *The New Granta Book of the American Short Story* (2007). Ford was elected to the American Academy of Arts and Letters in 1998 and received the *Kenyon Review's* Award for Literary Achievement in 2008. He lives in New York City and Maine and is at work on a novel, *Canada.*

Peter A. Fritzell ("Almost Out of Season"), native North Dakotan, accomplished golfer, Stanford PhD, and award-winning teacher, was Patricia Hamar Boldt Professor of Liberal Studies at Lawrence University until his retirement in 2003. Author of *Nature Writing and America: Essays Upon a Cultural Type* (1990), Fritzell has written essays, criticism, reviews, and poems for *Forest History*, the *New England Review*, *Philological Quarterly*, *Gun Dog*, *Sporting Tales*, *North Dakota Outdoors*, *Wisconsin Outdoor Journal*, *Thresholds*, *ISLE*, and *Gray's Sporting Journal*. He lives in Appleton, Wisconsin, but can often be found running bird dogs or scouting new cover near his northshire cabin in Springstead.

Bruce Guernsey ("The Dewbird of Sappiness"), a native New Englander, is Distinguished Professor Emeritus at Eastern Illinois University, where he was frequently honored for his excellence as a teacher and where he currently edits the *Spoon River Poetry Review*. A former Fulbright Lecturer in Portugal and Greece, his four poetry collections and seven chapbooks include *January Thaw* (1982), *The Lost Brigade* (2005), and *New England Primer* (2008). His prose has been published in a variety of places, including the *Virginia Quarterly* and *Fly Rod & Reel*. Guernsey and his wife, the artist/jeweler Victoria Woollen-Danner, divide their time between Illinois and Maine.

Jim Harrison ("The Dogs in My Life"), poet, novelist, screenwriter, memoirist, essayist, and roving gourmand, has published forty books since 1965, most recently a novel, *The English Major* (2007), a book of poems, *In Search of Small Gods* (2009), and *The Farmer's Daughter* (2010), a collection of three novellas. Since 2003 he has written a quarterly column, "Eat or Die," for the Canadian literary journal *Brick*. Harrison, whose work has been translated into more than two dozen languages, was elected to the American Academy of Arts and Letters in 2007. A native Michigander, he divides his time between Montana's Paradise Valley and southern Arizona, and shows no sign of slowing down as a writer.

Randy Lawrence ("The Other Man's Dog") has been a teacher for thirty-two years, the last nineteen at Hocking College in Nelsonville, Ohio. A contributor to the anthologies *Pheasant Tales* and *A Breed Apart*, his work has also appeared in *Gray's Sporting Journal*, *Game and Gun*, *The Double Gun Journal*, *Shooting Sportsman*, *Quail Unlimited*, *Muzzle Blasts*, and the *Pointing Dog Journal*. Since 1991, Lawrence has written the "Wingshooting" column for *Sporting Clays*. He and his family live in southeastern Ohio, along with his pointers, horses, mules, musical equipment, and, occasionally, the other man's dog.

Sydney Lea ("Blessed") founded the *New England Review,* which he edited from 1977-1989. His stories, poems, essays, and criticism have appeared in many periodicals, including the *New Yorker,* the *Atlantic,* the *New Republic,* the *New York Times,* and *Sports Illustrated,* as well as more than forty anthologies. He has held Rockefeller, Fulbright, and Guggenheim fellowships, has published eight collections of poems, including *Pursuit of a Wound* (2000), a finalist for the 2001 Pulitzer Prize, a novel, *A Place in Mind* (1989), and sporting/environmental essays, including *Hunting the Whole Way Home* (1994) and *A Little Wildness: Some Notes on Rambling* (2006). He lives in northern Vermont and makes annual hunting and fishing forays to his Maine cabin.

Craig Mathews ("Auggie Doggie") is the recipient of numerous conservation awards from Greater Yellowstone Coalition, Trout Unlimited, Madison River Foundation, the Nature Conservancy, and others. He and his wife Jackie own Blue Ribbon Flies in West Yellowstone, Montana, and are co-founders of One Percent for the Planet, an environmentally conscious organization of business alliances. Named *Fly Rod & Reel's* Angler of the Year in 2005, Mathews has published several indispensible books, including *Western Fly Fishing Strategies* (1998), and, with John Juracek, two volumes of *Fly Patterns of Yellowstone* (1987, 2008). Diehard devotees of German shorthairs, the Mathews couple hunt several different species of grouse and quail sixty days a year.

Thomas McGuane ("The Only Honest Way to Eat Poultry"), recipient of the 2009 Wallace Stegner Award from the Center of the American West at the University of Colorado, Boulder, has published twelve books of fiction, most recently *Gallatin Canyon: Stories* (2006), and a novel, *Driving On The Rim* (2010). His screenplays include *Rancho Deluxe* (1974), *The Missouri Breaks* (1976), *Tom Horn* (1980), and, with Jim Harrison, *Cold Feet* (1989). His sporting books are *An Outside Chance* (1990), *Some Horses* (1999), *The Longest Silence* (1999), and, with photographer Charles Lindsay, *Upstream: Fly Fishing in the American West* (2002). McGuane was *Fly Rod & Reel's* Angler of the Year in 2010. An award-winning horseman and working cattle rancher, he lives in Sweet Grass County, Montana.

Craig Nova ("The Flying Saucer"), novelist, screenwriter, essayist, memoirist, and blogger (*The Writing Life*), attended the University of California, Berkeley, and Columbia University. A recipient of NEA and Guggenheim Fellowships, he has published twelve novels, most recently *Cruisers* (2005) and *The Informer* (2010), and an autobiography, *Brook Trout and the Writing Life* (1999). His books have been translated into ten languages. Since 2005 Nova has been Class of 1949 Distinguished Professor in the Humanities at the University of North Carolina, Greensboro, where he dreams often about fly fishing Montana's rivers and spring creeks.

Howell Raines ("The Prime of Their Lives") was editorial page editor of the *New York Times* from 1993-2001, and its executive editor from September 2001 until June 2003. Winner of an individual Pulitzer Prize in 1993 for his article, "Grady's Gift," he is also the author of *My Soul Is Rested* (1977), an oral history of the civil rights movement; *Whiskey Man* (1977), a novel; *Fly Fishing Through the Midlife Crisis* (1993), a best-selling memoir; and *The One That Got Away* (2003), which covers aspects of his journalistic career. An Alabama native, Raines lives with his wife Krystyna, a journalist, in Henryville, Pennsylvania, where he is currently at work on a historical novel set in the South during the Civil War.

Bobby C. Rogers ("Hunting Close: On Bird Dogs and Lost Time") grew up in West Tennessee and was educated at Union University, the University of Tennessee at Knoxville, and the University of Virginia. His poems have appeared in *Southwest Review*, the *Southern Review*, *Shenandoah*, the *Georgia Review*, *Poet Lore*, *Cimarron Review*, and elsewhere. His book *Paper Anniversary* won the 2009 Agnes Lynch Starrett Poetry Prize at the University of Pittsburgh Press. He is professor of English and director of creative writing at Union University in Jackson, Tennessee. He lives in Memphis with his wife, son, and daughter.

F. Daniel Rzicznek ("Bad Habits") teaches at Bowling Green State University and is the author of two books of poetry, *Neck of the World* (2007) and *Divination Machine* (2009), as well as a chapbook, *Cloud Tablets* (2006). His poems appear widely in literary publications including the *New Republic, Boston Review, Gray's Sporting Journal, Orion*, and many others. Co-editor of *The Rose Metal Press Field Guide to Prose Poetry: Contemporary Poets in Discussion and Practice* (2010), Rzicznek lives with his wife in Bowling Green, Ohio, and hunts and fishes his way across northern Ohio every spring and fall.

Dave Smith ("How I Came to Live with Bird Dogs"), past editor of the *Southern Review* (1990-2002), has held fellowships from National Endowment for the Arts, Lyndhurst Foundation, Rockefeller Foundation, and Guggenheim Foundation, and has twice been a finalist for the Pulitzer Prize in Poetry. Editor of Louisiana State University Press's *Southern Messenger Signature Poets* series, Smith has published twenty-five books of fiction, poetry, criticism, and essays. His recent books include *Little Boats, Unsalvaged: Poems* (2005) and *Hunting Men: Reflections on a Life in American Poetry* (2006). A member of the Fellowship of Southern Writers, he lives with his wife, Dee, and new dog, Whizz (successor to Finn), in Baltimore, where he is Elliot Coleman Professor of Poetry and chair of the Writing Seminars at Johns Hopkins University.

Jeddie Smith ("A Good Southern Name"), a lifelong outdoorsman, attended college in Virginia and Louisiana, and earned his law degree from Louisiana State University's Paul M. Hebert Law Center. He works at the Louisiana State University Press in Baton Rouge, where he lives with his wife, Willa, son, David Jeddie "Jed" Smith III (who stands to inherit the family hunting tradition), and their Brittany spaniel, Jake. This is his first publication.

William G. Tapply ("Burt") hunted his native New England woods for upland birds for over half a century. Before Tapply's death in July, 2009, at the age of 69, he wrote about his hunting experiences extensively in such publications as *Field & Stream, Gray's Sporting Journal, Shooting Sportsman*, and *Upland Almanac*, as well as in two books on the subject: *Upland Days* (2000) and *Upland Autumn* (2009). He also has written a dozen books about fly fishing, including *Trout Eyes: True Tales of Adventure, Travel, and Fly-Fishing* (2007), and more than thirty novels, two dozen of them featuring Boston lawyer-turned crime solver Brady Coyne, most recently in *Hell Bent* (2008). Tapply lived in Hancock, New Hampshire, with his wife, writer and photographer Vicki Stiefel.